Psychedelic Modernism
Literature and Film

Raj Chandarlapaty

Series in Literary Studies

Copyright © 2024 Vernon Press, an imprint of Vernon Art and Science Inc, on behalf of the author.

All rights reserved. No part of this publication may be reproduced, stored in a retrieval system, or transmitted in any form or by any means, electronic, mechanical, photocopying, recording, or otherwise, without the prior permission of Vernon Art and Science Inc.

www.vernonpress.com

In the Americas:
Vernon Press
1000 N West Street, Suite 1200
Wilmington, Delaware, 19801
United States

In the rest of the world:
Vernon Press
C/Sancti Espiritu 17,
Malaga, 29006
Spain

Series in Literary Studies

Library of Congress Control Number: 2023950780

ISBN: 979-8-8819-0066-3

Also available: 978-1-64889-823-5 [Hardback]; 978-1-64889-885-3 [PDF, E-Book]

Product and company names mentioned in this work are the trademarks of their respective owners. While every care has been taken in preparing this work, neither the authors nor Vernon Art and Science Inc. may be held responsible for any loss or damage caused or alleged to be caused directly or indirectly by the information contained in it.

Every effort has been made to trace all copyright holders, but if any have been inadvertently overlooked the publisher will be pleased to include any necessary credits in any subsequent reprint or edition.

Cover by Yogitha Kasinadhuni, 2023. Color pencil Sketch.

"You must understand the whole of life, not just one little part of it."
Jiddu Krishnamurti

Table of Contents

	Preface	ix
Chapter 1	Introduction: The Problem of Studying Psychedelia	1
Chapter 2	The Meaning of the Aldous Huxley Collection to Studies about the Author's Efforts at Parapsychology	19
Chapter 3	Aldous Huxley's *The Doors of Perception*: A Critical Examination of its Contents	31
Chapter 4	The Mike Wallace Interview, 1958: Modern Prolegomena, and Positive and Negative Techniques for Understanding Thought Control	39
Chapter 5	"Matter, Mind and the Question of Survival": Aldous Huxley's Ascension to Psychedelic Form	47
Chapter 6	"An Attempt to Understand Things": Oliver Hockenhull's *The Gravity of Light* and Summations of Transcendence	53
Chapter 7	Our Dear, Beloved Acolyte and Muse: Laura Huxley's Theorizations and Query about Aldous in *Huxley on Huxley*	63
Chapter 8	Brave New World: Reader's Guide: A Synopsis and the Illustration of Narrative Fact to Illustrate Huxley's Grand Cultural Theory	71
Chapter 9	*Neal Cassady: The Denver Years* and Underclass Developments of the Psychedelic Epoch	79

Chapter 10	*Neal at the Wheel* and Beatnik Adaptations of the Classic Form	93
Chapter 11	*Hofmann's Potion:* Canadian and American Connections in the Growth of Psychedelic Form and the Possible Legend of Psychiatry	101
Chapter 12	The True Multiplicity of Perspectives. *LSD: The Beyond Within*	113
Chapter 13	Dr. Timothy Leary and the Popularization of Psychedelic Forms	121
Chapter 14	The Collective Body of Interpretation of Leary's Life, Work and Times, and its Relevance to Trends in Psychedelic Film and Literature	129
Chapter 15	A Shared Spotlight and the Messenger's Return: O.B. Babbs' *Timothy Leary's Last Trip* and Timothy Leary's Long Journey	135
Chapter 16	The Studied Portrait and the Looking Glass at Life's End: Dr. Timothy Leary's Special Relationship with Ram Dass in *Dying to Know*	145
Chapter 17	Understanding Ken Kesey	153
Chapter 18	Milos Forman's *One Flew Over the Cuckoo's Nest*: Countercultural Objectives	157
Chapter 19	The Merry Pranksters' *Tripping*, Kesey as Prophet and Countercultural Leader, and Pop Perspectives	167
Chapter 20	"We're We're Sadistic Crime": Neal Cassady Driving the Bus in *Magic Trip*, Re-Casting Beatnik Glories of the Road	177
Chapter 21	The Tomorrow Show and the Grateful Dead: Guitarist Jerry Garcia's Explanations about LSD with Ken Kesey	191

Chapter 22	**Americans and the Quest for Psychedelic Truth:** *Long Strange Trip*	197
Chapter 23	**Carlos Castaneda and Enigma of a Sorcerer: The Positive Value of Psychedelic Science**	205
Chapter 24	***The Gospel According to* Philip K. Dick:** *Narcotheorist Projections in the Science Fiction Era*	217
Chapter 25	**Truth, Doubt, and Penultimate Anxiety: Modernist Dictations of Future Truth in** *the Penultimate Truth of Philip K. Dick*	223
	Conclusion: Literature and the New Dynamic for Studying Psychedelic Films and Culture	231
	Works Cited	235
	About the Author	241
	Index	243

Preface

When I first revised my work on psychedelic literature to include documentaries, I owned up to a host of misconceptions. These changes broadly-offered the focal point of view: scientists such as Albert Hofmann and Timothy Leary treated mental health patients with drugs such as LSD, mescaline, and psilocybin, offsetting their symptoms and sickness. This finding, however, was overrun after testimonies from rock icons that included Ken Kesey, continuing to the point by 1968, at which LSD was used casually throughout the United States. From the guiding perspective of knowledge and social theories, psychedelic realism focused on alternatives to formalism and socialism, limiting neurological and psycholinguistic idea transmissions. Aldous Huxley's debut as a psychedelic thinker was with his 1953 publication of *The Doors of Perception*, crowning his role as a social-institutional thinker who advocated conscious revolution. This brought forth many possibilities, but as an introduction, I note that both Huxley and Leary were reluctant to advocate drugs as instrumental in changing society. It was with some difficulty, intellectual as well as political, that thinkers would envision a world where taking LSD, mescaline, and psilocybin constituted part of a legal and meaningful experience. Somewhere within the fault lines between communism and capitalism lay different perspectives that altered subjective lines of self-invigoration, perhaps to advance greater humanity but also to change the impact of democratic thinking. Huxley's belated ambition would not be for lack of evidence: he had, in his early writings, documented stories of the corruption and abuse in pre-Enlightenment England. Surprisingly, the chance of divergence was avoided, with the films offering many reasoned introduction points.

Antagonisms between experience and its translation present a more meaningful solstice of our learning: let us say, for instance, feeling and experiencing obfuscate many channels of writing and memory and complicate consumption's idea as a social metaphor of being. From this point of view, finding a blueprint for tripping would seem logical: it would, at least, tell us what the mind's processes told us about who we were, cosmically and physically. We ask the societal question: how open are we to the idea of drugs as begetting social transactions, underscoring a self-governance or super-governance that manages itself in our modern lives? This question rewrote many details, but themes and key evidence show that psychedelic learning was conceptual, and its text and discussion conform to authority, science, and even literature. The test was certain: previous drug-influenced writers, including the Beat Generation, had limited success telling why their uses were socially relevant. Scripture's relative absence suggested the obvious: why were we studying this? Is it not likely that drugs are consumed for pleasure and that humans depend upon their ignorance of drug interactions? But, then, responses were overwhelming: Aldous Huxley, Timothy Leary, Albert Hofmann, Ken Kesey, Jerry Garcia, Carlos Castaneda, and Phillip K. Dick undertook the tryst with meaning, to say that people's lives may be managed better than they were, with solutions to capitalist pathologies surrounding drug addiction. I found that vision, inscribed in religious histories and memories, may rebuild our senses and our resolute social belonging.

At the outset, it should be said that prospects for teaching authors who used psychedelic drugs are pleasantly broad, perhaps if only because classes and studies have ignored their potential draw at re-building and contextualizing a truly pluralist modernism that has considered the psychic and intertextual ramifications of guiding mental and social worlds away from repression, and away from highly limited Victorian doctrines that racialized and criminalized practices to uphold White dominance. Such efforts distorted humanism's limitless potential to re-configure the bane of empiricist-rationalist relationships that had, in their passive, un-rhetorical suppression of contexts and mental experiences, darkened and baned addict lives and helped to revive Victorian moral stamps during the twentieth century. FIU Professor Richard Schwartz had been plain about the human condition in 1992 when speaking about George Orwell's *1984* in a Cold War Literature class, musing: "Maybe love is the answer." Many in our generation did not take graduate courses on liberal authors. They so recalled no class discussion about drugs' apparent role in helping to build modernist theory as it skewers our attempts to remain Eurocentric. This reality obfuscates psychedelia's true discussions, wherein a logical, composed, and resonant interconnection with the modern psyche could liberate and manage the modern man in a model closer to his true inspirations.

With censorship's deep gaze counting the details, I only taught the subject of drugs in literature to undergraduates three times, almost all of it focused on the subject of marijuana. Student essays at Florida International University and the University of Texas, Rio Grande Valley, maintained the bland, sterile gauze of prohibitionist admissions and identifications of the drug user's "bad" social identity. Still, author discussions that include interviewed colleagues, plus engaging, endlessly broad archaeology of counterculture's new beginnings and Huxley's curt pedagogical appraisals when thinking about forms, signals that modernism held within itself a much greater breath and that it is time we turned to specific inferences and logical, meditative points reversing socialist-Victorian indoctrinations that debilitate the human subject, rendering them unresponsive to their existence's true dimensions. The project also posits the necessary debacle: the Beat Generation, who professed themselves as romanticists who praised errant forms and incomplete syntax. In these studies, I would like to underscore that psychedelic modernism, or its disciplinary study, promised us a supreme logic and a utopic necessity that might mitigate controls, self-control, interactions, and even social conformity's minutes as our guidance. Greater modernism lay open, with warmly positive themes replacing the dark, crude, and rueful decanting of romantic loss and inertia that wrote the Beat Generation's pages. Documentary films promise the width of the author's semiotic reinvention as cultural forces: Stephen Prince observes, "The spectator's understanding of the cinema is therefore explained as a matter of cultural conditioning."[1] Of course, re-interpreting the author or scientist would likely favor "pure" researchers who might then be explored and assumed to proponent a greater meaning to inquiries. Still, Denver-born adventurer, writer, and mystic Neal Cassady was within the lost literature. So, we will recount his legitimate studies and his engagement of countercultural icons to paint a new freedom that the film's sweep of talks and comments would underscore was unimagined in Jack Kerouac's halcyon days during the 1940s and 50s.

The book's purpose is to build psychological and societal relevance to the initial studies and experiences to derive commentaries, research, and authorial questions as the beginning points for greater studies of psychedelic drugs during the key period. More aptly put, this work will demonstrate psychedelic media's prevalence and interactive influence in our parallel discussions about consciousness, ideations, and spiritual freedoms through various mind-body techniques found in literary modernism. Key to examining both literature and films, which democratize archival learning and re-introduce decentered intellectual models, was our capacity to "earn tradition," as T.S. Eliot put it, through models and experiences, carving open the roots of inquiry to produce a modern idealism that could redress concerns of science, psychiatry, faith, and post-Empiricist intellections about humankind's experiences, memories, and collective actions. Huxley and the writers who followed him keenly eyed the apparatus by which knowledge and traditions grew to anoint pathways and mysticism that could redraw modern societies by rehabilitating human beings prone to Victorian moral and medical shackles. Several key components exist beyond simply memories, self-reporting, and documented surveys. Thinkers tried to understand drugs' rational principles, to say that they beckoned a new, romantic model of social and national control while giving us symbolic outlets for one's pre-rational inquiry and cognition. The purpose of this study, then, traces our initiation of psychedelic studies to introduce documentary films that include interviews and commentaries, together with studies and narrator summaries, to build modernist quests for knowledge and our psychiatric

---

[1] Prince, Stephen, "The Discourse of Pictures," 90.

certainty. Traditionally, studies of drugs were more confined to science, psychology, and crime to suppress a great deal of interactive content that could speak for both societal change and for mental, physical, and imaginative re-examination as cursors screening a new dynamic and also a repressed modern involvement in life. In our history, the case for the humanities engendered this repression, and books and published sources limit substantive content that could speak to learning, experience, and idea-proliferations in the decades after World War I that introduced psychoanalysis. Literary studies were limited to published works, ignoring more engaging and thoughtful data that could bravely spell out the author or thinker's accomplishment at breaching Victorian and socialist controls in psychology's critical re-examinations as a true science. This idea is accomplished when we use humanities reasoning and hard data to project a broader, more truly cogent psychology that includes drugs as part of a partial reconnection with recurrent Western philosophical anxieties. I believe that, however, twentieth-century literary authors related perspectives and rough findings to constitute equality with the domains of science and psychology. It was evident from this time that literature intended to conduct serious mind-soul investigations by examining characters, histories, and political-leaning commentaries. Though Danielle Giffort was vague on this point, "storytelling often crystallizes around particular figures of expertise who become performative images that can be inhabited. Motifs related to science, credibility, and ethics get attached to these figures,"[2] it should become clear that scientism and analysis pervaded the trippers' stories. Rock n' roll excursions carried scientific curiosity's basic pretense, or the curiosity to build their experiences and festivities around the psychological principle of enhanced humanity. It was also clear during Jacques Lacan's mid-twentieth century that literature as part of the humanities was shaded. It grew science's objectivity, filling us with empty conceptual frameworks that had beguiled nineteenth-century psychologists. Some attempt is needed to adapt music artists' writings and comments as they strove for common linguistic and cultural origins when uncovering psychedelic ideas and talent. This book, my third in the area of film and literature, devises communitarian and academic beginnings that could be popularly demonstrated, as they did not confine themselves to the abstract literary isolation: it will instead project social impact through authors, friends, and thinkers commenting on the crucial periods in the historical past and then in the twentieth century after World War I. Documentary films, as they gauged unpublished and posthumous findings of time and context, broaden our scope and develop historical themes and threads to help us understand interactive points in psychology's ascent,

---

[2] Giffort, Danielle, *Acid Revival*, 13.

extending its rays beyond Victorian models of control, suppression, and criminalization of Being. We can then say that a greater social context could be imagined and formed from the annals of time and archaeology of the mind and spirit, as these entries had been confined to obscurity and irrelevance. After all, psychedelic films as fictional narratives would be just that—likely to confirm our stereotypes through humor. Patricia Aufderheide states the obvious challenge with brevity and clarity: "A documentary film tells a story about real life, with claims to truthfulness."[3] Still, initial studies and the treading of philosophical rather than criminal ideas sharpen our angle, calling upon our objective focus to demonstrate the idea's development over time in this medium to grant drugs legitimacy. Suppose we are to ever gauge the seriousness of drugs as a social or psychological idea. In that case, we should follow instruction and reason, explaining it as a science consistent with humanities writing and forming inferences that speak to a greater, psychoactive leaning in knowledge directed towards dreaming and visions. We should also categorize and grade alterations of perspective to suit our abandonment of rationalism's confines that, in its root motions, criminalize experiences that traverse and modify the mind's actions. While I will situate these in terms of history, this project emphasizes the relative newness of discoveries and pretenses towards knowledge, building the rungs of Michel Foucault's "repressive hypothesis" as the basis for re-examining thoughts, inundations of meanings, and our psychiatric concepts. No historical period will be underscored, nor will anyone be managing philosophy or ideation system. Still, it is without a doubt that history, when lost, invites strategies to recover its contents. Our display of knowledge when courting psychedelics and their specific reference to hallucinogenic cults, religious texts, and aesthetic summarizations is uneven rather than broad, and the necessary keys to our understanding of shamanism's impact are broad, though thinly referenced. Still, this was not true for Huxley himself, and this fact re-opened popular literary discussions on Buddhism, pre-Columbian rituals, Hindu philosophy, and counterculture's sweeping modern re-invention of these in culture-freed contexts. Demonstrating the simplicity of American forms complements the initial meditations from Europe.

    A final note has to do with positions concerning the legality of drugs and their media. Because some of these writers rejected the idea of implementing the legal use of psychedelic drugs, a host of critics identify the elitist trend, suppressing democratic experiences that may inculcate greater learning and a wider appreciation of cultural contexts. Timothy Leary stated this authoritatively in an interview, saying that his political views about LSD, psilocybin, and

---

[3] Aufderheide, Patricia, *Documentary Film: A Very Short Introduction*, 3.

mescaline were "the same as the Johnson Administration."[4] Part of the book intends to demonstrate learning versus mainstream opinions and ideas about social change, speaking to our public ambivalence. Of course, published works identified social instruction and indoctrination. So, we will focus on the counterculture's surrogate idea-makers and their populist forms in imaginative mental pathways, bringing together modern experiences geared to de-philosophize psychedelic insight. Strong attention has been given to Huxley's inundation with Indian realism during the times, and thus, we could examine our pre-scholastic anxieties in documentary films. Positive cautions from Huxley and Leary's exhibit, where authors had refused to advocate legalization, durable findings contraindicating the tradition to suppose social and pluralistic realization. Penning history and historical truth, too, alters our social projections, opening the doors for critical re-examinations.

Moreover, the antagonism was basic, calling upon authors to detail the sensory and linguistic evidence, allowing psychedelic studies to, at last, comprise science. There ought to be sufficient knowledge and social information to build free societies with greater humanistic inclusion of one's conscious and cognitive responses to institutional controls. In short, responses did not depend on criminal hypocrisies but on the guiding sense that ideas and experiences grew towards greater inclusion. This expansiveness was not said in isolation: clearly, psychedelic documentaries made a strong, three decades-long association of chemists and scientists with the Sandoz Corporation, fully legal and based in Switzerland during the 1940s, 50s, and 60s. A partial outcome of this work will be connecting the authors to their larger modernist compendium as they, having taken mescaline as early as 1951, weren't given recognition for their findings and so assessed the modernist minute as one where mental and perceptual expositions initiated modern penultimate re-examination while facing social change as the precursor of the Earth's de-romanticization. The prohibition of hallucinogens was a Victorian stricture, and some attention ought to be given, too, to the examples comprising science from that period. Legality's facade was not at all a façade—clearly, thinkers and pundits built a syntactic awareness of drug properties, counting them to be part of legitimate psychiatry.

Socialist Beginnings: Transcriptions of Drug Use and Their Criticism

Criticisms and their partial fallout were blank and acrid: in Gus Van Sant's 1991 film *Drugstore Cowboy*, a young hippie scribbles lines on a paper and calls his acid trip "groovy." Socialist principles quickly developed, from this example, motions that criminalized drugs of all kinds, with German philosopher Karl

---

[4] *Dying To Know.*

Marx operating the obvious reduction in his synopsis of sense-perceptions destruction of the Self as it weakens one's soul:

> [...] the more the worker appropriates the exterior world of sensuous nature by his labor, the more he doubly deprives himself of the means of subsistence, firstly since the exterior sensuous world increasingly ceases to be an object belonging to his work, a means of subsistence for his labor; secondly, since it increasingly ceases to be a means of subsistence in the direct sense, a means for the physical subsistence of the worker.[5]

Evaporations of context, meaning, and abstraction, then, constitute socialist dictations that as "work" or as "being," drugs are delusion and take away our human subsistence: our organizations of thought, feeling, and sensation, then, are guided through drugs to be a kind of deterioration. Socialists aptly and cleverly annex the key inference. If we couldn't figure out what we were experiencing or what parts of our cognition we were developing, we were wasting our mental and psychic resources and thus were harming, not praising, our Being. I believe it is finally time to accept the truth of the fact that Drug War politics concerning LSD and other psychedelic drugs suppressed fairly immense rounds of potential data and mismanaged its content, bowdlerizing dreams and visions that, in a descriptive form, may have been intact had we joined them to our scientific approach. It is time to narrow our lens to appreciate that when we examine data without social codes designed to constrain them, we get finer examples that constitute the text's meaning and find that these journeys could have been meaningful if they had been studied and given greater relevance. While drug reforms may be critical, we might not attach the idea of happier, translocative lives that offset sickness. Instead, we demand social change when facilitating non-Victorian happenings to increase our awareness of cultures and experiences that society banned. We might also own up to the necessity of a "system" and gain a greater sense of human growth in complex times. When Hofmann warmly attests to his translation's meaning, we learn that ideas and principles are not tied to any one form of governance. By extension, spiritual and supernatural associations provoked Being's unvisited portions that grew democracy's institutions away from accepted norms. Psychology and psychiatry, at last, grew their pre-scholastic roots, projecting another repressed social livelihood. Visions and hallucinations aside, documentary films beget the building of social norms, and those tied to

---

[5] Marx, Karl, "Alienated Labor," from McNeill, William, & Feldman, Karen S., *Continental Philosophy*, 216.

memory and experience hold historical and pre-cultist meanings. So, was the exercise legitimate? Did drug tripping tell us something about the Soul, the moral, and the intellectual? I will examine as many critics as I do advocates: what is clear is that a knowledge base might have been greater had ideas and immersions not been tied to our cultural fantasy. This book's objective morphology then relates the impact of literature and literary ideations to our phenomenology. It, too, is as likely that metaphors and encoded symbols of Being told us of not just humankind's imaginative lapse but much more about individual and social urges to be and how they must be made compatible with society's pluralistic goals determining the Self's realization when tagged into everyday social contexts. Conversations, texts, and short synopses establish this literary trend. It was clear from the outset that psychedelia transformed literature's modernist outlook and relevance, broadened psychic angles meant to restructure man as s/he faced the tide of postmodern stereotypes that would forever moor humans to their corporate, capitalist, and fetishist estimations of purpose and involvement.

In writing my third book in the film and literature series about documentaries, I will say that several factors affect the validity of the documentary film that correspond to their perceivable weight in re-examining literary studies. There is, of course, the narration's caliber and specific textual and biographical examples that correspond to the film's contents. Using videography, interviews, and commentators will generally establish a tone friendly with textual, biographical re-examinations of fact and principle. Then, there is the authorial portrait, with inferences situating the writer, artist, or scientist against others in their field. When compressed into film, we might judge these as to whether modernist theory had successfully relegated and responded to powerful Victorian and socialist forces that stymied research's progress and that guided people away from the makings of science and ideation. Modernist fiction and music append the doctrine of form: we surmise that postmodern novels, including those of Thomas Pynchon, dealt directly with World War II soldiers' sex and drug activity, attaching Victorian models of moral and personal circumspection and posing descriptions that exaggerate prohibition's control in our self-expression:

> So when he disentangles himself, it is extravagantly. He creates a bureaucracy of departure, inoculations against forgetting, exit visas stamped with love bites (…) But coming back is something he's already forgotten about. Straightening his bowtie, brushing off the satin lapels of his jacket, buttoning up his pants, back in uniform of the day, he turns

his back on her, and up the ladder, he goes. In the last instant, their eyes were in touch is already behind him (…)[6]

Passages like these, from 1973's *Gravity's Rainbow*, underscore the writer's covert imaginations and, in its picaresque form as with Burroughs, who published *Naked Lunch* in 1959, re-attach conservative, Victorian moral prescriptions and interruptions of syntax, to connote authority's control of individuals. When applied to drugs and sex, postmodernism may aptly suppress the content of pleasure and introspection, hoisting the eternal, syntactic scaffolding of control beneath Pynchon's funny commodity fetishism. By contrast, psychedelic thinkers preserved and airbrushed themes, latently and rigorously, and constructed a new, functioning organism amidst the maze of modern life's many pathways. This work did not depend upon commentators and documents during that period; a key tenet of this exercise is that the authors' deepened psychedelic inquiries about culture and practice came from published or printed forms that stretched across their lives. The book itself promises greater objective content than found in the circulated forms of the larger Beat Generation, mired as it was in its humorous, fantastic dialects that, when examined, go up against the larger, objective conundrum. I justify inclusions about Cassady and other Beat Generation writers: studies on drugs come from many directions, and Cassady's poverty and abuse necessitate his synopses of drugs to rebuild the depressive person to illustrate possibilities and synthesize learning. As it turns out, critics have praised the format of Cassady's letters. We will underscore those relationships with the larger context. Author studies include, by and large, an examination of their letters and unpublished works: this gives us a positive sense of what ambitions the authors could not completely organize. At the same time, they built their repertoire of interactive works.

There are several people that I would like to thank in this ambitious new effort. Naturally, I thank the films' producers for organizing such clear content over nearly fifty years, and I would say that the time has come to examine content and intention for a didactic retreading of the basic facts as well as suppositions and analysis that could detail our understanding as to what science means. The book's authors are thanked for bringing so much useful material for us to read and growing these discussions about psychiatry and culture. Rosario Batana, Blanca Duran, Argiris Legatos, and Javier Rodriguez at Vernon Press are thanked for re-opening an engaging discussion about the positive change in philosophy and its registered influence on contemporary society. I thank Phillip Sipiora, Kurt Hemmer, and Richard Schwartz for

---

[6] Pynchon, Thomas, *Gravity's Rainbow*, 471.

encouraging my work. I also thank Kirsten Wilson for providing materials from The Aldous Huxley Collection and The Timothy Leary Collection at The Harry Ransom Center, with many unique and sustained examples of immersive ideas and experiences. Thanks also to the Pennsylvania State University Library for Ken Kesey archival materials, to Pauline Cochran at Borchardt, Inc. for Aldous Huxley materials, to Jami and Cathy Cassady Silva for materials on Neal Cassady, and the University College London for excellent source material on Ken Kesey and George Orwell.

I salute the changes in current laws that allow drugs to be part of the human health scene. Thanks also to my Mom, who mailed me the DVDs.

Raj Chandarlapaty

Chapter 1

Introduction: The Problem of Studying Psychedelia

At the Century's Turn: Models for New Thought and Inquiries into the Mind

Nineteenth-century Indian thinker, yoga student, and philosopher Swami Vivekananda once wrote, "All truth is eternal. Truth is nobody's property; no race, no individual can lay exclusive claim to it. Truth is the nature of all souls."[1] While this comment may attempt to de-realize Indian realism while promoting intercultural exchanges, it also situates the challenge of contradicting modern ideologies to profess ownership. Moreover, it re-opens the humanistic study of any society by drawing forth the imagination, the studies, and the collective actions of all the moments of the Earth's history. Capitalism, to bear this imprint, denies us meaning's non-ideological transference: this notion, having been brought forth to present our illusions about reality, gave us meaningful interfaces and yet denies any one form of knowledge control, to draw forth histories, estimations of one's being and consciousness, and thought-idea relationships that are many rather than one. Victorian societal problems grew from human orderings of perception and action, connoting man's legitimacy from realist determinations that weren't sensory and had not considered the brain's imaginative relapses. Vivekananda's statement interrupts and discards Western hegemony, whether aesthetic or ascetic. Interrupting German philosopher Immanuel Kant's general organization of fact and principle, Vivekananda points to the psychedelic theorists as spawning an intricate necessity that counters moral man's doctrine of separation and control when juxtaposed against ideas, dreams, and perceptions that cause us to question the acquisition of wealth, family, and possessions to constitute Selves.

Still, Vivekananda tells us with a wider intention: "According to Krishna [Hindu god], we are not new beings. We didn't just come into existence. Our minds are not new. In modern times, we are all told that every child brings all the past, not only of humanity but of the plant life."[2] This statement's broad angle means to redraw our humanities, to suggest mystical and imaginative relationships that pointed to nature's ascendancy in times of vision, and

---

[1] 100 Amazing Quotes By Swami Vivekananda.
[2] *The Complete Works of Swami Vivekananda, vol. 1.*

perhaps the growth of perspectives and life that may outgrow traditionally Victorian modes of inquiry into Selves. That our minds are not newly prefigured, their truncation and misdirection from the modern, political, and economic impetus to build societies. Within its positive civilizational relapse, drawing the lines of conscious meaning once again called upon humankind's myriad of repressed histories and our chances to exist in a greater minute of truth as abstractions speaking to what was primitive, native, and soluble in our experiences. Future histories beget humanity's declassification and impulse to live, create, and dream. The liaison was indeed special, favoring Huxley's ascension to worldwide notoriety. Indian, Chinese, Mesoamerican, and European histories and their identifying themes are interwoven, covering the sweep of thousands of years and the illusory matrix of meanings that devoted our attention to religious and political mysticism. A meaningful part of this work will examine instances that could speak to the complex array of philosophies and ideas that favor hallucinogenic similitude.

Meanwhile, balanced on Huxley's growing apparatus were George Orwell's self-examinations. Orwell had meditated on socialism in India during the 1920s, dropping it to favor more psychological estimations of man's powers and how they might be neutralized and redirected to posit humans´ literate, institutional dominance.[3] The two minds' concurrence operated Huxley's pinnacle of rebuilt romanticism and Being's errata that favored imagism, transcendentalism, and anti-politic, giving us the chance to cover psychedelic drugs' robust promulgation during the 1960s.

Philosophy, at a Glance: Aldous Huxley Versus Rationalist Suppressions of the Brain and Thought

Before we engage the body of very real, poignant discussions about consciousness, the mind, human perceptions, and philosophy itself, it is necessary to note that, except for the past few decades, philosophy has tended to exclude drugs. Drugs themselves aren't an integral part of modern philosophy. Even today, key discussions barely include any narcotic thinking. Our traditions in the nineteenth and twentieth centuries do not constitute drugs in any analytic or continental philosophy; psychologists, too, were reluctant to study them, tending to see no operative purpose in studying perceptions or dreams. While there were exceptions, Jacques Lacan was not one of them, so the genealogical reasoning was denied any such immersion. Huxley and later psychedelic thinkers faced the unspoken task of re-assembling doctrines and logic: his dependence on Eastern thought spoke to

---

[3] George Orwell Collection, UCL.

aestheticism but did not tell us as much about human functionality as we may philosophically guide it.

In my reasoning, courses in philosophy often expose the fake parable by which drug use was acquainted with "philosophy." Undergraduates have tended to ignore or make fun of analytic philosophy's real Victorian prescriptions, keeping philosophy safe and free of intoxication: Nietzsche's disparagement of philosophy and psychology also ensured a substance-free continental form that Lacan quickly copied.[4] Students at the American University of Afghanistan laughed at the discussions in the Contemporary Philosophy and Literature class during the Fall of 2015, throwing forth ideas to redeem their hashish smoking. However, a student named Abdul Mujadidi demanded that we recognize that Muslims held a philosophical tradition during the Middle Ages, even though some retorted that it was only aestheticism. Non-Western criticisms of European analytic and continental philosophies, then, call for our theoretical re-entrenchment in the dynamic world: for Huxley, Hindu, Buddhist, and Native American discussions approach their ethical and logical recognition in his spoken and interviewed statements and color Leary's writings to the tune of his controversial humanism, as we seek higher notes of self-absorption and comprehension. As a side note, Huxley also represented anti-racist generations of white ethnography, taking away racist dialogues that had kept non-Western archaeology and philosophy in their unrecognized obscurity. For this matter, *The Perennial Philosophy* did much to re-establish legitimate studies and archaeology on Hinduism and Buddhism.

Born on July 26, 1894, to a wealthy English family and later an Oxford graduate, Aldous Huxley exhibited many facets of a growing East-West interrelationship. He published *The Perennial Philosophy* in 1944 to stage the sympathy between visionary knowledge of life, the mind, and the soul and intellectual determinations of faith and truth, as it may be called religious doctrine. Covering many of the world's religions, *The Perennial Philosophy* was ambitious, textually rich, and thoughtful about the abstraction of deducible aesthetic principles. Partly because he was a writer who published short stories and novels, including those on remote cultures in North America, Europe, and Asia, Huxley navigated the post-dynamic between literature and philosophy that, though intellectual, favored non-material transferences of ideas and facts so that he might summarize the logical impacts of what was romanticist, or at least occurred before socialism's advent that prefigured technocracy. In the text's formal discussion, Huxley operated the principle of East-West aesthetic similarity. Our analysis will then situate Huxley's literary reality as much as his use of philosophical imagination's imaginative and religious turns, giving life

---

[4] Nietzsche, Friedrich, *Ecce Homo*, preface.

to conscious growth in the emerging human. This emphasis will expand his legacy beyond later works like 1953's *The Doors of Perception* and *Heaven and Hell*, which, in the final summation, were personal excursions and thus less scholarly.

Huxley's exchanges with India were many, but he also built a multi-ethnic fashion to include several non-Protestant cultures, welding Being and Truth into an enhanced format. These included Indo-American philosopher Jiddu Krishnamurti, who also advocated Being's selflessness; thus, Indian philosophy would be both ordinary and non-ordinary, spawning transcendent ideas. Still, a problem arises concerning this translation: What do our experiences mean, especially when we cannot transcribe them? What do they mean by our translation? Challenges to Huxley's general scholarship, which figured the idea that non-rational reality could be studied, and so might constitute society's true functioning, causes us to allow that works like *Brave New World* were fantastic and supposed to have no verifiable function in twentieth-century imaginations. We would then research the century's scholarly elements to construct what might be called a science and then postulate that this science counteracted Victorian models that repressed feelings, dreams, and sense-derived introspections. Religious themes should be carefully studied: when we say that conceptual worlds exist beyond our daily realm or that media confirms corporate/capitalist control of the direction of thought, epistemology might grow from man's collective path of visions rather than from capital- or writing-derived social theories. This factor was not without fierce battling from mainstream authoritarianism: in 1968, President Lyndon Baines Johnson angrily seared LSD as causing "the slavery of our youth."[5] The films include psychiatrists, government officials, and professors attesting to both the malfunctioning addict and his absence of principles. Binary historical visitations may cause us to appraise Krishnamurti's estimations of the mind and the self with greater freedom to resolve truth's paradoxes. In *The Flight of the Eagle*, he wrote:

> [...] We must give total attention—which is, after all, passion—to see and find out for ourselves if there is a way of life wholly different from our own. To understand that one has to go into several questions, one has to inquire into the process of consciousness, examining both the surface and the deep layers of one's own mind, and one also has to look at the nature of order, not only outwardly but within oneself.[6]

---

[5] *LSD: The Beyond Within.*
[6] Krishnamurti, Jiddu, *The Flight of the Eagle*, 69.

Based on this rough model for re-examining experience and life, we might conclude that Aldous Huxley, Timothy Leary, and Albert Hofmann were in a singular aspect successful at demonstrating this factor—experiments, be they rationalized or perceptually real, contrast perception and meditation, and thus superficial and intellectual realities. Still, we might translate the philosophical experience with fewer preternatural ideas. A new history and historical angles, including visions and dreams, change man's true social function. There would be nothing coincidental: Krishnamurti explored Vedanta's elemental idea during the 1920s, with or without drugs, but within realist criticisms of the social idea's generation. Strictly focused on man's interactions, he contrasts Huxley's critical remarks with Being's necessity, hence its possible translation onto modern forms. We should be more critical, too, of Krishnamurti's criticism of drugs such as LSD and marijuana: Krishnamurti synopsized man's lack of personal freedoms and the brain's self-manipulations towards escape, seeing their use debilitate man's impulses towards freedom and its redirections. He did not, as Huxley did, see the media's necessity or our logic of societal control through those media to achieve Being. Drugs, then, to Krishnamurti, were a replacing idea-mind configuration, whereas Huxley believed that specific drug consciousness could evolve the human specimen, removing avenues of product-object control from without. The two men agreed about the drugs' damaging effects but did not concur about what could be useful or applicable for a necessary mind-body continuum.

Situated in the expansive world context, *Brave New World* targeted new forms of communalism, vaunting the mind over products. It should be understood, too, that Huxley was careful not to step too hard on television, capitalism, or money as social media: we would, nonetheless, be amiss to suggest that he was not motivated by human reforms that could escape control brainwashing or more debilitating drug psychoses. Anti-drug psychologists and professors had criticized the LSD experiments, with one noting the absence of time in altered experiences. They pointed to drug use's physical dangers, including patients who "thought they could fly."[7] The purpose of our discussion is not to demonstrate the validity of states of awareness but to speak from the validity of experiences and changes in one's mind that could create social makings true to the human experience as it was. The idea, being post-Freudian, stresses this template of importance gauging how exactly the mind, when dosed, could revive human actions. This concept will give fruit to its irrational, dream-like contemplations that stem from an essential human need that capitalism, socialism, and Victorian modes of thought and social coding controlled, repressed, categorized as sickness, and took actions against to maintain modern culture's specific model.

---

[7] *LSD: The Beyond Within.*

Several of the films expose the dark side of our study and immersion: addiction, health problems, and hallucinatory experiences building schizophrenic forms rather than curing them are recurrent criticisms in the films' text. The social model determined whether a person was physiologically and mentally rejuvenated or deprecated: critics and pundits were keen to examine the interactions with this model to project freedom as a metaphor for building an ideal, prosperous social control.

Huxley and the World Stage: Anticipations of the Wallace Interview

Huxley brings his rationalizations to the world stage in his 1958 interview with Mike Wallace to note the positive impact of media in building propaganda in communist countries.[8] Hallucinogens and virtual media, then, advance the cause of freedom. This fact can be applied to Western and Eastern examples and could help express formal control of ideas and communities speaking of that identity. Still, comparisons were hard to earn because of the absence of personal data in transmitting experiences. Written memories did not, in short, tell us much about what we have learned or what inferences could be carried away from an idea. In Carlos Castaneda's 1971 work *A Separate Reality*, Don Juan praises a younger mescaline-taker by saying Mescalito had "taught him a song."[9] Paraphrasing man's subjective sense to be objective, then, may force us to identify societies tying drugs to addiction, to the destruction of brain-nerve impulses, and mental associations with corrupting or deluding experiences. Our exercise in studying drugs should be conceptual, considering the arrangement of ideas, words, and histories against capitalist-communist limitations on experience and the pre-rational, hierarchical arrangements of reason.

We might as easily borrow our dictum from Austrian psychologist Sigmund Freud to state that Western history, socialism, and other parts of the human experience were necessarily constructed out of the desire to curtail experience in our pursuit of social determinism. Freedom, of course, may cause us to form reasons about what constitutes belonging, pleasure, thought, and so on—man's intuitive adjustments, in support of "the system," necessarily direct persons away from core reasoning that our experiences are meaningful and ought to be socially translated, to draw forth existence that favors non-ideological, super-rational determinations of man's social belonging. Freud operated this crucial minute in 1899's *The Interpretation of Dreams*: "Every dream has a meaning, and dreams are designed to take the place of some other process of thought." [10]

---

[8] Aldous Huxley, Interviewed by Mike Wallace, 1958.
[9] Castaneda, Carlos, *A Separate Reality*, 147.
[10] Freud, Sigmund, *The Interpretation of Dreams*, 121.

Introduction: The Problem of Studying Psychedelia 7

By contrast, Wallace drew forth the resultant idea in the CBS interview: television could not be classified as bad or destructive.[11] But was there any supporting evidence that visions or dream sequences were, in some practical way, real and enough to promote our social ambivalence? After all, *Brave New World* as an experiment, results in the main character's deaths. Huxley was calm and deliberate on this point, suggesting that neither were drugs a problem in the United States nor that they had been studied enough to understand their uses in propaganda.

Much research has been done on the mind, and Kathleen Taylor's expert work *Brainwashing* tackled the problem of altered states as stepping-stones to dysfunction and external control. This work examines mind-control mechanisms as they were used in countries where dictators ruled, including violent actions as part of the general technique, examining the brain's vulnerability to methods of indoctrination and control. It may be necessary to admit that general psychology did not adeptly figure the advent of drugs into personal-psychic mechanisms or our rationalizations about health, character, social involvement, and conflict. These themes were first studied during the 1930s, figuring into a wildly incomplete, jagged pattern of humorist readings and vague aphorisms that did not estimate drugs as antidotes to moral obstruction gained from product-idea configurations. We may aptly ask, "Did the popularity of hallucinogens include a legitimate growth of civic and personal ideas in current societies?" Fear that we are historicizing behavioral trends may nix their universal relevance. Still, we might ask ourselves how developed or historically legitimate these inquiries were to gain a broader definition of drug use beyond Leary's first advocacy of their legalization before Congress in 1965:

> Leary: And I recommend respectfully to this committee that you consider legislation, which will license responsible adults to use these drugs for serious purposes, such as spiritual growth, the pursuit of knowledge, more in their own personal development. To obtain such a license, the applicant, I think, should have to meet physical, intellectual, and emotional criteria.[12]

There is ample evidence to suit the form of Huxley's fiction and short stories, and even in his private memoirs about England that extend as far back as the seventeenth century: a whole body of knowledge lay duly suppressed, sporadically navigated and doctored out of serious discussions about society, family, work, and visions. Were we, then, to derive a separate human functioning? In this

---

[11] Aldous Huxley, Interviewed by Mike Wallace, 1958.
[12] *Dying To Know*.

regard, documentary films produced several potential creators: they, at least, should be cross-examined to state how far the idea creators were from Lyndon Johnson's remarks, how many improvised conclusions ceded fact, and how cultural creations are historically consistent. A grain of importance was thus earned, as there are copious hallucinogen-friendly first-run films as inane and fantastic as *The Adventures of Harold and Kumar* or *Half-Baked*. Studying documentary films will add the logical principle's sincerity to spell out the practicum for understanding drugs in the light of the historical-cultural similitude hiding Victorian controls.

It would be incorrect to pen literary writers as not understanding the principle of inquiry when understanding narrative. More likely, however, we would equate the consumption of drugs with cultural, systemic, and perceptual overgrowth that held together a few interactive principles that withstood critical inquiry from socialist-formalist understandings. Supposing Immanuel Kant's naïve brilliance and Sigmund Freud's limitless imaginations do not alter the basic fact—translations of text and imagination, in their purest forms, hearken the senses that reference a pre-Victorian imagism and have us glance and glean cultural encodings that suppose theistic rebirth and an endless redrawing of one's visions and factual interrogations. Comparisons with twentieth-century British writer George Orwell are meaningful and draw upon the two men's travels in India and Southeast Asia, spelling out Orwell's stronger tie to brainwashing's role as a modern, not ancient, social necessity. In an unguarded sense, Huxley did not manifest modern or futuristic thinking when he proposed the vision's persistence. In the last sense, he did not unpack structuralism without attesting to the vision's formal brilliance as the socially redirecting factor. Therefore, it is at least possible to credit aestheticism found in the twentieth-century writers, bringing Huxley closer to a broader tradition that examined drugged experiences. For his part, Huxley envisioned a grandiose, overflowing romantic tradition of expatriate acolytes broadening the sides of consciousness. It is at least possible to say that his studies promote an inter-historical, rather than specific, notation of being. Literature, while not this book's focus, merits some re-estimation of our romantic thinking as the antidote to Victorian sciences that cement institutional supremacy. Intercultural dictums aside, it is a refreshed modernism and one convinced of learning's transparency. That science ignored its necessary studies will be answered positively through films to cover and relate logical principles to offset far-fetched reasoning that, when closely examined, will not tell us much after all.

Films and the Future of Psychedelic Science

A final principle to understand psychedelic theories is derived from film's agency, or rather incomplete transferences of knowledge that bear facts, discussions, and poignant visual examples building perspective on what should be noted. In context, the films are structurally very much like other documentary films concerning writers and thinkers in our time. Generous additions of closely threaded thought and introspection aside, I think that we ought to, at an early instance, favor the forms' popularization and psychedelic science's de-authorization. This is not an easily deduced objective: films operate distilled, pointed insights and memories about each author under their sleeve, using pictography and commentaries alike to cloak the author in the airs of potential brilliance and ultimate relevance. Robert Stam cursorily notes: "The critic must, therefore, be alert to the tensions between the directorial personality and the materials with which the director works."[13] It is rife in our angle of studies to presume the obvious: looting thinkers and writers of their materials, plus taking advantage of their collections and interactions, might diminish our sense of accomplishment. We are, it is certain, likely to attach disruptive rather than sane additions to psychedelic studies, bowdlerizing their content to favor dystopia-like outcomes. Whether subtle or composed, our amalgamation of visual, spoken, and intuited texts advances the writer's thesis while adding the humanism that criticism strips them of. More subtle commentary by friends, relatives, and admirers will accomplish the director's goal to make forms and facts popular. Because journals and letters in the authors' archival materials did not always support this general idea, an added thrust comes to making documentary films studded with the comments of friends and associates. In the early stages after the advent of the 1960s counterculture, it was important to document the ferment of these inquiries textually, thus adding to the author's reflections at an elder age with certainty about our psychiatric evolution.

The authors inhere private and public domains of greater abstraction and visual instances to harbor published notoriety that we call subsets of the work's meaning, bracketing films to comprise new, critical beginnings. Films about writers operated a controlled process rebuilding the positive hypothesis for examining new perspectives not reviewed during their times, narrowing into idealistic leaps contradicting and contraindicating socialist forms that deny us drugged agency during medieval and modern times.

I think, with findings from both the Timothy Leary Collection and the Aldous Huxley Collection, that scholars might comparatively assess the films, relating the authors' considerable work to fields of humanities and psychology and

---

[13] Stam, Robert, *Film Theory: An Introduction*, 89.

reconciling examples of public figures and correspondents who may then translate more rigorous historical studies. First, let us say that Huxley was a short story writer and essayist, and light projections of the author's political satire drew us to bold public readings and commentaries that comprise freedom, mysticism, thought control, and self-inflictions through drugs and propaganda. Yet let us admit that Huxley, as a commentator, could suppress theory and knowledge to accentuate his reluctance to change the public order. Suppression of content was implicit in the Wallace interview. In contrast, university lectures unveiled a more formidable anthropology and perhaps the recurring metaphor that was compressed into a single philosophical remembrance in 1953's *The Doors of Perception*. While it is true that Huxley did not sketch a psychedelic legend for Europeans, it is also true that his religious examinations were deeper, undercutting traditional conservatism in books like *The Perennial Philosophy*. Our task is not merely to ascertain what drugs could and could not do—or, more likely, what was the thinker's private dilemma and its typos, but to state at length the idea of twentieth-century humanity's intellectual growth away from pre-Victorian strictures placing identity in the hands of capital, and institutions in the hands of mass production, stereotypes, and financial prosperity. In doing so, we will parse our link to philosophies engendering repression as the social guiding principle. Huxley's liberated sense grew in the decades after World War I through his travels to India, Mexico, the United States, and Italy. Instead of expositions about the human subject, his short stories may paint exhaustions and illusory syntax to describe what exotic travelers may have experienced. Huxley recorded impulses to freedom and parapsychological excess during his travels to India in the 1920s. The operative prejudice, namely, that Hindu mysticism would be replaced with Mohandas Gandhi's austere, abstemious doctrine, told us that societies organize themselves to project more adventurous, internally dynamic modes of Being that socialism suppressed. When Huxley appeared before Wallace in 1958, neither did he condemn drug use nor did he fail to equate conscious control with the machinations of communism and totalitarianism. From this abiding sense, we may get a primer for more verbally dedicated commentaries from future psychedelic thinkers who were more advanced while promoting colorful and evocative details about LSD's worldwide popularity.

Films that relay the detailed work and prophecies of Swiss chemist Albert Hofmann come with specific points of emphasis in their documentary form: *LSD: The Beyond Within* situates Hofmann versus his British counterparts, while *Hofmann's Potion*, released fifteen years later, underwent the development of LSD scholarship and influence in medicine through recorded studies at Weyburn Hospital in Saskatchewan. We note not only the regional, psychiatric development of drugs but also the opined philosophical and personal brilliance of the detailed transformations. With this opportunity, it seems likely

Introduction: The Problem of Studying Psychedelia

that we might give attention again to Hofmann's sublime studies as our antidote to postmodern reasoning, which, it was presumed, would crush hallucinogenic studies. With these two films, Hofmann rejoined the hallucinogenic canon; there are ample pathways pushing the study forward and specific examinations of LSD biochemistry that will explain its rise to political-social stardom.

Films about Swiss chemist Albert Hofmann include *LSD: The Beyond Within* and *Hofmann's Potion*: they, mired with ongoing legal struggles to prosecute hallucinogen use, entail largely psychiatric discussions coupled with ample footage of drug-takers and patients in laboratory-like experiments. A good deal of footage cannot be relayed because, while numerous examples, they did not represent the angle the film's commentaries would have accomplished. *The Beyond Within* includes several experiments at a British hospital, where the patient is called upon to recall a phrase said at the time of dosage. It also includes footage of a woman who, under the influence, does not recognize "colors." In these scenes, several examples maintain the psychiatric parable, with positive and negative intonations about the LSD experience. Hofmann did not supervise these experiments and is largely absent from the film's second half. It would seem that, when combining the regions of Switzerland and Britain, we could partially transpose the idea that Hofmann was a *magus*. However, the film surveys European examples, collapsing several angles of drug debates and, if we shall, our excursions into the unknown. Nonetheless, *The Beyond Within* accomplished the details of Hofmann's stated romantic inscription found among his garbled written tales, situated in the forests of Basel: it is not hard to understand the film's essential prejudice, relating to us that Hofmann's vision or its partial poetics, recurred throughout Britain and Europe.

First-run DVDs that tend to the life and works of Ken Kesey consider at length his modernist objectives, as he was a serious writer with sustained literary origins that arose from the inspiration of writers during the 1940s and 50s. They may consider the makings of his storied drug trips and his unkempt fashion for presenting learning as the pretext for improvised experiences and casual, loose associations connected with the dissemination of lifestyles and attitudes among the counterculture's growing numbers. Kesey bore strong ties to Beat Generation writers, and his prose readings and specific inferences coincide with the maze of Jack Kerouac's rambunctious travels and experimentation alongside friend and co-conspirator Neal Cassady. Interestingly enough, Cassady is featured in some of these movies, and *Magic Trip* chronicles and re-values conscious archaeology to demonstrate what was a pushback to garbled tales of "the road" during the 1940s and 50s, and the sunrise of dream-intonations and meditations gained from colonialist beatnik adventures in America and Mexico. I will point my reference at the Beat Generation's many adventures if only to spell out both the legend and the increased findings that rebuild underground portraits in learning's dissemination, something that Kesey was keen to recast. Films such as 1999's *Tripping* paired Kesey's legend with what could be called a positive amalgamation of ideas and facts from the growing rock subculture. These accounts included pop stars and rock journalists and foreword discussions of text and imagination to more cynical and cautious post-rock heroes such as American writer Hunter Thompson, who published *Fear and Loathing in Las Vegas* in 1972 to document idealism's deterioration, and the gamut of post-modern inferential ideas rebuilding modernism's epitaph through drugs rather than its beatific innocence and suggested well-being. First-run films that Milos Forman's 1975 adaptation of Kesey's 1962 novel, *One Flew Over the Cuckoo's Nest*, may at least lend a touch of navigation to questions about authenticity. It is worthwhile to demonstrate modern regressions in Victorian psychiatry and Jack Nicholson's positive innocence when he argues for a richer, more involved, physically active patient population. In the Beat Generation vein, we might as easily find Nicholson reviving the cultural being through sports and the non-rationalized, healthy persistence when building function. What is important is Forman's guiding sense that repressive Victorian psychiatry *did not solve the conditions and problems of the afflicted, nor did they possess any symbolic engagement of patients.* Without touching the subject of drugs, Forman's visually dense series of metaphors and questions add the handle of our well-being through drug use: it suggests to us activations of being through pleasure and medicine's deteriorative stance as it did not consider the patient's memory value or his severe health problems.

Films, insofar as they include rock stars such as Grateful Dead guitarist Jerry Garcia, are, by nature, more imperfect translations of hallucinatory experiences that recall no written translation. We may, however, ask if the coordination of psychedelic experiences in rock performances called us to the historical portrait or what specific social metaphor lay in store when we unpack the deducible perceptual and visual meanings. Jerry Garcia's specific organization of his band comes through appreciably in *The Tom Snyder Show*, without relating particular ideas and with songs to guide us, I think it may be wise to count music history as rebuilding moral and personal codes when we project post-lifestyles, now functioning without Victorian guidance or aesthetic repression appending romantic selves. Because rock is not organic music, its inventions count the number of traditional influences in song and orchestration. Garcia's acid confessions were life-long, and there were, at least, in teleological terms, guiding senses that a less-than-amorphous meaning would preside over his partial resurrection of visions, dreams, and stories.

Numerous books detailing the Grateful Dead's life on the road, their pastimes, their experiences, and during the 1980s and 90s broadcasts on David Gans's *The*

Grateful Dead Hour enlightened us about the group's adventures and the estimations of the live show. Still, I could find no books developing their internal struggles to pair memory, learning, and imagination with sound and symbolism. Good analyses of the Dead's music limit themselves to the songs; with no knowledge about the fans' experiences or of the band members, we would be lost when assigning music's psychedelic characteristics, overtones, and thought-concept arrangement of drug taking. There are several fan experiences on Free Borrow, but none that could assess vision for our more passive senses. Tom Snyder's interview includes a collage of perspectives where a drunk Ken Kesey freely interprets the band's subjective content. My analysis will cover both the songs and interviews: with more in mind, it might even be possible to calculate the growth of psychedelic reasoning in today's rock n' roll generation.

Psychedelic generations reach their full summit and return full circle to questions concerning authorial and cultural anxiety of influence when we presage the ideas and mystic investment of American anthropologist and self-appointed shaman Carlos Castaneda. What is most important is tracing the legend of this very peculiar statesman who had adapted forms and techniques for the benefit of his followers. Castaneda reported that he studied the Yaqui magic culture for ten years but was still well within his critics' cross-hairs when they denied the Don Juan legend's legitimacy. It is well known, of course, when considering the impact, angle, and mesmerism of drugs such as mescaline and psilocybin, that we properly situate the academic world and that of cultural advocates and critics amidst their straight negations of content, forms, and inventions in Don Juan's collective prophecies and visions, and Castaneda's ministry that most Mexican scholars believed a fraud to secure the author's gains. *Enigma of a Sorcerer* will, through its commentators and devotees, explain the idea's level of competence and, if possible, its scholarly value while contested at many levels. When juxtaposing the two camps, it is valuable to note the partial trend away from straight criticisms that characterize socialist prose's negative pose. Frequent Castaneda critic Richard de Mille is then reintroduced within a narration that allows him to cut down many key points in the author's inquiries and include followers who state the practice's validity and supernatural attunement amidst the film's transcription of immersive gatherings. We might, then, understand in context how the film's specific scholarship and its tapping of shamanistic histories around the world held practical utility when we understood concepts such as life, death, soul, being, and self-realization. These composite ideas inform scholarship's pale; they are also, at length, ample ground for rebuilding Castaneda's detractors. So, we will take a closer look at the opposing sides and their valuation of art forms in the intriguing scene, with some inclusion of Castaneda's written texts. We come to the sunrise of an unpleasant thought, namely that Castaneda, either for gain or for personal emblem, was a spiritual leader to his followers until he died in 1998.

Aldous Huxley's Anticipated Battle: Brainwashing Versus Liberal Expositions about Drugs

When understood retrospectively, Aldous Huxley may dissect problems about the experience to suggest alternate and radicalized possibilities when confronted with intersections of thought and Being. In the CBS interview, he recalls:

> If you want to preserve your power indefinitely, you have to get the control of the ruled, and they will do this partly by these new propaganda techniques. The will do it by bypassing the sort of rational side of man and the feeling of his subconscious, and the deeper emotions.[14]

Huxley's program for enlisting others in the study and comprehension of drugs, to be sure, was extremely ambitious, considering positive and negative uses tantamount to reorganizing society and for power, control, and necessity. By contrast, however, we cannot say that he neglects the ascetic turnabouts or the high-channeled mental possibilities when re-examining one's psychic and personal involvement in trips, which stem from our extraction of memory and perception. When colleague and friend Jean Huston interviewed him, Huxley supersedes Freudian realism and interstitial formats of the mind and its memories to call upon a greater relationship and internal supersession of modern man's moral selves:

Under suitable research conditions, exploring the strange and other areas of the human mind is one of the things that has emerged, I think, in recent years. Not only is the maternal universe larger and stronger than we used to give it any credit for—but the mental universe is also larger and stranger than we give it credit for. If we carry about inside our skulls an extraordinary world, a visionary world, a mystical world, and the interesting fact about the substances is that they open the door and permit us without doing any harm to us, but this is the most extraordinary act by the new drug, without doing any physiological damage.[15]

Huxley, in his response to Krishnamurti's criticisms and Freud's expansive paradigm, thus democratized the process for engaging hallucinogenic drugs by suggesting a greater mental order and the absence of violence that

---

[14] Aldous Huxley, interviewed by Mike Wallace, CBS Show, 1958.
[15] *Gravity of Light.*

Krishnamurti claims separated man from his mental and physical engagement of the world. Moreover, this direction assumed that the world might be post-rational and that alternate possibilities inveigh real gaps of human comprehension and the sustenance of what was essential, one tracing *Atman* (Soul) to ideas, perceptions, and even dreams belying Eternal truths. This was not Huxley's lone focus—yet, we may ask if the many directions that beam from psychedelic immersion will broaden or narrow our grasp of consciousness and how telling thoughts are when stated in our rational minds. With mental-physical axes in mind, this book includes Huxley's explorations and perhaps his greater self-development, which was only partly achieved in *The Doors of Perception*. When we consider Huxley's fiction works, the greater effort is to summarize lectures, interviews, and textual examples to capture greater mental immersions pushing us forward from the repressive hypothesis. Much of this work will be devoted to modern man's positive angle. The perceiving mind's many diffractions and collisions of romantic-real experiences and data cause us to re-enter spiritual domains that modern authoritarianism censors. Ascetic man's self-perception, borne of the dilemmas of his twentieth-century rational inquiries, then causes us to borrow a greater chunk of mental immersion as the buying price for new histories, religious visions, and, if possible, transformations of Self-Society relationships. Huxley does suggest that this is a possibility and probably a necessity. Therefore, he cautions Wallace to present the dangers of drugs when controlling and manipulating one's ideas and assessments of Self. Gone were the days of the accusation of "dirty pacifist speeches": the Wallace interview orchestrates, with many answers to short questions, Huxley's mature form and his realization of man's essential problem towards freedom.

Timothy Leary and the Popularization of Psychedelic Practices

Studies of Timothy Leary replicate patterns for growing psychedelic study and immersion: they, calling on a more populist approach and a longer immersion in texts, experiences, and propaganda, might call into question the experiences themselves and what could be deduced from the findings. Though the focus of our study of Leary is bound to instances and footage from his formative period in the 1950s and 60s, criticism was aimed at him that forces us to give a stronger re-assessment: he was a checkered thinker and mystic who was frequently jailed for drug possession, adding to the sum of his output for nearly twenty years. Scholars will aptly point out that Leary was a professor who published in academic journals; Leary's study of Mahayana Buddhism and Tibetan Buddhism again references the Buddhism that Jack Kerouac first presented in 1958's *Dharma Bums*. What needs to be displayed is his positive form, around responses telling us about his willingness to outlaw LSD. If Leary had disowned activism, where other psychedelic figures had not, what was the point of his psychedelic promulgation and indoctrination? How clear were the relationships between religion and non-ordinary hallucination? We will, in short, find an able scholastic ground, with pundits on either side roundly discussing the proliferation of drug findings. We would be apt to point out that, in keeping drugs illegal, Leary chose the idea to create a separate and distinct thread of practices, learning, and territories, consistent with the underground presentation of the facts and generalist, not academic, inferences about them. Findings ought to be simple and not mired in neurological analyses. This raises the credit Leary gets for having organized such activities. President Richard Nixon's positive notation of Leary as "America's Most Dangerous Criminal" meant that Leary was a relentless, unstudied force: this moniker, I will prove, is false, with countless psychologists attesting to LSD pathologies contradicting Leary's teachings and prophecies. We will learn that hallucinogenic immersion produced challenges for psychology and brain studies: the techniques, normative enough, ensured a wealth of inferences about the mind and body that might cause us to view a more diverse practice, one not tied to any spiritual moment. Leary, then, could erase the necessity of Huxley's hypothesis: society would be organized around the principle of a single kind of immersion. I think revisiting the Beat Generation's archives also meant that this literary group's excursions with mescaline and marijuana were real, counting on aestheticism instead of science to display the tablets of learning. While this monolith was not fatal and could be considered scholarship by some, when we read Leary's own written works, we may add the questions that came from not considering his tapping of Eastern mystic texts. This overview will give us insight into how science and psychiatry could use these largely ascetic principles and inferences in contemporary countercultural development.

The left's cross-examination was harsh, choking the ferment: "Timothy Leary's dead," proclaimed the Moody Blues.[16] We may assume that lots of people did not understand Leary's scientific principles and had not thought about what they instead considered was indiscriminate drug use somehow tied to scholastic beginnings or about any one method that illustrated what the brain, or the psyche, had learned in the sessions. Therefore, more rigorous scientific estimations and of the news examples telling us Leary's very real, gnawing anxiety in coloring the words speaking to the mind's liberation reconcile theories with actions and thoughts among the multitude who had, by and large, been promised a good time. It would suit us to admit that anxieties were steeped in the rhetoric and the logical play of the time's contemporary literature. There are several instances in Leary's letters and archival materials where he struggled to efface the U.S. Government's deletion of his identity. One

---

[16] Moody Blues, "The Legend of a Mind."

crucial factor was the accuracy of the late psychedelist's positive pose, and we may believe that Leary's rhetoric, in his later years, was clipped to maintain a working identity.

Many works are available from the Harry Ransom Center: these will be examined in some detail when presenting the larger picture of what could have been a much more ambitious progenitor due to the universalist image characterizing the last ten years of his life. Mind/soul divisions of experience also depict the interviews and narration of other psychedelic thinkers, including Leary and Hofmann, while giving attention to the Eastern angle and what specific indoctrinations meant for an expanded modern Self. Unpublished materials may also be a barometer for how successful documentary films made the case for greater study. Furthermore, we ought to ask ourselves how advanced or objective the indicators of the writer's meditations and general perspectives were when pointing out the need for a refurbished psychiatry that considered the patient's subjective reasoning rather than criminal statistics that halted the redemption found in curiously formed ideations that were common to modern life. Ultimately, we will visit the titanic redrawing of world-views that is strangely common to our contemporary ethics. This theme, naturally, considers the patient, the hippie or Prankster, the beatnik, as a person who uses drugs to enhance and cultivate their positive world sense as the beginning of reformed societies. We shall find out, thoughtfully enough, that the commentators and writers had intended to change society, that their studies were inseparable from postulations about the new world order, and that political acumen was demonstrated in most cases.

Chapter 2

The Meaning of the Aldous Huxley Collection to Studies about the Author's Efforts at Parapsychology

Many published sources, as well as those in library archives such as those found at the Harry Ransom Center, target ambitious studies in film and interviews featuring Huxley as a futuristic progenitor who drew upon psychedelic immersion. To be sure, interviews target the conservative apologist who advocated greater internal/parapsychological meaning to visions, meditations, and psychic practices that grow human motions towards his conscious origins. In other examples, Huxley dissects socialist and communist evils, stating their role in furthering the spiritual exploitation of humans. The Collection miniaturizes Huxley's short fiction, interviews, and emerging grasp of the collective and East-West diagrams to project a consciousness approaching modern necessity with imperfect, slowly formed goals that spoke to utopia as a partial navigation of contemporary material and intellectual deterioration. These examples are useful to film studies because they identify key generalist themes about the human experience, its roots, and its difficulties as theorists meditated during the Industrial Revolution's decades. When studying films and documentary entries, we might allow that enough material pondered existence and inner states of awareness that they possessed a legitimate basis for societal inquiries to indicate the more mature work calling upon interviews, to sum up their essential content.

Studies in the general sense have emphasized the diffusion of art forms rather than the omniscience of human consciousness. They would benefit from complete research featuring Huxley's many talents that operated in an engine of relentless growth for his life. Situating close readings and essays that inspired the gifted young Englishman fully in flux from his travels might decipher an essential semantics, perhaps one less theoretical than we might have expected. To begin, we count the number of literary influences and also-riders to Huxley's ascension to fame in terms of the basic study—restated, diversifying spiritual consciousness and imaginations to raise psychedelic transitions, proposing a new beginning, an eternal underwriting force against socialism's growth, and more true rationalism interfacing with popular cultures during the twentieth century. Because Huxley wrote from the realm of visions, dreams, fantasies, and imagination's peculiar technologies, we should at least separate syntactic origins from their more theoretical ends to posit wider spiritual problems to freedom, the mind, and the latter's submission to modern ideologies. In this way, we guide anti-rational contentions to a greater understanding of Buddhist philosopher Dharmakirti's dual consciousness, which he first understood during his investigations in the sixth century AD. Gradually, we may decide whether ancient wisdom and immersions may dredge themselves out of realism's shackles. The inference was complex: socialist realism held its greatest influence in the 1950s, anticipating the destruction of brain impulses common to humans. At the same time, we might answer questions about psychology, literature, and philosophy, simulating a greater transcendence. Slowly but surely, mystic literary tendencies conferred certain achievements and our real operative purpose of making them modern.

George Orwell, Drugs and Modern Democratic Humankind's Future

Socialist realist criticism from contemporary twentieth-century British and American authors established an early tone for Huxley's musings about a non-ordinary utopia and the necessity of changing thought and responsibility from within. Among Huxley's compatriots was British novelist George Orwell; both had traveled in India during the 1920s and 30s, and both were puzzled by the meaning of idealism during their times. In a short story titled "Clink," Orwell laid the ground for comprehensive social re-examinations of man's responsibility and perhaps his conscious rendering of man's true nature, well ahead of his bestsellers, including 1945's *Animal Farm* and 1949's *1984*. Orwell summarized the purpose of laws and penalization by saying of the prisoners that, "It's not prison I mind. It's losing my job".[1] Orwell then retorts, "This is, I believe, symptomatic of the dwindling power of the law compared with that of the capitalist."[2] Of the brewer who lent the prisoners money that he would embezzle, he states about "the system" and its negative, grim estimation: "I think that his life was at an end, as far as any decent position in society went, was gradually sinking into him."[3] Summarizing drunken crimes, the jail's privations, the idiocy of one's transformations, and social participation's valuation over one's freedom, speaks to the West's dysfunctional moral laws and the criminal's success. Comments speak to military-industrial hypocrisies and manipulations, inverting hierarchical reasoning that placed value and prestige upon those who did not drink. The addition of a would-be informant selling out his life and subsistence tells us also that modern responsibility, though

---

[1] "Clink," From *The George Orwell Collection*, UCL.
[2] *Ibid.*
[3] *Ibid.*

filled with pages of instruction, indoctrination, and arbitration, did not answer the soul's conditions, as it had failed to organize conscious obedience by giving life to one's cerebral desires and the intellectual breaking of Victorian health and social codes. According to Orwell, what the intellect does is superior and more native to the Soul than the labors and obedience of the mainstream subject: criminals have, by extension, more right appraisals of themselves than those who keep them confined. Because Orwell was upset at being arrested for being drunk, he gravitated towards this peculiar immersion, causing us to think that crimes of the mind, the soul, and the body likely state us to be sentient beings. This inference was, perhaps, the true outcome of conservative, repressive moral and social codes designed to stop drug and alcohol use's evils—though it could, and should, be noted that "Clink" preceded US Bureau of Narcotics Chair Harry Anslinger and his concentrated dogma of narco-racism, thus targeting the reality that prohibition inveighed a fallacious moral case. Retrospectively, both Orwell and Huxley understand that society could not execute its will to manifest socialist realities and penal codes upholding moral reasoning about the subject's interdiction. In the final sense, we admit modernism, from beneath Orwell's looking glass during the 1920s, shadows and supersedes moral conservatism and socialism when it could project an ambitious and complex modern futurism that would rebuild modern man's institutions away from repressive dynamics.

Product-subject relationships are less true, with Orwell's underscored capitalism enshrining Huxley's defense of it when confronted with communism: free society would include man's freedom to dream, to use art and psychology, and to build the unconscious.

Huxley's Early Studies of Drugs, Religion, and Thought: Modernist Literary Beginnings

In *Storming Heaven*, Jay Stevens summarized the subjective problem of taking LSD as follows:

> But to use the drug for subtler ends called for an understanding of how ambiance was heightened in the psychedelic state: how certain pieces of music—Bach, for instance—came across under LSD as so holy it was almost as though God was humming the tune; while others—[Hector] Berlioz, say—made you sick to your stomach with sugary pretensions.[4]

Hallucinations might offer considerable freedom and philosophical referentiality when considering a trip's meaning. Perhaps wherein social, moral, and psychic

---

[4] Stevens, Jay, *Storming Heaven: LSD and the Dream*, 59.

data could produce a range of cerebral inculcations of fact and perception—it was also true that future psychedelic thinkers graciously extend Huxley's intertextual, international stance. In some ways, they were the outcome of his expatriate days. The dimensions of dream and vision lay wide open; I think, too, that this position should be evaluated when considering film as a way to demonstrate the conditioned mind's visual and semiotic agencies. Mind-body separations did not alter the considerable concentration of personal fact. Meanings might be controlled in the viewer's syntax and thought's private realms referencing history and brain modifications.

It should be noted that Huxley's understanding of perception is not completely tied to words or spoken phrases: there is a greater reach for visions and indoctrinations. Aldous Huxley's letters and unpublished short stories were not, then, infantile in any abiding sense but necessitate greater terminology and theory shoring up what would be seen as conscious errata and brilliance's self-reported moment that writers sought to encompass and that from which protestors and gatherings engender both psychodrama and self-rationalization to enshrine memory and vision for the benefit of a greater humanity. It might be said, then, at the outset, that stories and essays were consistent with the short fiction, bringing to light a cogent perspective looking for examples and more penitent indoctrinations shoring up the author's findings. Since it would be socially derived rather than the work of genius, and so confined to the microscope, the psychedelic film benefitted from the author's freed position. One memoir ascribes immediate, theoretically sound conscious investigations when Huxley reads German pharmacologist Louis Lewin, who published *Phantastica* in 1924 to introduce mescaline as part of a renewed pharmacology:

> By the time I had reached the last page, I knew something about the history, the geographical distribution, the mode of preparation, and the physiological and psychological effects of all the delicious poisons.[5]

Much archaeological meaning, perhaps in forms friendliest to cinematic transcription of drug trips and non-ordinary reality, rises from spirit-capital dichotomies covering Christ's ministry. Huxley had first written to Lady Ottoline Morrell in 1915 of his plans:

---

[5] Huxley, Aldous, "Good Conversation". From *Nash's Pall Mall Magazine*, December 2, 1931. From the Aldous Huxley Collection, Box 3, Folder 6.

The Meaning of the Aldous Huxley Collection

If, as seems probable, I visit my Texan brother next year, I shall certainly join his colony for a bit. I think it might be very good to lead the monastic life for a little.[6]

A quarter of a century later, on July 4, 1938, he wrote J. William Lloyd about the essential proclamations that he had learned:

"Cosmic consciousness" is probably a relatively common phenomenon which, as you say, may occur spontaneously. "Spiritual consciousness"—to give a separate name to the phenomenon—never occurs spontaneously, but only as a systematic weaning of the attention away from the cosmos as we know it—a killing of all cravings, in the words of the Buddha.[7]

Because the theme of religious inquiry was so ingrained in Huxley's writing and thinking ambitions, we might transfer some of its content onto futuristic writing and theorizations in a game of synthesis to forecast new explorations that may constitute something *Real*. Again, ideas and synthesis anticipating drug explorations appeared early in Huxley's letters, and historical studies coincide with the writing of books like 1932's *Brave New World*. In his 1932 essay, "If Christ Should Come Today," he operates a solid defense of Jesus's ministry, taking head-on illusions of spirit facing capital, laws, and traditions that exuded repressed mysticism. He is redolently sincere from the beginning, debunking Christian Neo-Platonism: "How can we reconcile the conflicting claims of letter and spirit? The answer is that we can't."[8] To dismiss scholarly inquiry means to make democratic happenings surround one's Spirit, drawing an enhanced subjectivity that no longer chained findings to words. Huxley did not hold these ideas alone, calling into question media and culture studies in philosophical works by thinkers such as poststructuralist philosopher Roland Barthes: "I don't share the traditional belief that there's a divorce in nature between the objectivity of the scientist and the subjectivity of the writer, as if the former were endowed with 'freedom' and the latter with a 'vocation.'"[9] We could speak to Huxley's works, as early as 1928's *Point Counter Point*, in which the main character summarizes art's purity and its special role in the contemporary modernism: "art moves you—precisely because it's unadulterated with all the irrelevance of real life."[10] In doing so, he would match his study's

---

[6] Sexton, James, *Selected Letters of Aldous Huxley*, 21.
[7] Lloyd, William, Aldous Huxley, *Selected Letters*, 352.
[8] Aldous Huxley, "If Christ Should Come Today." From *The Aldous Huxley Collection*, Box 4, Folder 1.
[9] Barthes, Roland, *Mythologies*, Preface.
[10] Aldous Huxley, *Point Counterpoint*, 7.

objective purity and strength against the Victorian Era's prescriptions, building testament to modernity's complexity and thrusting ascension as it sublimated its subjective indifference. In the time capsule's specific minute, Huxley tears down the Victorian aesthete: "real orgies are never so exciting as pornographic books,"[11] to cement a growing modernist sentimentality not far from that found in Kerouac's *Visions of Cody*, written three decades later. [12] He would then operate his inclusion's popular arc to deny realism to favor his studies: "The Communists are the most active enemies of spiritual values."[13] From this beginning, within modern man's suppression of contexts, he draws his most ambitious take on his spirit, including realms of memory introducing emotions, dreams, and visions:

> [Jesus's task] would be to make his philosophy as attractive and compelling as the old metaphysics based on the idea of a personal God.[14]

This excerpt liberates vision from legal and moral issue-bearers, yet is not complete in this breath: Huxley says that experience and uniqueness bore greater importance than clerical laws and ideas. In short, Huxley bypasses the Church to favor an eternal ministry conceived out of man's mental diversities and greater perceptual reach. Huxley also quotes G.K. Chesterton in the latter's essay, "How Christ Would Solve Modern Problems if He Were on Earth":

> I hide behind the hackneyed and wearisome evasion that Jesus of Nazareth had beautiful social ideals that died with him and that the Church had forgotten, perverted, or reversed.[15]

Chesterton goes on in Huxley's entry: "And so, by refusing to make rules for his generation, he left principles which are valid for all generations."[16] Presumably an answer to Friedrich Nietzsche's grilling of Roman Catholicism, Chesterton unveiled themes of freedom that were friendly with Huxley's collective hubris that determined much of his public representation of psychic ideations and nativity. Chesterton stated that Christian outreach and revivals of the Spirit, lyric, and physics did not spell out any collective idealism: "There is nothing in

---

[11] *Ibid*, 7.
[12] Kerouac, Jack, *Visions of Cody*, 76.
[13] "If Christ Should Come Today."
[14] "If Christ Should Come Today."
[15] Chesterton, G.K., "How Christ Would Solve Modern Problems If He Were on Earth Today."
[16] *Ibid*.

the Gospels about making the world a better place."[17] The summative point about Christ is at once an axis of idea-creation: "as soon as [people] failed to take [the advice of Christ]."[18] To state Christ's ministry anew, in the aftermath of legal and clerical destructions of the tenets of a largely romantic church that extolled the impact of souls, opens up centuries of scholarship devoted to dreams and visions that more correctly espoused what Christ meant to millions of people, and how that tied in with man's redemptive existence. Huxley, without symbols and themes to guide and with no pertinent evidence, when tying belief to moments in history, paraphrases these ideas in spirituality's enhanced projection, including the dimensions of mind, body, and thoughts through visions, psychosomatic control, and fulfillment when using drugs as a daily medium. Huxley's comprehensive, thorough investigation of British societies restarts when it states the Christian fallacy as the reason to examine visions and memories in casting conscious redemption as a greater, not lesser, effect upon the human race. Concepts and holy instances from saints, *per se*, were condensed into formal theoretical abstractions in *Heaven and Hell*:

> Along with preternatural lights and colors, gems, and ever-changing patterns, visitors to the mind's antipodes discover a world of sublimely beautiful landscapes, living architecture, and heroic figures.[19]

This was not to say that, in works like *The Perennial Philosophy*, Huxley did not reference saints, monks, and religious thinkers over time—though it is clear that examples in this text are weighted towards non-Western models.[20] Notwithstanding Huxley's greater studies exposing institutional injustice, too, his paraphrase liberates the printed page and posits new imagination, only to reconcile them with aesthetic *tropes* that escape German philosopher Friedrich Nietzsche's ascetic ideal, which points to repression or suppression of man's facts, and his proselytization. Huxley had envisioned a resurgent Christianity, fulfilling the modernist dictum for "earning tradition"[21] by transposing surreal or visionary experiences that rebuilt Christianity's battered, violent history through the revived tale of vision as the standard divine governance. Without deriving more from his literary reception's complex pathways, the opening pages of *Aldous Huxley: The Critical Reception* includes social change's ambitious framework.

---

[17] *Ibid.*
[18] *Ibid.*
[19] Huxley, Aldous, *The Doors of Perception and Heaven and Hell*, 111.
[20] Huxley, Aldous, *The Perennial Philosophy*, 161-211.
[21] Eliot, T.S., "Tradition and the Individual Talent."

> My aim is to arrive, technically, at a perfect fusion of the novel and essay, a novel in which one can put all one's ideas, a novel like a hold-all.[22]

Without enjoining the religious study of derivable experience, the film might also depend upon literary influences to direct research or posit inferential questions to apply psychological techniques over generations. We may find questions more appealing than answers, a key factor in growing psychedelic content. In an unpublished 1932 interview with Louise Morgan, Huxley introduces the abstract technique when confronted with modernist fiction:

> It isn't easy to think abstractly about a novel. It seems to me that I believe only while I'm sitting. I have a generalized idea, of course, before I begin. Then, everything relevant that I observe or read adds to that core of the concept. The idea acts as a sort of magnet, and all the appropriate things cling to it, like iron filings. Or take another figure. The idea is like a crystal in saturated liquid. The stuff gradually forms around the crystal, enlarging it. Mine arriving at the theme of a book is not unlike [Henri] Poincare's method of solving a mathematical problem.[23]

But cleverly stated the writer's unconscious dependence on their own "manner" and the subjective problem of deriving meaning and objective characterization from one's own words:

> One of the curious things about writing is the apparent impossibility of escaping from one's manner, You get into a certain way of looking at things, and it's extraordinarily difficult getting out of it.[24]

Within the same moment, Huxley explodes into a modernist theory about fiction writing: "Sometimes quite unconsciously, the theme for a novel takes conscious form with me, all of a sudden."[25] Thus, Huxley's partial embrace of modernism carried with it the anxiety of both re-creations and objective narrations: to build psychedelic studies, then, his primary problem was letting go of omniscience, or aptly, his attempt to resurrect the objective thinking pose about experience's disparity and diversity. Huxley nicely reduces differences between conscious and unconscious direction, forcing forward questions of man's mental organizations of experience in the general effort to navigate beyond his subjectivities. At other points in the interview, Huxley targets

---

[22] Watt, Donald, ed., *Aldous Huxley: The Critical Reception*, 2.
[23] Aldous Huxley, interviewed by Louise Morgan, 1932.
[24] *Ibid.*
[25] Aldous Huxley, interviewed by Louise Morgan, 1932.

writers of imaginary characters as "mute" and "blind" while assigning journalism's partial relevance, which may impede future writing, but within a modernist conundrum that ensures a special, de-materialized process presuming a special conscious relationship bringing together theme and memory, and therefore our difficulty at rendering experiences accurate or calculable. Modern people´s positive skills and the growth of their objectives would take special note of the antinomy between memory and feeling, building vision and experience as with the printed word. The task, too, to synthesize disparate and alien consciousness and characterizations might form a greater angle of imagistic and synthetic self-creation, mapping journeys of the mind and spirit to move against reality to suggest deeper, more underscored conscious psychological origins. I think meaning and text operate a gradient of knowledge in the films that cannot be tied to any one metaphor of personal meaning, signaling growth and questions where there might be, in the realist sense, few alternatives to derive meaning with no author. Documentary film studies then apply and reject authorial interpretations as often as they might embrace them or give them meaning. Huxley's study was ambitious, to clear the ground very early to foment the author as thinker and researcher, re-organizing human consciousness to tie together the romantic and modernist instances of twentieth-century society.

A final thread in examinations of these films discusses literature and the didactic form for teaching fiction and writing to foreword literary discussions onto the cinematic presentation. We might as well gather the abiding sense that literature influenced knowledge and its scientific debate; we would also be quick to note the contrapositive, that literary studies truncated fact and were, therefore, less applicable to psychedelic studies. In an unpublished essay, Huxley trumpets the form's virtuosity but accents this finding with a dialectical tendency to state thought-referencing as building awesome, controversial predictions about the Western people´s quest for *Umwelt* from beneath psychology's depths:

> I have mentioned the remarkable gift of [James] Joyce for hitting on the not just instantaneously and effortlessly. In his youth he had read widely and alternately, not for more aesthetic pleasure, still less for instruction, but with an eye to the author's vocabulary and his handling it, and thanks to a positively elephantine memory, he had forgotten nothing. [26]

---

[26] "Two Studies of Joyce Method, by Aldous Huxley and Stuart, Gilbe," *Aldous Huxley Collection*.

Studies of writing's vocabulary naturally enhance and develop a strong focus on the technique for representing knowledge and effectively counteract the negative development through twentieth-century fiction, which in turn masks and misrepresents the times due to the author's subjective development of themes and place. Of course, Huxley was robustly aware of his time's literary trends. In this article, he paraphrases Joyce's rejection of fellow British novelist and poet D.H. Lawrence, and we may thus testify to fiction's "fantasy" or isolate the techniques of writers such as Lawrence who drafted roguish male characters while dismissing and prevaricating man's modern necessity.[27] Published versions of this tendency were harsh, as found in *The Perennial Philosophy*. "Language is a main source of the sense of separateness and the blasphemous idea of self-sufficiency, with their inevitable corollaries of greed, envy, lust for power, anger, and cruelty."[28] In this light, Joyce's special acumen dramatizes the modern concept's deep agency and necessary synthesis of ideas and themes, promulgating its authority when relating modern consciousness and social responsibilities. It may, too, signal Huxley's academic sense that inquiries would not cease with his life and that learning erased the author's prejudices.

But there is a runoff conception: when writers value vocabulary, they might engage histories to express a more analytical tendency, grasping language's scientism in knowledge's disparate exhuming to profess archetypal reasoning in statements of fact. The film, too, may require that we embrace this tendency: as psychology was still embryonic, we would depend upon language's insight, not its passive reference to ideas and practices. The converse is true: Nietzsche did not stress writing nearly as much, calling upon European man's Greek origins in *The Birth of Tragedy* (1872) to deflect questions about modern man's authenticity.[29] The greater leap presumed in Joyce's commentary and self-analysis rebuilt tensions and anxiety when pursuing psychosocial learning. We may suggest a more concrete beginning and a broader survey calling attention to repressed histories as the beginning of re-examining truth and fact. We are likely to presume that Huxley operates a distinct modernism depending upon his notions of art to start examining psycho-science. This point greatly inflates paradigms related to psychedelic drugs. There will be considerably more, and documentary films and re-imaginations of text and interviews depended more upon the transformation's accuracy, perhaps connecting parallel historical instances initiating our social re-examinations.

Active syntax would become important to Huxley and his friends. Moreover, the absence of knowledge, too, at the beginning of modernism, may force us to re-

---

[27] Lawrence, D.H., *Lady Chatterley's Lover*.
[28] Huxley, Aldous, *The Perennial Philosophy*, 134.
[29] Nietzsche, Friedrich, *The Birth of Tragedy*.

evaluate how humans came upon their ideas, and thus their classifications and separations of truth and agency when commissioned to recover those facts. Let's now turn to the essential question of objective re-examinations of film and the films' distinct tendency to modernize idea-conceptions as we approach the new era, to not only reflect upon these findings but to state its importance during post-socialist times, calling upon the fruit of an endless populism which could fracture, and therefore redirect, authorial findings at his life's end. Because published examples include the abstract truth's grandiose format, "religious experience is something more direct and illuminating, more spontaneous, less the homemade product of the superficial, self-conscious mind,"[30] some attention must be paid in films documenting what Huxley himself had learned from the process of immersion, and add to this the question of what people could learn from his inquiries. Fusions of literary, biographical, and psychological realities are documented in science's positive growth and its necessary interface with pundits and scholars who stubbed out positive science's outgrowth to state its rational origins instead.

---

[30] Aldous Huxley, *The Doors of Perception*, 70.

Chapter 3

Aldous Huxley's *The Doors of Perception*: A Critical Examination of its Contents

There are many good reasons to underscore a humanist examination—meaning, an inspection of Huxley insofar as it concerns his literature, philosophy, and psychology studies, imparting the objective truths—of his 1953 treatise, *The Doors of Perception*. In sum, the explication of complex mind-neural and body-sense understandings of the drug mescaline breathes a centuries-long examination of literature, art, religion, philosophy, and psychology. We mean to understand Huxley's essential work about drugs as part of psychiatry in a study of visionary impulses and histories, and so the comparative East-West axes of our determinations of mind, spirit, and body to reveal truths that forecast an expanded human functionality and its systemic control. Because what Huxley proposed was so grandly revisionist about human experience, and because these impulses towards sense-control spawned visions and memories in our analysis of existence that had been roundly expressed, it becomes necessary to examine what Huxley had discovered in detail.

At a glance, Huxley builds his case for re-examinations of mind, dreams, and visions through drugs by substituting in a religious analysis that calls upon their determinations about the soul and the mind, and in doing so, partially escapes the necessity to institute objective terminologies characteristic of a science rigorously. Thus, defining what greater rational functioning might be becomes necessary, and why mescaline was instrumental in joining religious and scientific histories through the medium becomes essential. Scientifically speaking, Huxley patiently explains the drug's pathology in truly romantic terms, conjoining the specimen's scientific undertaking:

> When the brain runs out of sugar, the undernourished ego grows weak, can't be bothered to undertake the necessary chores, and loses all interest in those spatial and temporal relationships that mean so much to an organism bent on getting on in the world. As Mind at Large seeps past the no longer watertight valve, many biologically useless things

happen. In some cases, there may be extra-sensory perceptions. Other persons discover a world of visionary beauty.[1]

And then carves objective truth and knowledge into the form of one's intoxicated expression of the senses:

Mescalin raises all colors to a higher power and makes the percipient aware of innumerable fine shades of difference, to which, at ordinary times, he is completely blind.[2]

Though Huxley waxes in a conflicting pattern about Christian treatises agonizing Christ's vision as a metaphor for supernatural perception, and indeed has Christianity compress and suppress these sense-judgments. At the same time, Buddhism accepted and courted them. He lends imagistic powers analogous to mescaline in art and literature. He recasts the experiential journey through perception to constitute greater weight when considering Christian Europe and America. Although Huxley is clear, too, to give deliberative importance to the mescaline-taker's navigations, "they are visionaries all the time." Huxley is also clear to negotiate his religious transcendence by saying at length, after listening to music, "Would a naturally gifted musician *hear* the revelations which, for me, had been exclusively visual?"[3] Huxley's effort to state romantic man's growth stemmed from socialism's tide in our disciplinary knowledge, re-annexing his trend away from scripture: the sounds of instruments could be as divinely meaningful as what was spoken or seen. By lending this kind of legitimacy to eighteenth-century classical composers, Huxley partly accomplishes humanism's transcendence of religious dogma that had meant to confine and delimit the mind's boundaries, thus re-negotiating the role of the arts in one's culture, story, and intellections about the meanings of existence and experience during changing times. Divorced from the pane of naturalism, Huxley underscores a repressed growth of human actions and spirit, speaking to man's moment of transcendence of his rational-social systematization from beneath his Victorian eyelids.

The Doors of Perception and Huxley's Critique of Modern Souls

The Doors of Perception subsumes the posture of discovery under the nest of a thoughtful realism that re-appraises the human condition and the failure of socialism and Victorian science to refresh it: "Most men and women lead lives

---

[1] *The Doors of Perception*, 26.
[2] *Ibid*, 27.
[3] *Ibid*, 49.

at the worst so painful, at best so monotonous, poor and limited that the urge to escape, the longing to transcend themselves if only for a few moments, is and has always been one of the principal appetites of the soul."[4] Noticeably, Huxley maintains the critical mantle, pairing "transcend" with "escape," and refers the impulse to the begetting of "artificial paradises": thus, Huxley professes drug use's managed importance, and institutional supremacy over quests for spiritual and supernatural meaning that could not be quantified and studied. He then maintains the Victorian dictum to appraise rational existence as necessary and compelling while allowing that existence to be special and mystifying for all humans. Without raising hairs of speculation about Eastern philosophies, he re-affixes the Orientalist template in 1953:

> In their art, no less than in their religion, the Taoists and the Zen Buddhists looked beyond visions to the Void, and through the Void at the "ten thousand things" of objective reality.[5]

Though Kerouac summarized this concept in his letters and novels, we should be able to understand the depth of Huxley's scholarship, which tends to dreams and visions to the multitude of extra-rational happenings constituting an expanded mind and one that possessed both a greater deliberation and satisfaction that Sigmund Freud, perhaps in his Victorian minute, was less likely to say was essential to human governance. For his part, Freud did not advocate abandoning Christian rationalism or religious dogma as a necessary time-bearer. His testaments in *The Interpretation of Dreams* kept dreams and reality separate. We give the credit to Huxley, not to Kerouac, who had taken mescaline on several occasions in 1951 and 1952, because of the able, naturalist synopsis that had now amalgamated centuries of cyclical growth and diversification of the emotions, thoughts, and feelings in the arts and humanities. We may also affix our historical testament: Kerouac and the Chinese texts he generalized about glorified drug use and shamanism into the makings of language, philosophy, and spiritual growth as early as third-century philosopher Ge Hung, of whom translator Jay Sailey notes: "It is obvious throughout [Ge] Hung's writing that he favors civilization and refinement over a sort of a return to a state of idealized primordial bliss.[6] For his part, Kerouac's free translation of psilocybin mushrooms appears in 1961's *Book of Haikus*,

---

[4] *Ibid*, 62.
[5] *Ibid*, 47.
[6] Sailey, Jay, *The Master Who Embraces Simplicity*, 312.

> Mao Tse Tung has taken
>
> too many Siberian sacred
>
> Mushrooms in Autumn.[7]

and this constitutes a sort of modernist literary refinement of shaman ideas and mingling, with School of Visual Arts Professor Regina Weinreich observing: "Kerouac occasionally played with the seasonal reference to make a non-haiku revelation haiku-ish."[8] Abstractions such as these point to the obvious: shamans and scholars had used drugs to build language and knowledge, not to tear them down: drugs, then, constitute some of the basis for language, calling our attention to unconscious themes that have guided our perspectives throughout history. Still, Huxley's examinations underscore Christian indoctrinations that were not heresy at all: "awareness was not referred to as ego; it was, so to speak, on its own."[9] Of course, it's easy enough to base the ego upon socialist taming and subjugation of man's desires, wants, and subversions of moral purpose through drugs and drink; Huxley's specific, didactic moment praises responsibility to God over commitment to man, hearkening a much greater window of collective understanding that might produce greater patterns of happiness in today's secular world. Still, when Huxley tenders the role of drugs in social policy, he quickly cuts down drug prohibition as though using a sword: "a man under the influence of mescaline quietly minds his own business."[10] This matter-of-fact relay of the drug's effects and role in a person's life ignored schizophrenia's alleyways. Though he alludes to them and catalogs drug misuse in his interviews, he presumes that the long-term administration of drugs carries with it the science of control, both moral and systemic, in the management of patient lives. Curt appraisals of alcohol, then, present the dialogue of roguishness and sickness that told, in their Victorian tedium, that society misgoverned humans and that a more elastic control might allow us to build human life as one that can be a gradual utopia. Huxley's straightforward moment, at the science's behest but far beyond its administrative control, positively secured his gains as a thinker and the absolute moment of realization that was original and not borrowed from any academic part of psychiatry then. He, in his mescaline dreams and historical summarizations, broke with scientific-Victorian suppression of drugs by cutting down nearly all of their pathology. Huxley then subsumes his mescaline discussion under the guise of

---

[7] *Book of Haikus*, 16.
[8] *Ibid*, xxxi-xxxii.
[9] *The Doors of Perception*, 52.
[10] *Ibid*, 65.

the humanities' complex, animate re-conceptualization at a crucial instance in twentieth-century history: "The non-verbal humanities, the arts of being directly aware of the given facts of our existence, are almost completely ignored."[11] The final shadowing of purpose, which does not distinguish between vision and auditory perceptions, made connections between perception and writing, assuming the mantle of perceptions and dreaming as the true width of our existence, guaranteeing studies that would truncate or alter primarily literary studies enshrining theism as a social, rather than individual, doctrine. Thus, Huxley gave his hand at unveiling a dramatic humanist liberation to study and discover the roots of a much greater cultural expression that could be traced to Victorian culture's rejection of the senses in product-object relations defining status, class, outlooks, and perspective. The hallucinogenic idea's supreme democratism teased us with metaphors of civilizational belonging. Still, there was more to be discovered, and psychology studies should at least advocate the mind's much wider depiction as a modernist beginning. It is with that note that modernism had purportedly shrunk meaning's inscription under the guise of modern man's precedent institutions to state the call for greater humanity and transcendent minutes as our beginning for re-examining God, humankind, Nature, and culture as more resonant forces that could build people away from reason. By extension, we might at least underline the exercise's limitations: Huxley was not calling for a greater modern examination of European and Asian phenomenology, as these were now tied to socialist-nationalist dictations of truth. Instead, he quietly made the case that religion and mysticism could be channeled through this open-ended portrait of what ideas and perceptions could mean to us now. Without effacing the sure simplicity of Buddhist and Christian inquiries that preceded the Middle Ages, Huxley appoints the referential width of the human experience as our true humanism.

These ideas, in short, would be precursors to the coming counterculture of a synthesis of claims and unfinished academic dialogues over thirty years. Not surprisingly, Huxley annexes the discussion to his literary evolution by drastically limiting the discussion of other drugs such as marijuana, cocaine, LSD, and psilocybin: he offers no tributes to the development of these sacred drugs, stirring it in the monotony of postmodern boredom to anoint his special discoveries. His expression, then, in *The Doors of Perception*, operates new rhetoric and new scientism. It is not to be confused with other modernist writers who had dug deep into their imaginations to hypothesize about the influence of drugs. A posthumous warning would come from American expatriate writer Paul Bowles, who in 1975 said of the coming postmodern

---

[11] *Ibid*, 76.

fiction that had annexed drugs to its historical discussions: "It's too much to have to swim around in that purely literary magma for the time it takes to read a whole book. The cynicism and wisecracks ultimately function as endorsements of the present civilization."[12] The world of letters, and specifically those of the Beat Generation, would adopt the task of writing drugs into prophecy during the 1950s and 60s: William S. Burroughs had, by 1953, published *Junky*, his first novel about drugs, but had summarized the content of narcotics very briefly and did not give audiences the prolonged nuance of his discoveries and ideations, remanding most addicts to street life, cops, and rehabilitation centers. Thus, Huxley's admonition when addressing drugs' humanism was brave and central to modern expression.

Conclusion: The Case for Future Studies

As a partial history, *The Doors of Perception* bequeaths no sacramental, mythological, or cultist examples from Mexican and Central American Indian cultures, where mescaline is said to come from. Instead, Huxley subsumed quotes and overview from Dr. Charlie Dunbar Broad, who had synopsized: "Every individual is at once the beneficiary and the victim of the linguistic tradition into which he has been born—the beneficiary since language gives access to the accumulated records of other people's experience, the victim in so far as it confirms him in the belief that reduced awareness is the only awareness and, as it bedevils his sense of reality so that he is all too apt to take his concepts for data, his words for actual things."[13] Broad thus equates drug use with learning and with connecting with the larger society, yet mars it with the individual's isolation and perceived lack of inclusion in it. Still, Huxley robustly translates Broad's intention for meriting purpose: "Temporary by-passes may be acquired either spontaneously, or as the result of deliberate 'spiritual exercises,' or through hypnosis, or using drugs."[14] Broad accomplishes the hallucination's universality for Huxley in investigating mescaline's peculiar pattern that deprives sugar to the brain and, hence, the counterculture's professed wish to transform society by building psychic bridges across continents and classes. "Exercises," it seems, accomplish countercultural immersion's tenability: anyone can learn the art of tripping, and any psychic organism can build history and memory into meaning through its uses. Huxley's witticism pares drugs down to mescaline and peyote, and his ambitious translation thoughtfully established Mexican tenacity in its pastoral cultures that had rejected urbanism. Therefore, it could be surmised that Huxley,

---

[12] Halpern, Daniel, "Interview with Paul Bowles," 100.
[13] *The Doors of Perception*, 23.
[14] *Ibid*, 24.

when targeting the specific drug interactions, notes that all hallucinogenic drugs could be paired with actions and experiences that could be said to be meaningful through illustrations of guardedly active techniques.

Not quietly, and from the ivory temple speaking loudly, then, *The Doors of Perception* shows how science and psychiatry could accomplish, in the modernist tense, what Kerouac and his Beat followers could not: the organizing principle, and thus the psychedelic learning's objective sense without romanticism as its literary guide. I think, for example, it should be understood that Thomas De Quincey's 1821 book *Confessions of an Opium-Eater*, which paraphrases opium use among nineteenth-century citizens, was unfocused and not meant to draw objective realization and, therefore, posited drug taking to be inferior and subject versus Victorian moral consciousness.[15] Building an organized study principle, one not bound to aphorism and humor, allows us to posit drug use as meaningful, controllable, and transformative. Beat entries, riddled with anecdotes, jokes, and revelry, would not build true objectivity in the indiscriminate use of drugs. Huxley's concentrated, fairly simple study of the ancients and the moderns does this. We may, then, see the world's visionary histories funneling into one moment of totalistic modern necessity and proliferation. We will likely boast decades of concrete studies that could execute the tradition of repressed learning at the crucial historical moment as we contrast Huxley's written underscore of the essential Being and its professed introduction and videography in the films.

---

[15] DeQuincey, Thomas, *Confessions of an Opium-Eater*.

Chapter 4

The Mike Wallace Interview, 1958: Modern Prolegomena, and Positive and Negative Techniques for Understanding Thought Control

Aldous Huxley's May 18, 1958 interview with CBS anchor Mike Wallace introduced many positive tenets about the psychedelic conundrum. The interview, stated in a global context, found Huxley explaining mind control techniques to the audience, distinctly exploring propaganda techniques. This interview is remarkable in that it presents drugs in the vicinity of freedom and overpopulation, which crushed institutional governance while advancing modern necessity and overtures called for in the technocratic era that tends away from socialist methods of idea production and idea governance. Positive rifts in the interview's first minutes between capitalism and the imagination told us about the more intuitive transformation: Huxley, when prompted, says of *soma*: "It is a very versatile drug, to make people happy in small doses." Though quick to quash comparisons with narcotic drugs—*soma*, of course, was a re-invented term referring to the drug cannabis that was consumed in India— and to state that illegal drugs such as cocaine "lead to terrible results physiologically and morally,"[1] Huxley and Wallace operate a surprising, if carefully controlled rubric, giving the use of drugs considerable negotiating thrust:

> We may have drugs that profoundly change our mental states without doing any harm. I mean, this is the real pharmacological revolution that should take place.[2]

Still, while posing the question about drugs, Wallace sneers and says under his lips, "fuck them."[3] Despite *soma*'s identity in Hindu lore as the cannabis plant that pleased the god Siva, cannabis is not mentioned, nor was there any

---

[1] *Ibid*.
[2] *Ibid*.
[3] *Ibid*, 1958.

aversion to then-current rhetoric penning illegal drugs as being harmful. At the outset, I think it should be recognized that, despite the mechanisms for controlling rather than liberating people that Huxley returns to, the live interview stood as a considerable freedom and saw Huxley testify to his leonine projections. Its content tells us to admit that contemporary writers and thinkers were not given the liberty on television to speak about controversial subjects. Wallace does not try to prevent Huxley's findings: his tone, beckoning more study and development of social progress, coincided with Huxley's positive endorsements of capitalism, television, and democracy as guiding modern forces. In his turn, Huxley gives us a powerful case to foretell our understanding of complicated world processes and human-idea processes as necessary, driving, positive, and, most of all, *free*. Huxley's point coincided with postmodern and postcolonial restatements about human regulation while crushing their regressive cultural content drawn from product-subject relationships. The Wallace interview was ambitious, foreboding, and internecine, with content that spelled out the psychedelic generation's rise. Huxley suggests that capitalism and democracy can be positively manipulated to dredge human ambitions and aspirations against the soul-expression's curtailing under the Soviet-ruled Iron Curtain. In another guiding sense, the interview accomplishes what was denied to author-poets such as Jack Kerouac and Allen Ginsberg—inquiry's legendary continuities and perhaps the seriously commended dialectic of social transformations that move within humanity's social pyramid.

Huxley comments at length: "I do think that, first of all, there are several impersonal forces which are pushing in the direction of less and less freedom, and I also think that there are technological devices which anybody who wishes to use to accelerate this process away from freedom."[4] Taylor states the concept of freedom more physiologically, and with her focus on individual subjects: "freedom is rewarding because it implies control. We become extremely stressed when our sense of control is threatened: freedom, therefore, involves the absence of stress."[5] Situating this concept, at once friendly with Leary's engine powering rock re-invention and communalism, shatters socialist-formalist fetters that target product-subject relations. Further, the interview's bare rendition, versus President Dwight Eisenhower's Republican government, signals the grand re-introduction of foreign perspectives to guide America away from industrialism-authoritarianism, at once a romanticist and postmodern idea-divide that builds a refreshed purpose consistent with American democracy, without screening institutions such as government, religion, and capitalism to find our inspirations. Therefore, the Wallace

---

[4] Aldous Huxley, interviewed by Mike Wallace, 1958.
[5] Taylor, Kathleen, *Brainwashing: The Science of Thought Control*, 200.

interview was significant because the ideas should be understood and not misrepresented in the media. Organic momentum was denied to Jack Kerouac on *The Steve Allen Show* in 1959: no effort was made to realize aesthetic ruminations without sense or idea-significance, and no effort was made to understand the fruition of these ideas from working-class immersions in culture and experience. Strongly truncated content became likely enough for 1960s writers, including Norman Mailer. To present the modern Hipster meant to cloak many ideas and indoctrinations in garments of censorship, offsetting graphic representations that were unclear or morally suspicious. Literature as a whole had labeled the modern subject to be one who was depraved, insincere, corrupt, and transitory: modernism's respected column of works included F. Scott Fitzgerald's "Babylon Revisited" in 1932, simply telling us that the notion of paternal love is not real and that the pretense itself is probably dissolute.[6] Broadly stated, modernist outcomes also told us about suppressing one's rustic power and instincts, as with Arthur Miller's *Death of a Salesman* in 1949.[7] Huxley, then, performed society's supersession with no literary investigation, projecting findings and responsibility that had not endured their American transformation.

In the interview, Huxley calmly and deliberately operates techniques for inverting and repatriating American democracy at Pax Americana's height during the 1950s. The supple approach, wherein the larger world's rigors and social dynamics are easily and metaphorically anchored within notions of crisis, was unknown to many Americans in the 1950s. Polished filming techniques heralded counterculture to progress before the days of its inception, and that the conditioned mind using drugs was a legitimate entry, which did not characterize drug-taking activists' ejections and testimony in post-World War II generations. Huxley's messages operate with surprising clarity and functionality, spelling out the growing world's managerial and spiritual problems while steeped in the Communist shadows. Wallace asks, "How does overpopulation work to diminish our freedom?"[8] In doing so, he operates the classic formal minute of American responsibility and the innocence of this responsibility. Willing to address the world's concerns, the American journalist supposes the author's problems in democracy's light to funnel growth and family as anchors of a just society. Wallace also asks why we should not follow fertility and development as traditions operative in the modern world. Huxley's answer, astute and focused on themes of individual freedom as Malthusian economists had perceived them, synthesized growing threats to liberal political conformism:

---

[6] Fitzgerald, F. Scott, "Babylon Revisited."
[7] Miller, Arthur, *Death of a Salesman*.
[8] Aldous Huxley, The Mike Wallace Interview, CBS, 1958.

Well, in some ways. Experts in the field, like Emerson Brown, pointed out that in underdeveloped countries, the standard of living is falling, the people have less to eat and less per capita than they had 50 years ago. As the position of these countries is economically, the situation becomes more and more precarious. The central government takes over more and more responsibilities to keep the ship of the state on an even keel. And then, of course, you're likely to get social unrest under such conditions with, again, an intervention of the central government.[9]

Huxley intones: "One has to look at it, of course, from the biological point of view, the essence of biological life."[10] He then retorts, "As technology becomes more and more complicated, it becomes necessary to have more elaborate or hierarchical organizations. And incidentally, the advance of technology has been accompanied by an advance in the science organizations."[11] To link brainwashing and thought control as stemming from increasing communist-scientist organizations of Being could suppose the logic behind narcotic drugs' partial vindication: as freedoms wane, previous models of being ought to be expanded and nurtured, albeit within the loci of control. The point was not easily achieved: Krishnamurti would bellow with certainty about the goals of a modern person freed of violence and prejudice: "with a mind that is very clear, that has tremendous energy." Negative-toned examples such as John Frankenheimer's *The Manchurian Candidate* would appear in theaters shortly afterward, retelling us John Condon's 1959 novel about the subject of brainwashing as a complex indoctrination of torture, and featuring prominent actors such as Frank Sinatra and Angela Lansbury to document conspiracy's winds when manifesting mind control. At the film's outset, a dope, drink, and whore-taking troupe is summoned into combat, captured, and made into a Korean brainwashing experiment that "would force them to do things they consider morally repugnant."[12] The tactic would add more horrid graphics over the decades, culminating in Tim Robbins' severe terror and paranoia when taking "the ladder" as an Army soldier coupled with terror's graphics, sicknesses, and familial guilt in 1990's *Jacob's Ladder*.[13] Still, positive sympathies for man's emotions, dreams, visions, and privately nourished consciousness could be understood from Huxley's spoken commentaries about brainwashing. Huxley is not tone-deaf to Wallace's questions, noting that man's intellectual interdictions were borrowed from poverty, totalitarian government structures,

---

[9] *Ibid.*
[10] *Ibid.*
[11] Aldous Huxley, The Mike Wallace Interview, CBS, 1958.
[12] Frankenheimer, John, *The Manchurian Candidate.*
[13] Lyne, Adrian. *Jacob's Ladder.*

and strictures, truncating man's conscious pattern to introduce the wheel of modern growth and subsistence. Couched in this formal debate, Huxley veils questions of the modern man through a direct link with socialism as the negative. The basis for greater democracy, or democratization of knowledge away from socialist realism, spoke to American culture and counterculture. In this light, Huxley's interview re-introduces the world, its necessity, and its tribulations at a time of great realization and fulfillment in the United States. Huxley also restates the world's necessity and the idea's necessity to grow and prosper as we further human existence. This is done without visiting political realism's specter—and, in context, the Vietnam War, which counterculture would oppose as a potential epitaph of Pax Americana. Man's positive goal was to liberate experience, consciousness, the spirit, health, and interactions—the mind, as it was firmly possessed and conditioned to deprive humans of their sustenance, would instead grow and shake off the constraints of the twentieth century's rigorous conscious indoctrinations. Huxley's statements before Mike Wallace promised democracy's new spirit, friendly with many American ambitions, concepts, and ideas that had been less considered at the American republic's outset. Huxley's hostile tone also tells us of the waiting social necessity that courted American ideas and manifestations of this enhanced truth. Where future hippie thinkers entertain the contemporary minute's progressive nihilism and unlikely social immersion, Huxley paints transformation as regenerative, a continued underscore of his novels and letters.

The text interview does not cover Huxley's travels but suits Huxley's self-generation as an author and thinker. For his part, Huxley panned Gandhi's pietism and told of its quest to neutralize human thought, practice, and necessity.[14] Restated, Huxley was a tireless advocate of the ancient Asian man's traditions, techniques, and peculiar subjectivity as forces against neutralizing socialist gradients. For him, ideas were counteracting the mind's destruction and pain found in thought-control annexes in the Soviet Union and China. He states that the Orient's necessity partially guides how widely different traditions activate modern man's quest for Being and humanity. In this interview, Huxley also willfully re-translates Orwell's identification of the decline of Western institutions and practices that fulfill the logic of freedom, building the pages of *1984* to spell out the spirit's violent destruction and imprisonment under Ingsoc's axis. Huxley's modern grasp of the total pandemic, then, was worldwide. He spoke with patient clarity, supporting basic ideas and notes thought of during his early years as an author. In this way, a peculiar egalitarianism welds its way with modernism in his surrogate, but not undefined, evasions of modern man's

---

[14] Aldous Huxley, The Mike Wallace Interview, CBS, 1958.

destruction—more succinctly, the destruction of his institutions and the guiding hands of control.

Clean, linear expositions of thought leave less to hide—when approaching thought control and brain control, a very subtle yet well-tempered discussion, Huxley calmly laid the case for conscious exploration and redirections. It should be said that Huxley had, in the first sense, thought concretely about brain impulses and managing problems stemming from implementations of thought control, quietly making the case for more outstanding study and controlled experimentation by identifying personal and social avenues of growth that transfix lab experiments to build our record of the mind's pathways, surmising our extractions of memory, facts, and dreams to project a dynamic resolution that may improve human conditions. At this point, Huxley's pulse on Wallace's questions was discerning and reasoned: "You're being persuaded below the level of choice and reason."[15]

Comprehensive grasping and even the evolution of human identity is carefully identified in our society and others in an unaltered translation of modern contexts favoring non-systemic growth, which naturally favored capitalism and Christianity:

> You can read in the trade journals the most political accounts of how easy it is to get hold of the children. Then, they will be loyal brand buyers later on. But I, but again, you don't translate this in political terms. The dictator says that we are loyal ideology buyers.[16]

With this as our historiographical beginning, our specific knowledge about the nervous system directly interacts with complex totalitarian indoctrinations, traversing the commercial-military-religious history to trace indoctrinations to a closely configured rubric of words, thoughts, and directions that presume a lifelong relationship. Huxley's advantage at this point was not new: Arthur Koestler was clear to point out brainwashing's success as a technique of truth and agency in 1940's *Darkness at Noon*; still, Huxley was not pressured or on trial and did not feel the pinch of certain death as Rubashov did in the Soviet *gulag*. Engaging thought's neurological avenues points to a sophisticated rational dialogue written to be systemic in many examples. I have found that in today's universe, excellent work such as Kathleen Taylor's *Brainwashing* directly correlates the absolute concreteness of deprivation as the mitigating factor: "Humans with orbital frontal damage become oblivious to social and

---

[15] *Ibid.*
[16] *Ibid.*

emotional cues and some exhibit sociopathic behavior."[17] Restated in context, it is evident why Huxley operates such a clear, almost lucid, and scintillating case that Leary, Hofmann, and he could attest to. Psychedelics were employed to re-equip drug addicts and psychiatric patients. Moreover, specific totalitarian examples of conditioned moments of destruction were close at hand in the years following World War II. They caused us to know how indoctrination's verbal and physical abuse could explain recurrent pathologies. Shouldered with the examples of China and the Soviet Union as his partial composites of brain manipulation in its complete forms, Huxley widens the picture to include Western societies and the redundant programming of ideas that, for many, comprise human experience and direction. He says about brainwashing, "It's not the shotgun method like the advertising method. It is a way of getting hold of the person playing his physiology and psychology. But he breaks down, and then you can implant new ideas."[18] Huxley's abstraction of thought as a part of the social and moral process surpasses Freud's method for identifying man's conscious struggle to foretell Western democracy's eclipse and our manipulation of ideological, repetitive controls staging man's functionality and living attributes configuring the mind, and that the mind manifests itself in the body, to its social expressions of Being.

Locating the negative locus of control and subjugation requires that we admit modern social programming and "socialist realism" did not prepare the individual for society but instead marked them as a continuing subject responding to control, which crippled reason to favor ideology, again directing this angle at West and East alike. Conscious control through television and social norms did not cause Huxley to abandon television but to proscribe its living role, extending modern democratic individual aware collective problem. Statements from George Orwell were bald, prefiguring socialist realism's advent: to break free from the Ingsoc Party, one must "distribute habit-forming drugs."[19] In this way, Huxley heralds the light of man's possible romanticism and organic necessity, posing visions, feelings, and dreams as antidotes to the chains of control, helping people function without repression or abuse. Locating television, then, to be a brain-expanding instrument called upon physiology and psychology to suggest neural links to brain associations that are positive and natural, is referenced in agrarian histories and religions and transfixes social responsibility's aphoristic constructions. Huxley does not directly suggest this, yet anchors modern Beings' adversity through examples that connect socialism to democracy or instead to technology's role in

---

[17] Taylor, Kathleen, *Brainwashing: The Science of Thought Control*, 162.
[18] Aldous Huxley, The Mike Wallace Interview, CBS, 1958.
[19] Orwell, George, 1984, 163.

organizing society. In doing so, he anticipates Leary's non-corporate immersion and themes of nativity and transcendence, ones that at least had thought of Ralph Waldo Emerson's "Nature" and so worldwide transcendentalism's joyous amalgamation.[20]

In short, the identification of methods of brain control was aptly synopsized by Huxley's then-new title, *Enemies of Freedom*. Without gaining the McCarthyist resonance of this title, Huxley, in this interview, operated a mitigation of perceptible and academic truths that told of future sciences, courting a robust, intriguing start for psychedelic studies and that offset modern man's neutralization. Avoiding references to German philosophers Karl Marx and Martin Heidegger, Huxley courageously extends futurism's tryst to spell out humanism's unique, endless rediscovery through psychedelic forms. *Soma*, though not to be confused with cannabis derivations in India, forewords twentieth-century literature's ambitious decades, heralding conscious change and modulation from ideals connected to ancient drugs to answer the jet-set cavorting through drugs in early twentieth-century European expatriates in the pages of Huxley's fiction.

---

[20] Emerson, Ralph Waldo. "Nature."

Chapter 5

"Matter, Mind and the Question of Survival": Aldous Huxley's Ascension to Psychedelic Form

Much can be made of Aldous Huxley's May 10, 1960 lecture at the University of California, Berkeley lecture series: the one hour, seven-minute proceeding attests to visionary philosophy's history, notes its cementing engagements in the emerging Western psychology, and roundly attempts to delineate a ground from where academic experiences and studies rebuild the proliferation of Western analytic philosophies during modern times. The lecture lends itself open to many interpretations: evident throughout is Huxley's adamant tone that there are aspects of psychology and philosophy that ought to be studied and remembered and that techniques to understand philosophical histories were symptoms of our casual, twentieth-century engagements, consistent with our mushrooming parapsychology studies through drugs. While the obvious is emblematic—drugs weren't discussed in this medium--understanding the dent left by Victorian modes of repression calls our attention at once to Huxley's thesis that drugs employed more outstanding redemptions of our psychic Being and to visionary study's legitimacy as it traverses our cerebral re-arrangements of the mind-body distinction found in the Western analytic philosophies.

Huxley, for his part, did not separate the historical periods in which these studies were researched, nor did he note any one thread of meaning that could organize and direct our attention. These characteristics—of the region, historical periods, philosophical origins, languages, and overall contribution to psychology studies—are left out of most of the lecture. Still, we will glimpse Huxley's much greater penitent analyses that pervade works like *The Perennial Philosophy* and *The Doors of Perception*. It is enough, of course, to say that drugs were only a subset of Huxley's very ambitious conscious studies. It is more than sure, though, that re-opening analytic and psychological examinations for twentieth-century American history expanded philosophy's historiography, and at last, the meeting point of analytic and continental philosophies re-anoints modernist studies that act against mechanisms of conscious control. Huxley performed all of a master historian's qualities: he is succinct with information, building his case with very able, consistent authorial studies. This trait was not unique: Nietzsche had performed close studies of Greek origins, coolly and thoughtfully surveying disciplinary studies during the 1870s; we are apt to think that the literate acolyte draws more from the evolution of concepts than anyone guiding perspective. But Huxley is adamant about the guiding point of mind-body exceptionalism: "It is the mystics who have usually proved to be right about the facts."[1] He also supposes intellectual man's rationalist bind, in terms friendly to capitalist-socialist corrugations of the specific pathways enjoining psychology and science to favor the mind's criminalization: "Descartes postulated the relationship of mind and matter in a much more limited way, mind as being related to matter, whose essence is extension, and each mind being completely watertight and separate from other minds."[2] Socialism and totalitarianism, it would be said, rest comfortably with Descartes' ploy to separate, categorize, and rationalize brain and body content. In doing so, he rejected communalism, communication with the outside world and death, and dreams that transposed the irrational or incompletely formed thoughts. To pair rationalism with romanticism may suppose a debate that evolved and grew over time, but to say that from Descartes that the whole process is defunct and untrue gives credence to Victorian incarcerations of the mind in forms such as insanity, drug use, and anti-rational visionary practices in all the religions as well. But we ought to be quick to append Huxley's studies by noting that others had treaded the topic of mystic perception. Jiddu Krishnamurti's 1920s experiments with the Theosophy group, for instance, were recorded in *The Years of Awakening*:

> Is there any proof of religious faith—proof of the doctrines of transubstantiation or reincarnation? Where can one draw the line between faith and credulity? Is not faith the name by which we dignify our conviction of the truth of some unscientifically proved doctrine, and credulity our derisory word for such belief in others?[3]

Interrogating religious faith and the forms of spiritual transmigration had meant, then, accepting some part of the notion that visions and indoctrinations from the Spirit were not, in the scientific sense, true: it meant a return to empiricism and to the scientific principle of verifying fact and perception as the basis for understanding what could be called "truth" or the truth of man's physical existence. Still, Huxley quickly accomplishes the task's difficulty: "People with a vested interest in a certain kind of philosophy find it almost impossible to accept facts which go against that particular philosophy."[4] At one

---

[1] Huxley, Aldous. "Matter, Mind and the Question of Survival."
[2] *Ibid.*
[3] Lutyens, Mary, *The Years of Awakening*, 244.
[4] Huxley, Aldous, "Matter, Mind and the Question of Survival."

point, he summarizes his enemies' intent and conscious control's hostility during the late 1950s. Personalizing this relationship meant to state at once the suppression of perspectives, the antagonism against the mind's legitimate growth and subjective talents, and psychology's truncation or coercion of them to achieve particular goals. It also assumes, by contrast, that a hallucinogenic cult forms scholastic indifference and certainly poses this challenge to future countercultural thinkers. Thus, we can establish the regionalism and person-object conduction of visions and dreams to say that they inhered a redundant process that modern governance did not abstract. Huxley then greatly expands the meaning, content, and inferential production of meanings gained from studies of psychology and philosophy when attributing perception:

> If ESP (extra-sensory perception) is a fact, and I think it is a fact, then there would seem to be some reason to suppose that survival is a possibility if, for example, it is possible to establish some communication between people without the intervention of bodily science, and without intervention of the sense-organs, then at the face of it, it is possible to imagine that some kind of survival after the death of the body may be possible.[5]

Huxley does not operate, in short, a definitive note on this rendering, instead opening the doors to mind studies that employ vision, perception, dreams, and finally, death. De-objectifying physical science suggests that visions and hallucinations attend conscious expansion, and extractions of their content could build in us a more significant objective, humanitarian sense. This change raises the relevance of modern studies that point to expansion, democratization, pluralism, and the proliferation of human intentions. Re-treading ESP (extra-sensory perception) at this point in psychology studies attests at once to Freud's instrumental role in building psychology studies, navigating the tone familiar to liberal studies that consider perceptions that aren't common to the rational, material mind that depends upon sense-objectification. Projecting "beyond death" again means to re-anoint psychology studies in this direction or to project conscious reaches in our mind that extend beyond our sense disciplines but rather depend upon the intellectual sense's supremacy and its beliuuved status since they hold no physical component. He then ties ESP's concerns and those of visions to the brain's necessary function in life and death: "Because we know now by experience that an apparition appears to give information, [and] maybe not what it seems to be, something riddled into existence, an incorporeal personality, but the creation of the percipient may

---

[5] *Ibid.*

simply be the percipient picking up out of the psychic medium some kind of information."⁶ Comments like these promote the idea that consciousness inhered a broad imagination's generality and its wider sense of cultural inclusion in the modern problem. The modern human subject, at once responsible for disparate human histories, conscious movements, and the tailwinds of modern super-organizations into Martin Heidegger's universal moral purpose, called upon the intellect's transcendence of death, the body and the human intention that derives sense-information anticipating death and rearrangements of the mind-body and mind-divine relationships. Huxley was, of course, clear to pen the mystics as knowing something truly operative. By that same admission, he is adamant to point out the studied diversity of visions during medieval and modern eras. He notes, "I think in the cases of critical apparitions have been studied as early as 1882 and recently by Dr. Luisa Rhyne of Duke (University), by Dr. Wornell Hart who was at Duke. This, too, lends itself to the same kind of interpretation."⁷ When turning the page to the human condition's responsibility and to the duet of mind-body distinctions that tend to organize social consciousness, Huxley sharpened his point to suit conscious promulgations and the intellectual-sense supremacy when processing visions, dreams, and ideas gained from abnormal perceptions not tied to sense-object perception:

> This subliminal mind is not cut off from all the other minds, but it communicates somehow, with all other minds, the kind of psychic medium that we are in a certain sense-like crystals floating within this media, communicating with other crystals floating with this media [...] the medium, *Verwachsen*, accepted this view, maintained intrinsically, and it was not, in fact, omniscient now because, for the the benefit of the animal who has to survive on the surface of this planet, we cannot be omniscient because we were so full of irrelevant information that we should not be able to get out of the way of cars on the street.⁸

Typing "relevant" and "irrelevant" information allows us to see rational thought's penitent control as it was tied to notions of the Body and the extraneous nature of perceptions developed from visions: we may then hypothesize socialist humankind's suppression of Being in its manipulation and control of it. The idea that the subliminal mind could transfigure and transcend this modern structure, one that shut out the relevance of the brain's processing of sensory

---

⁶ *Ibid.*
⁷ *Ibid.*
⁸ *Ibid.*

and daily data, assumes that the mystics had opened the doors to a greater humanity, an abiding sense beyond sense objectification and avenues of mental processing that required historical expression. "Surface of this planet" again states that colonialism truncated conscious experience to suit economic goals; this aggravated the psychiatrists' response as they bring together meanings from history, time, places, and the solitude of man's subjective dreaming and seeing. Omniscience again gives us a chance at wholeness, a union of mind and Body favorable to worlds beyond socialist planetary objectification and freed of the peculiar science fictions that reduce the brain's novel qualities and storehouse of repressed knowledge. Visions could express the soul's freedom and greater reach into conscious human expression. Huxley summarizes the psychologists, including those such as Joseph Needham, who "doesn't feel at all that there is any necessity like the evidence to compel us to physiologize psychology,[9]" and William James, who makes the distinction between "productive" and "transmissive" studies, labeling the transmission of ideas and impulses "only a little more popular."[10] Huxley's general intention to link philosophy and psychology with studies about the mind's visions and dreams thus causes him to note the increased conscious functioning in examples freed from socialist dictations of thought and action. In his redoubt of the psychology profession's evolution, Huxley takes advantage of concrete epistemological studies and their advancing ambivalence, causing us to suppose that questions and conflicts necessitate study. It, too, is clear from this ambivalence that human experiences might be expanded and developed with greater understanding and meaning.

The proliferation of psychological technologies and treatises must be given some credit in funneling Huxley's peripheral studies, ones not tied to any one historiography and therefore distilling a greater, more operative content in modern, technological times. But "The Question of Survival" consummately builds and enforces the necessity of parapsychological and psychoanalytic studies to do what he seeks—to find a common civilizational point of origin consistent with Being's synthesis that may, in its sublime pose, offer us a glimpse at man's greater moment of realization. Huxley made it necessary to study the brain and the senses without touching the subject of drugs to broaden our scientific conceptions. To state that science was not supreme and did not hold enough objective answers to modern man's condition meant that greater interrelationships between Mind and Body could demonstrate what was true—the growing responsibility of psychology studies that should

---

[9] *Ibid.*
[10] *Ibid.*

consider documenting visionary theories that are consistent with greater parapsychology that could illustrate man's true existence.

Chapter 6

"An Attempt to Understand Things": Oliver Hockenhull's *The Gravity of Light* and Summations of Transcendence

Introduction

Imdb.com wrote the following label for *The Gravity of Light*: "Aldous Huxley: The Gravity of Light incorporates rare archival footage, computer rendered 3D animation, speculative fiction, and selections from his essays."[1] The complex array of interviews, footage, and staged undertakings of the dream of understanding truth amidst the modern era's spelled chaos is at first narratively disparate and remote from the psychedelic journalist's eyes. Renditions of study, coupled with Huxley's guiding comments, traverse his entire writing period and tell of his British origins to evince meaning from the study of his lectures, notes, and interviews. At the outset, it should be stated that Huxley had publicly engaged in psychedelic theory and praxis well before *The Doors of Perception*'s pages. The enhanced picture, gravitating as much towards Huxley's early works, expostulated classical psychedelic dimensions to be the necessary modern epoch. With short tales by sojourners seeking to understand, the collage of footage and commentaries unified and lengthened the thinker's portrait when caught in the insight's specific function and the multi-dimensionality of new theories anchoring study and query.

Commentaries from Huxley, when said to be authoritative and specific to the task of reorganizing modern man, bolster his accomplishment, spelling out a greater minute of contemplation than the later psychedelic theorists and engraving a sense of persistent authorial responsibility to the task. Studies by Huxley's followers, too, widen influence by challenging their traditional exercise and agency. In more basic terms, the notion that Huxley's thought could be studied was pleasantly accomplished and that the imaginative epoch carried away deductions specific to man's social and neural ills. Hockenhull's visual referencing of the fiction, with factories and specific technological devices interfacing with today's generation of hippies, projects an internal realism and a kind of concrete dreaming which may, then, guide us to psychedelic inferences

---

[1] Imdb.com.

inhering wisdom from works like *Brave New World, The Perennial Philosophy,* and *The Genius and the Goddess.* Literary inferences favoring Huxley's short stories, expanded studies, and detailed imageries and ideas into a new, concrete modernism, injecting fact and illusions into the mold of interfaces between pre-Marxist and modern idealism.

Gravity of Light, as it abolished scientific racism, assumes the light of a greater Huxley agency during modern times. Quite methodically and with grandiose intertext, this film told of Huxley's hallucinatory interactions and realism with visual- and text-defining metaphors consistent with our current state of psychosocial knowledge and, therefore, more succinctly echoed tales found in the "Leary Generation." Borrowing from tenacious futurism that bred occultism with the acquisition of Hindu metaphors of meaning, *Gravity of Light* narrates humanity's learning problem, away from Huxley's central texts and soaked in the twist of the Self's individuated projections, Huxley's unpublished materials, and his private reminiscences. The film, too, assembled this learning's confidence, far from authoritarian dictations and free to suggest the future man's *necessity.* Sifting forms of knowledge causes us to become comfortable with the anti-racist standpoint: I think that, when giving this film to future generations, the author's social realism may instill in us a broader conduit to indoctrinate us while using the author's terms and meditations.

A look away from the camera, too, stations a greater application of facts and principle; Huxley, in this posthumous setting, has no responsibility to conform to mainstream ideas and their necessity, further complicating the modern problem of freedom. Patient, sour, and thoughtful, modern applications of man's necessity and careful psychological examples of control replace public forms, whereby capitalism and Christianity illustrate the uniquely positive American democracy and its tendency to discard totalitarian instructions. *The Gravity of Light* did not represent Huxley's early travels or rather the penitent inspiration's sustained infancy: Blacks aren't included in the letters, and an angered David Odhiambo struggles with his ancestor's racist past. Odhiambo re-learns that Huxley's family kept enslaved people and glowers when asked to adopt his ancestor's message. From another angle, citizen groups, too, assaulted Huxley's "treacherous and disloyal way" and the writer's "dirty pacifist speeches,"[2] projecting conservative ire at what was perceived to be his opposition to American capitalism-imperialism. It can be said that Huxley's stalled momentum savors his literary moment, where there is no decisive appraisal of the facts of his studies: still, in an interview, he stated modernity's collective problem to be his collective message:

---

[2] *Gravity of Light.*

We have to attack on all fronts. I mean, we have to attack the individual human problem. I mean the psychology, physiological, and social fronts. I mean, attack the general social problem, its organizational fact, and individual training and education.[3]

Hockenhull notes at the film's beginning: "The project is not about a chronology of Huxley's life but his ideas."[4] In perusing this kaleidoscopic work, we find that the main screenplay operates a meshed threading of three specific narrations: one, Huxley's interviews, which patiently and authoritatively made a case for conscious change and control; two, the visual metaphor and its specific iconographies that project space, industry, and psychedelic development of imaginations and realities; and three, several screened plays where actors try to find meaning and certainty in Huxley's ambitious cultural and theoretical program telling about future societies at our specific instance of totalitarian crisis. Exhortations from white-robed, chubby Jean Huston, chanting in Greek, loosen critical extolling of the author's many-angled *hubris* when explaining what may seem a great scientific project. Relatives and friends elicit several angles of Huxley's parable, such as science, life, and moral and intellectual control—venturing into new countercultural forays at moments but focused on Huxley's specific vision of the modern man and his new window of conditioning that positively redrew the human experience. Actors and relatives, then, ponder the author's statements and philosophical entries that we must remember, building a strong nativity to the implementation of psychedelic *praxis*. Hockenhull then thrusts the key metaphor upon us: "Technology accelerates our progress, but this is often only a progress of acceleration."[5] Still, Huxley's idealism transfigures technology, industry, illusion, and self-representation as human archetypes, building simulations of the process by which moral, perceptual angles are closely identified, building a non-colonial portrait of the long inspiration that was becoming popular for the first time. *Gravity of Light* gives credence to Huxley's travels around the world and the author's public forms, including the Wallace interview, measuring Huxley as a thinker who has mused the fate of man's conscious identity and responsibility during his writing career. In the film's visible and spoken depth, he stands atop those meditations to suppose civilizational necessity and ahead of projections of thought control, together with drug use's positive interdiction as our necessary regulating media to re-structure post-capitalist outcomes in the human mind, body, and spirit.

---

[3] *Ibid.*
[4] *Ibid.*
[5] *Ibid.*

Huxley on Brainwashing, Totalitarian Control, and the Mysteries of Thought-Liberation

The narration of Huxley's interviews and speeches gives particular attention to brainwashing as a social technology, steadily building the case for an enhanced consciousness favorable to developing free consciousness as that stemming from the stigmatized tendency to hear, see, and know visions and hallucinations. Huxley synopsizes the persistent danger:

> Well, I meant that I described what medieval is a scientific cast system and that it was controlled not by force but by manipulation of the mind and body, and I would think that it is true that impersonal forces are pushing us in the direction of central totalitarian control. It looks as though the totalitarian regimes of the future will not be based upon terror because they have other means that I have described as brainwashing and propaganda.[6]

A few minutes later, he rekindles technology's effect as a key factor when spreading the reach and life-denying factors in government-controlled brainwashing:

> To a considerable extent, it's being done; brainwashing was already a fashion thing yesterday, for example, with a man who did much of the basic research for the work in this subliminal projection. He said it projected no great threat. But he said the technology is on the march, and we shouldn't doubt that within a few years, extremely effective methods for using this. And for persuading people to do things without their knowledge.[7]

When taken in context, the two statements add up to the Wallace interview's poetics, yet here, in this context, they are situated beneath technology's formidable stamp in modern life. To fan conspiracy theories, Huxley operated on the notion that ruling governments had controlled and neutralized psyches, gearing the way for greater idealistic development of the brain and psyche. As it was consistent with Huxley's historical inquiries, he uses the idea of technologies and experiences that could, once again, liberate the psyche from its totalitarian calculation in the superimposition of the controller's ethics. The Wallace interview appeared different: these minutes, and the supposed myriad of hallucinations and modifications of character and spirit, were within the urgency to fight socialism. Here, however, *Brave New World* operates the

---

[6] *Ibid.*
[7] *Ibid.*

necessity of controlling and counter-strolling man's happiness or his positive enunciation of dreams, ideas, and feelings. Huxley also hearkens to medieval times—this focus parallels his interest in psychedelic drugs, even with forms that stated their cult use to control and modify the supposed dialogues of the Spirit and Mind. Steeped in this rhetoric, Huxley equates the modernist dynamic with being a fighting force internally and through drugged media. This paring down of reason, it could be said, gave life to greater abstractions from the primary work, *Brave New World*.

Modern Meditations and the Intensity of Modern Revelations

Simple rhetorical arrangements of visual, spoken, and narration from the author and actors advance the key intellectual ideas of works such as *The Perennial Philosophy* and *The Doors of Perception*: a clear chord is struck, favoring philosophy over literature. Despite many references to *Brave New World*, no attempt is made to tell of drug use or parapsychology as dystopia and, therefore, not worthy of study. Interviews, too, document social change's relative urgency, as the author might have understood it. While Huxley's comments are many, some interviews underscore changes in human intellection and its belonging, erasing Victorian capital-social determinations. Huxley did not appear, at first, to be interfacing with colonialism as a metaphor for non-ordinary experiences. Instead, *The Gravity of Light* is a complex interface judging personality versus the task of understanding a greater sense of Self and, therefore, a more advanced, internally monitored reality. No direct links are made to the ancient philosophers. By introduction, Huxley talks about the current human situation from plain precepts of man's redemption away from the rigors of social and written control. In tandem, responses to *Brave New World* were designed to unseat modern notions of continuity. As a masked man appears on the screen, and as a dog looks up, Huxley reads aloud his letter to George Orwell dated October 21, 1949:

> Dear Mr. Orwell, the nightmare of *1984* is destined to modulate into the nightmare of a brave new world. The change will be due to the heartfelt need for increased efficiency. Thank you once again for the book.[8]

As Hockenhull poses criminal meditations and creation's innocence away from reason and human governance, Huxley then states his chasm of memory. The future would involve the new order's penitent suffering, stripping humans of their much-adorned relationship to capital as his agent of truth. Bypassing romanticism—meaning, in this case, the adoption of what was inhuman,

---

[8] *Gravity of Light*.

feared, and silent—meant attaching a much broader necessity that could ultimately value hallucinogenic studies meant to re-form the human race. Narrative opinions connect with Huxley's text in this fashion, as well. When Odhiambo muses about his ancestor, slavery, a breakup with a girl, and her benediction to seek life again, a big screen extols in electronic letters: "The disappearance of place replaced by the simulations of the screen replaced by the eternalizing heaven."[9] Then, sustained examples of conscious creation tied themselves to Huxley's philosophical inquiries. Commentaries from notables like Dr. Huston Smith, a University of California professor, state the author's heroic minutes: "[he] counted the ways and means to become transparent, transcendent, this was Aldous Huxley."[10] Smith then translates what the author might have been more reluctant to do—state the literature's relevance to Huxley's posthumous inquiries: "Books rich with ironies. Show the contradiction of the human condition."[11] Hockenhull, too, performs the feminine transition of identities through the author's conscious arrangements. While eating with a friend at a Chinese restaurant, a woman opines: "Well, I always ended up in relationships with older men, like I thought that they had something to teach me, and, uh, it got increasingly more difficult."[12] To state modern humanity's tensions through literature and progeny, then rebuilds Huxley's conceptual universe for today's technocratic generations, duplicating the human hierarchy in *Brave New World* to say that futurism was related to concepts and characters in his primary works.

All this is not to say that Hockenhull's videography was not penitent and meaningful. There is a visual screening of factories and countercultural fashions and the elderly author's spoken and photographed mystique while he is honing his perspective. Using classical and rock music at different points and American hippies or radicals socializing or in the photographs, Hockenhull inferred that ideas conceived in the 1920s were and are adaptable to spell out human growth. Hockenhull also finds Huxley attacking his critics from the lens of a philosopher and thinker. When browbeaten for his "pacifism," Huxley offered: "The notion that one can educate people without any attempt to educate the psychophysical instant seems radically absurd on the face of it."[13] As Odhiambo types out the words, Huxley delivers the following warning:

---

[9] *Ibid.*
[10] *Ibid.*
[11] *Ibid.*
[12] *Ibid.*
[13] *Ibid.*

> Looking back over my years of schooling, I can see the enormous deficiencies of the system, which could do nothing better than my body, the military drill, and compulsory football. Nothing better than my character in prizes, punishments, sermons, and pep talks. And nothing better than my soul, a hymn for bedtime.[14]

Rock transferences, too, are smoothened and meet with the convincingly modern videography: as the Beatles are capsuled, a hippie woman with a kaleidoscope is surrounded by chemistry formulas: "The Beatles seemed enjoyable, fashionable, liberty, experience in taking drugs."[15] There is no reasoned link between the two cultures, only that ideas and shards of self-conception through drugs had merged in the eternal, imaginative moment of humanity's conception. There is also no effort to propose any true relationship: inferences are, then, free from the author's pundit status, welcoming new parapsychological additions. Nonetheless, Huxley operates his role as the counterculture's possible godfather, gainsaying a breadth of practicable experiences and inner struggles that correspond to drug taking as a conscious agent and social controller. He points out:

> Since it permits, under suitable research conditions, an exploration of the strange and other areas of the human mind, man is one of the things that has emerged, I think, in recent years. Not only is the mental universe larger and stranger than we used to give it any credit for—but the mental universe is also larger and stranger than we give it credit for.[16]

He then adds his prescriptive comment with a total air of freedom to say that our means for governing and nurturing society envisioned the legalization of drugs:

> If we carry about inside our skulls an extraordinary world, a visionary world, a mystical world, and the interesting fact about the substances is that they open the door and permit us without doing any harm to us, but this is the most extraordinary act by the new drug without doing any physiological harm.[17]

Huxley, when prescriptive, notes that whole areas of the human consciousness must be studied and that the avenues of the Mind and—specifically the brain—require the use of drugs to underscore the relevance of man's meditations and

---

[14] *Ibid.*
[15] *Ibid.*
[16] *Ibid.*
[17] *Ibid.*

unconscious directions that may give us a greater reach in building societies exuding happiness, control, and self-direction. Rock does not permeate this film, but the import of ideas points the arrow to the coming of layman countercultural synthesis. It should be understood that this was *not* the first counterculture of the 1930s, as seen in the surrealists—clearly, the examinations point to the template of ideas and social/cultural inferences that would be the 1960s counterculture. Huxley's positive breath was, then, to demonstrate that these cultures and their axis of social determinism were organized into the affair with meaning and relevance. Society ought to change, and drugs were an agent when building that change. With this notation, Huxley nixes Victorian realism's social determinations and prohibitions: it is worth commenting that he had seen their malfunctioning wheels in his studies. Huxley then charts the direction of new countercultural media, activity, and proselytization within a note of unspecified idealism.

Through visual media and interview vignettes, *Gravity of Light* establishes the psychedelic scholar's embryonic necessity and the origin of that necessity through examples of quantitative analysis. To begin with, clearly, Hockenhull's film established a welcoming tone to the hordes of the new countercultural generation, and one that had not fully digested surrealism as it stood in the 1930s. At one point, visual scenes advance emblems of cerebral possibilities by sparring digital psychedelic images from a kaleidoscope, while disco and Indian classical music samples alternate, and the narrator notes that the images "give you any number of reasons to approach a practical infinity, a mathematically seasonable strawberry field."[18] At another point, an anonymous woman's commentaries about "the belief in a spiritual reality underlying the phenomenal world"[19] is the subject of the author's direct translation of suppositions about hallucinatory meaning and perception, staging light to be our key metaphor:

> also a great flood of light, the experience of unappreciated light, which produces a unique solidarity between the experience and the universe, which gives a tint of the basic rightness of the universe, understanding such a phrase that occurs in such a drove of a characteristic of the conic theory.[20]

In context, we can understand why Huxley's comment is grandiose and that Hockenhull uses author snapshots to generalize about visionary experiences that are individual, regional, and local. Nonetheless, in these passages,

---

[18] *Ibid.*
[19] *Ibid.*
[20] *Ibid.*

attention is given to the hallucination's systemic rearrangement of brain- and perception- waves in a matter symbolically analogous to Albert Hofmann's acid trips. Without engaging in tripping's practicum and social organizations, Huxley issues the transference of beings with the ultimate goal of transcending man's current political aptitude. *Gravity of Light's* streamed incandescence in its visual examples, peppered with the 1940s, 50s, and 60s instances of the technocratic, prism-like technological imagination in our times, over-suggests the strength of technological and global transference onto new psychedelic theorists. With an overlook of nuclear factories, scientists conducting experiments in labs, complex plastic and computer gadgetry, and Huxley's occasional voice, pronouncing the sermon-like shroud of intact philosophical rambling, *Gravity of Light's* scenery and videography profess a systemic and measured modern move into the domains of science and technology. Guiding themes, too, gave force and inference to future studies, suggesting new brain-body relationships that cause us to suppose greater societal application.

In short, estimations of psychedelic drugs' worth were brightly caparisoned with color and grave, ominous meaning in *Gravity of Light*, with the recurrent maze of postindustrial gloom situated against what should be called the author's optimism. Staged through the avenues of the 1960s and 70s, *Gravity of Light* calls upon the author's influential paradigm, situating learning without the benefit of "new" studies. This stress does not question the film's content and themes: most documentary films about writers and thinkers are clipped reasonably to avoid mainstream competition and their ideas and themes that could neutralize the film's meaning. The stress upon Aldous's heritage is incomplete and suggests future studies and immersions, interfacing with realities borrowing from the socialist moral imagination. Dense with images and filled with anecdotes, *Gravity of Light* states an authoritative problem and instances of the problem's solution.

Chapter 7

Our Dear, Beloved Acolyte and Muse: Laura Huxley's Theorizations and Query about Aldous in *Huxley on Huxley*

Classical violinist, wife, and writer Laura Huxley died in 2007, leaving us an immense library in California and numerous examples of her devoted study to her husband's theorizations and nativity quests. Accomplished and gifted in her own right, Huxley in *Huxley on Huxley* chooses to discuss Aldous rather than herself for most of the 60-minute piece, released in 2000. Nonetheless, she states many riddles, ideas, and summarizations of Aldous' text to glorify the prolonged epistemological experiment—indeed, here was our quest. Situated amongst notables that included Ram Dass (Richard Alpert), Jean Houston, Huxley's children, and many others, *Huxley on Huxley* displays and retells the wide, garbled tale of psychedelic learning from family as well as from introspections garnered from Aldous's books. This richly diverse tale and meditative interviews that feature Aldous's primary works begins with the story of Laura's career as a classical musician and her adaptation to the forms of the American jet-set. Narrator introductions give us clues about what was learned and how we might understand it without philosophical study. All this was not to say that the film is not scholarly—still, lighthearted remembrances color the screenplay, as an older and very comfortable, welcoming Laura stresses the key points in Aldous's inquiries to suggest what they might mean with or without books. Directed by Mary Ann Braubach and narrated by Peter Coyote, *Huxley on Huxley* proudly demonstrates psychedelic science's idea-creations, giving the author's wife time and place to illustrate Aldous's many findings and his ancillaries.

In scenes that include the author's grandchildren, nephew, and friends, Laura Huxley re-attributes her husband's emphasis on the importance of his studies, the need for societal awakening, and the indescribable impact that Laura peruses and admires. With a lisp and a pronounced accent, Laura confidently tells the tale of her husband's accomplishments and his education's synergy, discussing in a very relaxed tone, conscious estimations as she stars the moments of her relationship. Remarking about her Los Angeles home and chuckling when the mountainside headed by the sign "HOLLYWOOD" stands on the patio, Laura opines: "Always it was very interesting what I was doing.

You'd have some passion that told me for some things."[1] Yet when describing the scholarly apparatus concerning LSD, Laura was emphatic and determined: "You can believe it, eternity is a real thing, it's real as shit. Which was a very strange thing for me, right? Because it was not in his vocabulary."[2] Huxley's predecessor, Sigmund Freud, had identified the study's positive trend and, thus, knowledge's longevity and endurance when he examined the unconscious:

> The interpretation of a dream cannot always be accomplished in a single sitting. When we have followed a chain of associations, it does not infrequently happen that we feel our capacity exhausted; nothing more is to be learned from the dream that day. The wisest plan is to break off and resume our work another day: another part of the dream's content may attract attention and give us access to another stratum of dream thoughts. This procedure might be described as a 'fractional' dream interpretation.[3]

From the passage's contents, we may suppose that Laura could reopen many of the studied ideas of her husband and might use her interview inquiry to re-examine texts and ideas. What we find, though, is that Laura attests to the power and necessity of Aldous's studies without starring any essential practice as developing knowledge engines. With various media clips and shots of key articles about the author's work, Laura attempts to describe what could be called the simplicity of the study's needed overtures, allowing other family members scholarly input based upon the author's private commentaries. *Huxley on Huxley* also lends a secondary role to Laura's career as a musician and her books, all published after Aldous's death in 1963. She pledges continuity, vividly enjoying the openness and her seven-year marriage's seemingly charmed nature. We are not given instances of Laura's role as a thinker: coy, composed, and thoughtful. Laura lends general impulses to the steam of non-ordinary theory. She describes certain LSD experiences, including administering it to the dying Aldous, but leaves open the melting pot of practices, inspirations, and religions that drove his imagination.

At a Glance: Caretaker, Hermit, and Literary Accomplice: Laura Huxley and Literary Communities in California

The film's layout encourages further studies and considers Laura to be the comfortable inheritor of Aldous's knowledge and property. Repeatedly calling

---

[1] *Huxley on Huxley.*
[2] *Ibid.*
[3] Freud, Sigmund, *The Interpretation of Dreams*, 526.

upon the shelves of books in Aldous's library, she casually lays stress on them, later describing her yoga practice and having the grandchildren demonstrate individual techniques for self-awareness.[4] Guest appearances by Ram Dass and John Densmore—the Doors' drummer, and hence references to Laura's comment about "doors" as being an interchangeable metaphor with discovery and awareness—give learning a broader expression and proudly suggest future psychedelic drug-takers indoctrinations. Without directly engaging with the Leary camp, Laura befriends Dass, discussing the author's steadfast opinions and pronouncements about the future and society's potential reorganization. Without question, Laura's relationship with Aldous is enacted with the learning potential in a brave new world that advances conscious change. Ultimately, she is that learning's recipient, while she convinced Aldous to continue building that learning's outreach. Laura also recalled the partial *salon* that operated during her time, where guests, such as noted Russian composer Igor Stravinsky, were led, emphasizing Aldous's conscious persuasiveness while Igor got drunk at a luncheon.[5] While the film's visual anchors are not far-fetched, the compendium of interviews and commentaries builds a more concentrated engagement of literary and parapsychological ideas, weaving intertext to raise the idea's necessity. *Huxley on Huxley* is singular in spelling out the emphasis on the author's relevance and the grand social narrative that his books and interviews stressed. Though spoken messages weren't literary, conscious change had pervaded the humanities and avenues of social realism in their overview of the social experiments and the narrator's description of narcotic properties. Though Dass and Densmore were part of the living fabric, other drugs were not, and this truncates author studies as our guide to what studies were conducted.

As we turn to film examples of Aldous Huxley's life, times, and the derivable message when society approached his ideas, we may be encouraged by the ideas' profound statement as those that made modern humanity. We also accept the guiding literary sense that ideas and concepts, and thus their expressions and representations in the new psychology that expands socialist dictations about human agency, could be revisited without colonial dictations of White learning and re-identification of that which minorities could not use, to say that modern man was sympathetic with pre-Victorian goals that envisioned the unknown, and therefore its anti-racist determinations of the agency. A gifted writer and philosopher herself, Laura posits the following after three generations of countercultural pundits had transformed hallucinogenic studies and practices:

---

[4] *Huxley on Huxley.*
[5] *Ibid.*

> LSD doesn't do anything at all. LSD only opens doors that are inside of us. There are hundreds of doors, sometimes one part of us can comprehend, and the other cannot.[6]

To say that LSD was a generalizing experience and that it promised irregular or sporadic points of wisdom re-attributes drug use's historicity. Still, Laura's portrait concerning knowledge is attached to that of her husband; while Aldous's nephew, Piero Ferruci, says that "she was a celebrity in her own right,"[7] the film's text turns to the following Aldous quote: "approaching conception and pregnancy with inner peace and reverence for life to enhance the development of the future child."[8] Key metaphors confirm the perspective's unity and meaningful rethreading of Aldous's studies and prophecies. Laura also explains the details of her assistance of Aldous, "I did everything that came,"[9] then describes her transformation of former wife Maria, who succumbed to breast cancer in 1955, "[I] guided her to her death using the rituals described in the Tibetan Book of the Dead."[10] ."[11] She describes her career, her courtship, and lastly, her administration of LSD to Aldous, including the dose he took when he died. Networks of relationships are summarized with confidence, perhaps with Aldous's simplicity and progeny and even the literary impact of his ideas during his last years.

The narrator's biographical re-introductions, too, state Aldous's convincing tenor, including his statements about life, polity, and social governance. As a March 24, 1948 letter of praise comes from an Italian producer, we are given an instance of Aldous's thoughts: "The man is being subordinated to his invention."[12] The narrator underscores his commitment to human rights, noting the following:

> In 1958, they traveled to Brazil. Huxley spoke on world peace, warned of the destruction of natural resources, and environmental problems he called 'crisis in man's destiny.'[13]

Extending the biographical tale to the existence operated a natural step for psychedelic studies; nonetheless, at least partially, the philanthropic angle may cause us to build momentum for studies that re-assess man's societal projection

---

[6] *Ibid.*
[7] *Ibid.*
[8] *Huxley on Huxley.*
[9] *Ibid.*
[10] *Ibid.*
[11] *Ibid.*
[12] *Ibid.*
[13] *Ibid.*

and the necessity of modern morals and life-changing governance that can produce anchors such as freedom, well-being, internal processing of existence, and religion. Laura, the commentators, and the narrator return to the author's larger context, stating his public engagement in the world, not local, examples of human necessity and conscious interpolations. Laura is clear to build the foil, noting that JFK's death was on the same day as Aldous. But the film's reality is clear: the many intertwined themes depended upon the study's meaningfulness, its re-evaluation, and socialist realism's criticism of it as a neutralizing conscious factor concerning anything that could be called our needs. It is not an easy point: Malthusian economics anticipated life's adversity, and German philosopher Karl Marx gave credence to models of social control restricting the body and the spirit. Enough time is given to the thought accumulation and Laura's role in keeping it active. Calmly and with some deliberation, Laura operates prophecies as an extension of her husband's.

Huxley on Huxley features commentary from friends and lovers about the subject of taking hallucinogenic drugs. Friend Huston Smith was assertive about social transactions concerning drugs: "Humphrey Osmond, a great chemist, told Huxley about the powers of mescaline. The experience was reported in Aldous's book, *The Doors of Perception.*"[14] The screen later turns to a published article in *Clinical Psychology: Introduction by Lise Ostergaard.* Recorded in the typewritten page, the writer notes: "One hundred and 67 participants, 26 intellectuals, 73 professionals, 27 drug addicts."[15] The experiment's complexity and representative deductions were clear to the viewing audience, crossing social class to understand the mind's inner workings when dosed. Smith notes thoughtfully: "This was a time when the substances were legal and respectable."[16] In retrospect, we may wonder why substances were banned when studies permitted patient use and their psychic indoctrinations. It is likely that, instead of admitting the studies' value, Drug War paranoia had obliterated these findings. Would it likely that the author, having confirmed his studies' impact and communicating a viable angle for their uses, employs them to be part of a global theory? After all, Dass's summary is not inclusive and upends the point: "We wanted to save these chemicals for the use of the learned people."[17] Still, Laura is adamant about intellection's necessity, or rather its role in our path to realization, in the instance of Aldous's death on November 22, 1963. She said, "And I knew he wanted the same for himself. It was so clear that on the last morning, he was dying, and so he said

---

[14] *Ibid.*
[15] *Ibid.*
[16] *Ibid.*
[17] *Ibid.*

to me, 'Give me a neat piece of paper.'"[18] The audition provides Aldous's sole moment of redemption: "Aldous, strangely, could hear he was dying, and usually the house was very quiet."[19] She preserves the moment's uniqueness and Aldous's penitent separation from the fiction that modern science is a purely socialist medium. A hearing may operate a different, specialized cognition in the drug's administration. Confession's absence also restates the vision's completion as outlined in *The Tibetan Book of the Dead*. Attention to body, spirit, and conscious awareness is then related to Aldous's auditory tale: one's perceptions of life and its meaning, then, are tied to man's non-visual perceptions and intriguing tales about self-perception and its navigations of one's experience. Laura adds after President John F. Kennedy's assassination, "when he played music, and he went on, to a final pause. And so it was an extraordinary death. With almost a smile on his face."[20] Stating artistry and media as limits of human consciousness protects and emboldens vision in the final moments. Laura operated, then, a considerable impulse to conscious freedom—she is not the trip's subject but shares its enjoyment for herself and with us. With Walter Cronkite on television telling of JFK's death, the memory adds unity and color to Huxley's studies that opposed socialist realism—perhaps, at the moment of a new Era, and transcendence to guide Huxley into death's non-material light, the basic mission of *Bardo Thadol* in dying subjects is accomplished when eternalizing the human moment. We are only to guess about the world's future—one that may no longer stigmatize or denigrate the use of non-ordinary reality in our lives, duplicating death's reality when called upon as a historical metaphor.

Laura Huxley and Modernist Re-Formations of Thought

Restated, Laura Huxley in *Huxley on Huxley* performs the task of synergizing and complementing Aldous Huxley's studies, publications, and personal phonemic utterances that found their way to the press and published research and interviews. This was not an easy task: Jacques Derrida clearly outlined in 1976's *Of Grammatology*: "In an original and 'non-relativist' sense, logocentrism is an ethnocentric metaphysics."[21] But the pleasant, warm tone of Laura's restatement does more. Without misrepresenting the author's accomplishment, Laura expands and relates to the social avenues of her husband's prophecies without deconstructing him or spitting back any anti-authorial content and

---

[18] *Ibid.*
[19] *Ibid.*
[20] *Ibid.*
[21] Derrida, Jacques, *Of Grammatology*, 79.

practices memory's compassion ably for viewing audiences. Numerous outtakes that include friends, too, tell us a narrative tale tying together many moments of biographical agency. With its myriad reflections and comments from scholars and family, *Huxley on Huxley* commends Aldous's earliest inquiries.

Chapter 8

Brave New World: Reader's Guide: A Synopsis and the Illustration of Narrative Fact to Illustrate Huxley's Grand Cultural Theory

As we have alluded to in our reading of *The Gravity of Light*, Huxley provoked many enemies who attacked the seriousness of his lectures, and these speeches lengthened the author's notoriety. When posed with the rhetoric of psychedelic cultural theory, these comments cause us to entertain the author's concentrated response that was not open to free interpretations and indiscriminate drug use. I think, should we allow that the "first" counterculture of the 1920s and 30s was intellectually more rich and thoughtful in literary senses, we may then see the visual, aural, and physical strategies of the second culture deriving its phonemic thought from the pages of the first one, telling us of a gradual thinking process towards the unknown, controls, and psychedelic discovery's textual minute. It should, then, be argued that *Brave New World*, first published in 1932, was a more important work than 1953's *The Doors of Perception* and that literary records will paint greater moments of self-immolation to guard knowledge's positive secret, namely, that what is unveiled will change modern lifestyles and attributes. *Brave New World*, as it heralds society's positive change, takes on totalitarianism's conscious suppressions: it speaks at a pivotal moment when much of the world faced the dangers of identity suppression and had sought a conscious connection to spiritual truth. Perhaps, too, this work challenges democracy to represent our traditions, ideas, and communion as standard-bearers of human communities formed based on human rights. The natural question, "Can this work be taught?" is significant in its pretense: modernist literature is not sequential but depends on Being's abstractions.

Overview

Brave New World: Reader's Guide gives us a dry, atonal narrator amidst a PowerPoint presentation; the bullet point renders each chapter's contents, characters, and specific values as they engage each other. Theory and characterization are explained aloud at different points; Huxley's futuristic theories comprising alpha- and beta-characters and the world order as its result are explained. Science and propaganda are given their due, but, in short, the film suits quick fiction learners, providing enough information to understand Huxley's private theoretical sense about the characters and their outlook on their society. Huxley, like Orwell, penned his future fantasies in England, and no attempt is made to counter-surface the novel's geographies.

We must assess how successful this film is in teaching the novel and what sense of counterculture's pretense to living ideation is successful. Of course, *soma* use and sex are duly recorded in this reading, with the operative point that different types of people may learn to realize function by courting other classes. If anything, these two concepts appear to indicate that class mobility is a direct function of *soma* activations; no attempt is made to link the drug with cannabis, perhaps because the novel was published in 1932 before writers had studied the drug. Still, one may suspect such a connection: the drug's mild alteration of time and purpose indicates that Huxley's futurism was not so, instead depending on contemporary imaginations rather than studies behooving future scientism. No effort is made to purport visions or specific hallucinations in their physical forms; still, *Teaching the Brave New World* relays the work's character relationships and their real and surrogate justifications.

I think some effort must be made to confirm the film's statement at the outset, "By the time you're done, you'll be an expert on *Brave New World*."[1] Given the use of a toneless, unaccented narrator, our attention should be focused on the novel's complexity and its unique role in staging what could be said was modernism. In context, teaching angles for this prominent work require chapter discussions of character and action to be replete, filled with conceptual information, and filled with more derivable learning than could be found in critical summaries like *Cliffs Notes*. Explanations should also be comprehensive, targeting Huxley's root theories that go into the book's writing. Again, historical anomalies and the replication of themes and ideas found in Huxley's times require our attention to facts and description to be accurate and complete if we are to advance the novel's ambitious futurism, or rather, future societies embracing new life forms. A last point of query for this film underscores the visual angle to ask if it is appropriate to the task of the work's teaching.

Brave New World and Suggestions for Future Study

To begin with, and before we engage the chapters, I think it is useful to gauge the meaning of visual elements on the screen with this film. At the beginning,

---

[1] *Brave New World: Reader's Guide.*

a seventeenth-century document appears on the screen to document studies done by Huxley's family members in Britain. The screen reads:

> Fustily, which they make use of to cheat wives withal very lazy and wholly unaddicted, only necessity obliges them to follow husbandry: they are malicious, quarrelsome, and scurrilous (...) are generally lascivious and beastly drinkers. They wallow over one another like swine.[2]

The narrator introduces Aldous's grandfather, who "was an early champion for Darwinian evolution,"[3] and then Aldous, who "in 1921 edited the journal, *Theme*, a well-known literary publication."[4] When introducing *Brave New World*, the author calmly tells us: "We see in the book many of Huxley's interests at the time: individuals struggling against the collective, their detestation of popular culture, and Huxley's psychological intersects, especially conditioning, growing industrialization that he saw on his own."[5] *Brave New World*, then, documents the Western world's social and intellectual miscegenation as the presumptive fabric that expresses what was beyond modernism and what the mind's ideas and configurations tell us about the resilient quest for utopia across continents and in our unredeemed, bygone colonial histories. In this setting and with descriptions of plot, character, and setting, we may see how Huxley's modernism directly and flatly contested American poet-philosopher T.S. Eliot's pretensions, as the latter had laid out in 1922 the West's destruction and re-christening in *The Waste Land*. Huxley seemed keen to express modern man's mature ambitions and included *soma* and sexual competitiveness in the institutional game for control and personal expressions depending upon the will.

Tracing Huxley's roots to anti-socialism infers for us that he attempted to envision a world that had completely rejected most forms of socialism and that the characters struggle with authorities that deny them their ambitions and more naturalist sensibilities. Numerous concepts, of course, are spelled out. So the adult characters' basic plot is to grow beyond socialism's instance and presence to mirror counterculture's growth during Huxley's efforts against socialism. Short analyses are, in the mirroring sense, adept at spelling out Huxley's true goals. In one instance, the narrator asks us why Huxley tells the story of *Brave New World*, trying to show "technology's use in manipulating people, the rights of the individual vs. the survival of the society, happiness at

---

[2] *Brave New World: Reader's Guide*.
[3] *Ibid.*
[4] *Ibid.*
[5] *Ibid.*

odds with freedom."⁶ Writing's simple, clear principles are presented to make Huxley's embryonic form: our general idea, then, powers the discussion while looking at the problem of maintaining one's humanity in the face of technology's essentialism, forwarding discussions to the keystone of control as our metaphor for social change. It must be said that without the model of control, alpha- (strong, romantic) and beta- (intellectual, acquisitive) characters would not grow to function in this world and would find themselves at the mercy of totalitarian forces aiming to crush man's real impulses towards freedom. The novel's four main characters, Bernard, Lenina, Helmholtz, and John, have frequent relationships loosely roped around their ingestion of *soma*, which again holds no historical reference and is, at some point, an indirect reference to cannabis.

Brave New World's Characters and Written Text: Projections for the Future

The narrator notes the following during a reading of Chapter 5: "Bernard admires and is jealous of Helmholtz: he can relate to Bernard but is also annoyed by him. Bernard respects Helmholtz's ability to write; he's also envious of his form."⁷ The narrator then states: "Chapter 5 gives us a further look at how society relaxes and increases its energy"⁸; a photograph of smoke billowing from a refinery accompanies a plane journey where they fly over a phosphorous recovering factory.⁹ The narrator's introduction of jazz directly pairs with the group's shallow conversations; as the screen features a photograph of jazz saxophonist Coleman Hawkins with trumpeter Miles Davis, Huxley's basic remark is revealed: "It is worth noting, too, that without a sense of the rhymes, the rhythm of the music is just as cultural propaganda as anyone else."¹⁰ This was a unique bend when building modernist form, as many modern writers attributed meaning and sublimity to jazz as an art form, and as many pundits ranging as far as British poet Wystan Hugh Auden admired its take on worldwide conscious re-imagination. Naturally, should we dismiss the weight of Black forms in composing modern ethics, we operate the form's duplicity when it means to be White and Romanticist. Huxley's specific comment, in the context of contemporary music theory, would be answered: in *Music Reviews*, Le Roi Jones attested to the anti-racist breaking of forms, "Coltrane will leap over these boundaries, forgetting completely his 'sophistication' and assume for some major moments the naivete of the profoundly creative artist."

---

[6] *Ibid.*
[7] *Ibid.*
[8] *Ibid.*
[9] *Ibid.*
[10] *Ibid.*

Nonetheless, Huxley's comment illustrated his greater ambition to restructure life and humanity in our coming utopia since there would be romantic growth beyond the vein of jazz's *déclassé* situation. Of Bernard, possibly the most intellectual of the characters, the narrator says, "he never succumbed to the feeling of togetherness that everyone else seems to feel, seeing visions of height and tension and turns it into an orgy."[11] *Soma*'s disparity was activated by jazz and industry and reduced many aspects of belonging by projecting popular indifference to meaning and belonging, while the other *soma* takers felt togetherness. Bernard's specific hallucination means to pair the destructiveness of drugs with meaning's superficiality in music such as jazz, which paraphrases Black, not White, consciousness. At the same time, togetherness advances pictures of the mind's potential revolutions. These, when paired with Bernard's intransigence about his time's ideas, mount "energy" to comprise a more essential, conscious force in our redrawing, with no symbolist intellectual norms which, when crushing the weight of popular music and culture, had restricted man's symbolic growth. In this way, an adept modernist portrait featured the characters struggling with Being's modern problem, advancing Huxley's notion that current models of culture and culture-modified existence had stunted natural human growth. At least from the modernist angle, *Brave New World*'s narration affixes the modern splintering of perspectives to confirm capitalist dominance, its totalitarian impulses towards socialism, and failed human efforts to change society through drug use. Numerous attempts, then, are made to build into realism the total social change that Huxley demanded.

Character sketches of the novel's main characters attempt Huxley's positive fashion for cris-crossing their stated attributes and lending considerable freedom to paradigms of meaning and interplay. When sketching Bernard Marx, the narrator clearly states that, despite being a psychologist, he "often succumbs to petty emotions."[12] The perceived oddity of an educated, skilled worker bearing infantile characteristics complicates the Freudian paradigm of positive psychological understanding. The narrator continues: "he feels like an oddball in this society."[13] The dual angle of psychic reflection and the mirroring of identity is further complicated through the lone female character, Lenina, who is "a young and pretty Beta."[14] The narrator then reads: "She has a trip plan with Bernard in the Savage Reservation (New Mexico), and her end-line attitude and conditioned behavior will bother Bernard and later annoy John the

---

[11] *Brave New World: Reader's Guide.*
[12] *Ibid.*
[13] *Ibid.*
[14] *Ibid.*

Savage.[15] Though Lenina eventually has sex with Bernard, John, and Henry Foster, here are attempts at cris-crossing identity and manifesting negative exchanges and uncertainty to make possible post-Victorian extensions of the "love triangle"—in this case, "love quadrangles" suiting love's complexity, and the anxiety of mismatching personality types in a world where identity is bargained for as much as it is established. Complex character sketches such as these restate the pandemic, where romantic love has died, and adult persons bear needs, not emotions or beliefs. The narrator adds about the purely romanticist John the Savage: "John is an extremely moral person, building himself up to a strict code, inflicting punishment on himself when he's failed to live up to that code."[16] Bernard is cross-examined in *Love and Station* by Helmholtz Watson, who "writes propaganda and teaches" but who "feels alienation and can relate to Bernard."[17] Helmholtz and Bernard battle for political recognition, and Lenina directly implied the fault line in modern society between knowledge and power, or at least between intellectual reason and political coercion. The relationship, or rather the antagonism, was natural and, for Huxley, a fulfilling part of modernism's precipice, feigning destruction and reorganization based upon the studied human subject. The reader's guide gives considerable narrative weight to Lenina's character, supposing that women might operate modernism's tendency to overbear its hotly contested pretensions of transcendence.

In Anticipation of Dictators: Mustapha Mond

Of Mustapha Mond, "one of the ten World Controllers,"[18] the narrator opts for an identity close to the dictator's familiar portrait: "he will understand the world, at the end of the book, saying that it's a choice between this world or absolute destruction."[19] How closely Huxley modeled Mond against contemporary dictators like Vladimir Illych Lenin, Josef Stalin, or Adolf Hitler is questionable. Mond is more savvy and willing to court intellectuals and public figures when synthesizing his control, and the narrator offers the following: "Yet at the same time, he sympathizes with John, Bernard and Helmholtz, and their desire to make something better, more liberating."[20] I think that, in context, *Brave New World: Reader's Guide* did much to salvage diplomacy and idealism in the wake of powerful communist and fascist

---

[15] *Ibid.*
[16] *Ibid.*
[17] *Ibid.*
[18] *Ibid.*
[19] *Ibid.*
[20] *Ibid.*

ideologies, whereas British authors such as Arthur Koestler and George Orwell did not: breaches and intertwined riddles confirming love, station, and meaning suppose a more sophisticated world control that was unnoticed in the world at large, or instead a managing control far superior to that of dictators during the 1930s. Because *Brave New World* was published in 1931—two years before Hitler became Chancellor of Germany, it becomes evident that the film demonstrates Huxley's gift for extending positive chances whereby consciousness, at least theoretically, may grow with the help of educated people. Both *Darkness at Noon* and *1984*, by contrast, authoritatively state the domains and indoctrinations of moral and personal repression, giving much less ground to the liberal proliferation of thought designed to counter them. Also significant in Mond's control is his manipulation of the other men when securing power, rather than crushing his enemies, and parapsychology's persistence and oversight of modern man's conscious development centuries after Hitler and Stalin had killed millions of Jews, soldiers, and dissidents. *Brave New World* satisfies Huxley's time warp to envision the counteraction of man's suppression from within as it forecasts authority's adaptations of knowledge without disbarring its content.

Conclusion

At a glance, then, *Brave New World: Reader's Guide* is detailed and builds the plot summaries using critical terminologies and character descriptions to build Huxley's positive image as an idea-maker who had "discovered" *soma* and the drug's possible interface with a truly modern consciousness where idea-control had in theory matured and overtaken the capitalist-industrialist world, transforming it. The movie suggests that the main characters' paths and ambitions propose a greater world where ideation and self-development through drugs were strangely, but universally, active in some crucial way to suggest a final confrontation with authority that demonstrated what personalities of different types and origins had learned during their experiments and travels. All this is not to say that *Brave New World* is not constructed, but that it bore an ingenious context and that the confusion and conflict told us the maturity and focus of Huxley's social ideas. Futurism, too, may answer questions about the socialist/fascist debacle, far from romanticist excursions found in Huxley's short stories.

Chapter 9

Neal Cassady: The Denver Years and Underclass Developments of the Psychedelic Epoch

Several ideas are contrastive in Neal Cassady's biographical films, and enough venues of the critical reception tell of these. Quite in contrast to the affluently studied Huxley, Beat Generation writers came from poor or middle-class families and would tell of their travels, jobs, and anxieties more than their work's pages. *The Denver Years*, through commentators such as David Amram, Tom Noel, and Jerry Cimino and the narrator himself, advance Cassady's elastic moment: his friends had brought his prolific stature and development of psychedelic ideas into texts, whereas he never enjoyed a writer's or thinker's status. *The Denver Years* chronicled Cassady's roughened childhood and his parents' erratic poverty during the 1930s. It should be noted that the film's effort at canvasing a geographic, personal history from the 1940s to the 60s coincides with a wide range of American writers, from Jack Kerouac to Truman Capote, and no clue is given about what, during the impoverished period, sparked American psychedelic writing's positive fireworks. Without a college education or an audience to write to because Kerouac had adapted and published the techniques of drug immersions and reflections, Cassady was referred to in the film's text as a "muse." Dense notation and description found in Cassady's letters, though, speak to his level of inundation and transcriptions to reveal that Ginsberg, Kerouac, and other Beat notables drew many pages of their work from Cassady's persona and that Cassady was the time-honored basis for many treks to Mexico where they smoked marijuana and ate mescaline.

The Denver Years pulls together an excellent overview of Neal Cassady's historiography, his origins, his conflicts, and his travels; the basic format of visual accompaniments in the form of buildings, family and friends, sketches of downtown Denver's streets and neighborhoods, and cartoons of altered states and even pop translations of the ideas that became the Beat Generation while running alongside spoken readings of Cassady's 1972 novel, *The First Third*. Directed by PBS Director Heather Dalton and spanning three decades of Cassady's life in Denver, this film underscores and relates poor Americans' meandering spirit as they envision psychedelic drugs to be antidotes to the ills of Victorian social and institutional repression. Drugs still operate a subtle point, but the writing imagination's specific location supposes Cassady's enhanced function through drugs, and thus, vision's impact to restructure and rebuild depressed entities.

From the Letters: Profile of a Writer, Mystic, and Eccentric

We would be historically relevant to note the paradox and the supreme tension between pathologies and discoveries, forging a counter-voice to elite pundits such as Huxley, Leary, and Kesey. To start with, we find in Cassady's letters that Kerouac had referenced mescaline use by 1952; such entries are noticeably confined to pot in Cassady's own published letters. Still, Kerouac encouraged Cassady to write, only to discover that Cassady would die before his monograph, The First Third, published in 1972. Within the "novel" and its specific footage, narrative archaeology, and commentaries to ground the tale, we find Cassady sought meaning and Being through drugs as the antidotes to his poor life. We also find, posthumously, that a broad range of reflections and ideas came from Americans who had lingered and suffered in annexes of capitalist-socialist depression, denied skills and knowledge because of their poverty, hunger, and neglect. *The Denver Years* attempts to raise Cassady to the status of psychedelic progenitor and as a thinker who had assessed his deficiencies and possibilities for personal growth. Binary ellipses between identity and function in one's social experiences were Cassady's spoken-of brilliance, with family members extolling his virtues in his persuasions and life. At the same time, friends and colleagues echoed his uncrowned, unpublished achievement as a potential muse, spreading his doctrine of Love without qualms.

Unsurprisingly, *The First Third* pointed thoughtfully to poor life's gnawing problems and deteriorative fashion, and like Huxley and Orwell, anoints the idea that human beings could be rehabilitated through drug use:

> The Army life further awakened Neal (Sr.); thrown into induction, he had neither smoked nor drank; now he began doing both. He discovered the existence of whores, and in a short time, contracted a disease to which they are prone.[1]

Three decades later, he appears to ditch his friendship with poet Allen Ginsberg, stating the following about the potential psychedelic immersion they had become casually accented towards:

> You rave about "objectivity" and "sacrament,"—I've got that, it's only I felt unable to live and commune that way with you (or anyone) that has

---

[1] *The First Third*, 12-13.

motivated my seemingly false attitude toward you. So, you see, we must understand and move on.[2]

Because Cassady was poor throughout his life and justified himself as a traveler, and because Beat Generation writers had endured the pages of "sacrament" by this time in their writings, Cassady likely envisioned an independent direction for ideas and imaginations that involved taking drugs. It continued letters to Ginsberg and Kerouac documenting Cassady's sublime prose and his prized stress on intoxication as an elevated, greatened state that interfaced with "the road" and its connections. The Cassady family's specific biographical examples, together with those that screen Denver as a host city for the myriad of activities that will, in their course, advance resonant instances of depression, opportunity, and anxiety. Denver is caught in the depressed time's barbed wire and its peculiar inspirations, with the film juxtaposing the rise of clichéd institutions and complexities common to poor neighborhoods alongside the inventive contrast to modern man's tactic for making it in love and society in the changing, post-Victorian world that was spreading its rays of invention through working-class, poor creations of spirit. Because these were comically and depressively arranged in post-Beatnik writer Truman Capote's 1966 non-fiction novel, *In Cold Blood*, where beatnik adventuring was a license to murder and to cash bad checks, we may believe that an abundance of stories spell out modern American man's struggle with inventions and idea-creations as mechanization and urbanism developed, challenging the twentieth century's widespread agrarian unhappiness.[3]

Neal Cassady's Anxiety of Authorship: Detailing the Beginnings of Modern Man's Psychedelic Problem

In a March 17, 1951 letter to Ginsberg, Cassady coughs up the opined direction of the Beat Generation by succumbing and relenting the task of writing a book: "The real reason I don't write is because there is so much to say and if I begin I get hung detailing everything, and that's too goddam much work."[4] Letters to Kerouac, such as the one sent concerning Cassady's trip to Los Angeles on February 13, 1951, marked the tone for a modernist progenitor. The letter, filled with color, light, transcendence, and urban movement and place, set the tone advancing Kerouac's growing fictional ramble and his modernist tightness calculating the forms of his inner tremors and the joys of his human spirit.[5]

---

[2] Cassady, Neal, *Collected Letters*, 37.
[3] Capote, Truman, *In Cold Blood*.
[4] *Collected Letters*, 286.
[5] *Ibid*, 284.

Kerouac's "spontaneous prose," in its shrouds of ambition and devotion, absorbed this inference when *On the Road* was published in 1957. These ideas were humorously and depressively recast around when he would write *Visions of Cody* that year.

Within the larger circle's elastic context, it remains to be seen what specific ideas accomplished the Beat Generation's attention to drugs and what we could learn from Cassady's excursions, which were prolific and spoke to his life skills' rehabilitation and his quest for knowledge awareness that poverty, intoxication, and insecurity had riddled and subjected at many points. As friend Jerry Cimino talks next to a scrolled copy of Ginsberg's "Howl," which proudly announces the group's immersion with "peyotl solidities,"[6] we are led through the specific textualism and videography of both Cassady's family and Denver itself, contrasting and linking the city's prosperity with the persistence of "houses of ill repute" and a stream of drunkards and homeless citizens roaming Larimer Street. In these instances, the engaging, tricky, and reflective Cassady has confirmed Huxley's basic hypothesis: a society borne of the body's deterioration would find new avenues to express itself.

In a series of letters to Allen Ginsberg and Jack Kerouac during the last days of 1950, Cassady executes penitent anxiety and composed rebuilding of transcendental realism with drugs, tightening and broadening the perception of what American philosopher Ralph Waldo Emerson may have more generally applied to the philosophy. The letter to Kerouac partly expresses a "t"(tea) dream and the ambiguity of discoveries that build the sensation of light and color as gradual forces in one's actions. The letter to Ginsberg appears to be his closest engagement, with examples telling the difficulty of psychiatric facts and the broader use of the senses to realize one's social and personal Being. Cassady's rustic-fenced abbreviation of Emerson's ideas about "Soul" and "Nature" are told with abstract sincerity:

> "Soul" for the man who has advanced from mere living and feeling to the alert and observant state is an image derived from quite primary experiences of life and death (…). A soul image is never anything but the image of *one* quite definite soul. No observer can ever step outside the conditions and the limitations of his time and circle, whatever it may be that he "knows" in itself, involves in all cases choice.[7]

Such intonations of what sprung from an Emersonian axis of perception and reflection may tell us that Cassady's program was ambitious, focused on

---

[6] *Neal Cassady: The Denver Years*.
[7] Cassady, Neal, *Selected Letters*, 212-13.

perception as the reviving cultural force that enlivened one's anticipated Being and physiological and neural growth to counter depression and sickness. These glowing reports would add to the question of whether or not Cassady understood transcendentalism better than Kerouac, who hung poetic foliage and meter to beautify and christen his verses. Still, an abiding moniker for dope-tripping would also be examined in scientific detail:

> "How does one begin to go about finding out what a dope addict feels, thinks, or would want to confess, objectively?—i.e., how does his clinical scientific method peer into the addict's being? How can one begin to know, let alone write about the conviction that precedes any confession, how they came about?[8]

Tailing William S. Burroughs's studies that would bear fruit a few years later counter-illustrates Cassady's particular venom when he places marijuana above the lens of introspection to advance a wider psychiatric dream that considers Cassady's specific theories about interaction and meditation sequences favorable to a non-Victorian-psychology that did not separate mind and body. Based upon these examples, we dourly ask ourselves what *The Denver Years* could tell us about the author's accomplishments and place in psychiatry. By telling the frame tale as an amalgamation of urban depression and alcoholism and then of delinquent man's functional revival through crime and revelry, we raise American psychedelic culture's spectacle above the poor man's depths of suppression, and thus his remanding to repressive psychiatry. With a deeper wound in Victorian dictations of science and control, we could then expose a greater materiality and drug use alternative to the violence and abuse common to poor Americans. *The Denver Years* laid the formidable ground for excavations of working man's tenacity and ambivalences: the 1 hour, 28-minute tape gave us numerous examples and sub-narratives that spoke to Huxley's general inquiries about history, society, and doctrines of control, brushing past the cautionary tale that Orwell favored.

From his Friends: Unsolicited Praise

As in other psychedelic documentary films, *The Denver Years* includes the narrator's historical generalization of fact: "Neal Cassady can be the foundation for the Beat Generation, and set the wheels in motion for the founding of a counterculture, and that would open up the floodgates of freethinkers to

---

[8] *Ibid*, 201-2.

follow."[9] Comments from Beat friend and musician David Amram are equally ambitious, exhuming the dimensions of mythology:

> We'll have a whole new picture of a new person who influenced not only Jack Kerouac but many other people. And an authentic American original and a mythological figure of the insane, kleptomaniac car-thief speed driver will be replaced by an extraordinary person.[10]

Still, comments from Cassady's wife, Carolyn Cassady, state the film's intentions more thoughtfully and to the point of extracting and building psychedelic insight. Carolyn first tells of the belated author's fundamental idea of the impact of travels, drug tripping, and so on: "he was way ahead of everybody."[11] Still, Carolyn is quick to guard the would-be writer's identity and *ethos* when talking about Kerouac's monolithic novel, On the Road:" (Neal Cassady) hated Dean Moriarty because he felt that Kerouac was celebrating parts of his character that Cassady was trying to overcome."[12]

Amram is adamant on praise, suggesting a greater involvement that begets science and speculation: "Almost anything he did within anybody makes a vivid memory, and they would take whatever—he was such a vibrant guy, brilliant personality."[13] As the tape gradually situates portraits of Cassady and his Beat Generation friends hanging out in Denver's burgeoning landscapes, passing by his Larimer Street haunt and happily talking about the church group's imaged memory of churches, Amram stresses the impact of Cassady's imaginations, memories, and conceptual understandings on coming generations and its fixed poetic transmission of ideas and adaptations friendly to drug tripping. "Brilliant," certainly, supposed accurate translation of psychedelic histories and visionary ideations: it meant that Cassady had calculated much of the narcotic impact of his friend's writings and could abstract those ideas. "Overcoming" his narrated Self means his immersive depth and what could be learned or acted against in one's manifestation of Being. Carolyn does not allude to the focus of Cassady's research and philosophies, accentuating their importance without unveiling Cassady as a scholar. No excavation is given of books he had read, so there were purer vagrant origins that escaped psychology studies.

---

[9] *Neal Cassady: The Denver Years.*
[10] *Ibid.*
[11] *Ibid.*
[12] *Ibid.*
[13] *Ibid.*

Neal's Origins, Childhood, and Religious and Personal Experiences

The film's historiography, centered on Neal's origins and includes excerpts from *The First Third* to document his extensive ethnography, stylistic technique, and generative ideas concerning his hometown, Denver, both illustrate down-and-out sublimity and are trained to execute his narrative technique, one that supposes his ability to write about drugs and the drugged narrative that stresses place, emotions, colors, and human sympathies. Reasoned in narrative contexts, Cassady's emulations of buildings, technologies, and adaptation attempt to capture the period and cast forth the illuminative technique involving drugs that could revive human characteristics from the real-life dungeon of Victorian scientific control. The mechanized dialect's situations are common in *The Denver Years*: the narrator reports that "Neal, Sr. bought a Ford truck and built by himself an unaccountable constructiveness, neither anticipated nor repeated a top-heavy household, a sloping roof, the truck's 2-ton bed," turning its image into a cumbersome truck contraption that illustrated the adaptive talent of Neal's father.[14] The movie's narrative then turns to the difficulties and hardened Great Depression Era setting, zeroing in on Larimer Street, church rehabilitation programs for alcoholics, whores, and homeless people, and Cassady's special, contrived devotion to writing and study. Specific examples of Cassady's narrations, heavy with material description and familiar, penitent Beat stresses on emotion and feeling, are found in his thought-colored walking of Denver's streets:

> We went up to 17th Street, to the newly created Federal Reserve Bank with its passive marble square yard, and the left turn along the block of Arapahoe Street poorhouses that I later feature noisy sheet-metal shops and motorcycle showrooms and garages and up to Champa Street, with the mighty colonnade structure of the post office. I made paradox of the puzzling proverb carved in its granite caution against too much rest while offering it freely—desire rest, but desire not too much. I scampered in a weakening run of the pleated sides of every enormous column fronted Stout. Across California Street, go in the alley behind the basement church, the Holy Ghost, where I once served a year as an altar boy without missing a day.[15]

Neal Cassady: The Denver Years, in its arrangement of buildings, fronts, and street signs, casts the reading as a kind of "trip," forwarding questions about Beat authenticity. In short, Neal's transcendences base themselves on the city's

---

[14] *Ibid.*
[15] *Ibid.*

material constructions and vastness that curiously provoke his emotions and biographical wisdom. Written alongside Kerouac's diction in his "spontaneous prose," they elicit similar didactic forms of civilization's aliveness and perception and the subject's humble inclusion. Many analogous passages can be found in *On the Road* and *Desolation Angels*: what is clear, of course, is that Cassady's specific, individual personal identity creates meaning and width to his navigation of the city's streets. We would be apt to point out that memory-producing visions document the elder Beat's invention of the technique ahead of Kerouac. We could as easily suppose that writing and dreaming are antidotes to a poor life, rehabilitating the human imprint through drugs at a later stage of one's life.

By professing Cassady's historiography and personal life, *Neal Cassady: The Denver Years* attempts to compress, and therefore intensely correlate, the story of his imagination and potential written ability to engender the basic facts of his poor life: alcoholism, beatings, physical poverty, and irrational, pained inspiration. His suffering, restated in basic ideological terms, contributes much of the liberating force of his ambitious, dense studies of human thought, evolution, and psychiatry. *The Denver Years* patiently traces the young Cassady's travels, his stays with his father and brothers who beat him, the dingy, depressed Denver streets, and the vagrants and working poor who lingered on them as winos and prostitutes. A key binding of the detailed data of Denver slums occurred when he experienced hallucinations, presuming that Cassady later took drugs to re-examine and transcend his specific descents into pain from his half-brother Jimmy's beatings and amidst the years of total neglect:

> These claustrophobic experiences caused another reaction. Even more unusual, less easy to explain the reeling of my senses caused, I imagine, by an off-balance wheel rolling around with close clearance increasing in tempo, set up a loose fan-like vibration as it rotated in an ever-tightening flutter.[16]

The screenplay then turns from a cartoon of a man with coils running around his face to a picture of William S. Burroughs, surmising the following:

> Both Cassady and Burroughs believed that these childhood nightmares evolved into a drug-induced hunger to recapture the strange fluidity of time.[17]

---

[16] *Ibid.*
[17] *Ibid.*

Though Burroughs's childhood may cause us to underscore learning's controversial nature when it is through drugs, "megalomaniac tendencies were located in the child's internal struggles,"[18] we may note the working-class Cassady details his greater burden of experiences, pain, and symbolic utterances. Specific textual examples that recall "fluidity" and "time" resurfaced Cassady's peculiar sense of absorption and even the Soul's attempt to recast its understanding of life through drugs. More aptly, it recurs with Huxley's concept of the debilitation of man's psychic senses and the idea that drugs might rebuild them. But the pair with Burroughs also bore testament to his childhood terrors and Cassady's secret wish to understand parapsychology to redeem and cherish what remained invigorating about life. It also bears herald to the post-Victorian man's depression and sickness and to the mind's violence, which could destroy modern man's intention.

More robust and warmer perceptions occupy the fore when the movie focuses on Cassady's attempts at school, his period as an altar boy, and his troubled education due to his "lack of family discipline."[19] Still, his wife Carolyn intoned summarily: "he didn't believe in any of the dogma. Then, of course, he had been brainwashed in such a—a young child, and he

Never lost that feeling of being poor and a sinner."[20] Carolyn's comments anoint the portrait of Neal as a spiritual seeker, speaking to the beatnik resonance of a deeper, underclass piety that subsumes ideas about dreaming and transcendentalism. Collisions of impoverished materiality and suffering with one's spiritual examinations may give us a clue as to why Cassady chose to exposit and sermonize his debuts with drugs, stealing, and folk mythologies that found him tripping, hearkening "the road" and its redoubtable glory as his adopted, yet timeless emblem. Cassady's partial translations of Christian faith and belonging build human impulses to freedom and proselytization through drugs: they weave the cloth of his coded translations of experience that Kerouac would soon adopt.

One might attend to the literary portrait, raising and estimating the value of Kerouac's side comment in this film: "Neal is a colossus, risen to destroy Denver."[21] This "destruction" may be more of a conquest, one that is literary, epistemological, and spiritual. His prose did not record this manifestation: *Visions of Cody*'s paragraphs, style, and characters document a depressed, desperate, and longing child far inferior to engaging the cultures in downtown Denver, a softened and miserable child who feigned love for the scene. Perhaps

---

[18] Chandarlapaty, Raj, *Seeing the Beat Generation*, 130.
[19] *Neal Cassady: The Denver Years*.
[20] *Ibid.*
[21] *Ibid.*

the literary picture, spiritual involvements and drugs, and resilient attention focused on "the scene" and "the road" and other monikers of Beat Generation ecstasies and partying shadow a sometimes progenitor who sought to redraw the characteristics of modern American society through devotion, hallucination, and libation. At this point, breaking of familial bonds opens up one's perspectives, and our attempt at composing histories that attend to the technique for expositing a more hallucinatory narrative and symbolism that might change how people looked at society's different avenues, a talent Kerouac had exploited and perfected. "Destroy," naturally, also assumes Kerouac's referencing of domains that told of Cassady's ascent above the cages of destruction and isolation to reveal his growing maturity as he could not be debilitated. In truth, *The Denver Years* may also lend us the denial of progenitor status as our beginning to understand questions concerning Denver's verbose pathology. How did we, in a modern Era, replace the revelries and sickness of alcohol and prostitution with those of drugs and more ambitious sexual promiscuity to state the chosen aesthete to be the revived moral and conscious message-bearer? Tracing the width of this series of discoveries might cause us to recognize that knowledge and religion could unshackle itself from socialist realism as a changing force that, through drug use, bore the mark of a wider idealism. Noel replies warmly, if somewhat haughtily: "Yeah, we probably should celebrate Neal Cassady in Denver. He's possibly America's greatest car thief."[22] Without contrasting Noel's comment with the obvious grist of the literary reality—countless authors, ranging from Kerouac to Capote, had grilled characters as criminals with vague, grandiose ideas about travel and libations to be had through crime—we as easily read *The Denver Years* and its image-laden snapshots of readings from *The First Third* as a kind of conclusive evidence that the mind's interlocutions and its aggravated links to psychology could broaden and brighten modern man's social functions, to the point at which skill and ability can help us draw new universes familiar to intellectual appraisals of human social needs and their controlling impulses. In short, Cassady builds American dynamics, in some ways wider than Huxley, but also resiliently targeting winds of growth, development, and social and personal freedoms that decades of solid American prosperity had built with no correlatives in Europe. By calculating depression's extreme depths, *The Denver Years* builds the case to examine psychedelic drugs as antithetical to the human spirit's control and domination—an idea that Huxley first wrote about in his short stories.

---

[22] *Ibid.*

Re-Visiting 'The Scene' in Cassady's Denver, at Mid-Century: Jazz and its Influence, and the Beginnings of Beat

The Denver Years illustrates aggressive videography and ethnography of Denver, counting as essential Neal's relationships with girls, stealing, jazz clubs in Denver's popular downtown, and road trips to New York City as early as 1945 to meet, among others, Jack Kerouac and Allen Ginsberg. Tom Noel notes the antiracist tone of jazz clubs quite thoughtfully: "whites with some idea of what Black life was like."[23] The narrator notes the appearance of Miles Davis, Dizzy Gillespie, Billie Holiday, and Nat King Cole at bars like the Rosonian, saying: "Bop sounds could be heard echoing all along the Welton Street corridor."[24] David Amram noted the following Beatnik tension: "[Kerouac and Cassady] didn't have any calm, they sat down and listened, appreciate what they're doing, whether you're in Japan, Europe or Five Points. You could become part of the music."[25] Amram introduces the attention foregrounding Cassady's writing form: "His famous Joan letter to Kerouac is an extraordinary piece of literature."[26] Kerouac attests to the burgeoning literary anxiety, saying that the December 17, 1950 letter was "the greatest piece of literature ever written."[27] Jiminy Cimino notes the narrative tension between the two writers: "What if you took that style, and you made a novel about it? And that created bop prosody because Jack Kerouac wrote the way Neal Cassady spoke."[28] The positive, unanimous detailing from friends and family members tells of considerable intellectual talent, and with that, abstractions of theme and ideas to rebuild romanticist attentions to form through street, material, and humorous indifference to, and consummation in, the living world centered on "Beat." Facing modernism's drugged technique, thereby escaping its borders to build a heroic, hyper-perceptive thrust, counts drugged experiences with moment, place, and meaning accelerations. Neal's wife, Carolyn, cross-examines Kerouac's rise to fame and stardom—it becomes clear that collaborative techniques for talking, thinking, writing, and rebuilding could offset the parameters of a more Victorian perception that would tend to ruin and depress the modern subject.

The Joan letter, with its pervasive references to sex and pornography, is perhaps gustily praised for its risqué *genre* and tastily sensual meter. As the basis for Ed Bates' 1997 movie, *The Last Time I Committed Suicide*, it represents

---

[23] *The Denver Years.*
[24] *Ibid.*
[25] *Ibid.*
[26] *Ibid.*
[27] *Ibid.*
[28] *Ibid.*

the acceleration and positive accenting of modernist form to compete with modernist greats such as D.H. Lawrence, Henry Miller, and Georges Bataille as harbingers of America's renewed sexual revolution during the mid-twentieth century. This content's letter palates the healthy, pornographic smut of self-representations that illustrate the spirit's triumph:

> It was a Sunday night, so no work. I waited outside the 16th and High Street apartment till my parents left and then went in and fell to it. I had all my clothes off and in a living room, and she was washing my cock in the bathroom. [...] Here I was nude, with no clothes, and all exits blocked. I couldn't stay there for what if the old gal wanted to pee? Most older women's bladders and kidneys are not the best in the world.[29]

What is not, then, our abiding question is exactly how "sexy" Cassady's specific entry is, but why Kerouac recalled this short piece to be the best work of literature. Cassady, working from job to job, having occasional and intense relationships with girls, and suffering from beatings and the law, comprised a conversational and intellectual force that Kerouac and Ginsberg drew upon in their writings and valued to be the basis for the technique of Kerouac's "spontaneous prose." Drugs, then, are not only intellectual rehabilitation but give us a much denser and wider sense of man's sensory pendulum and his private ascriptions to spirit through Cassady. In its narrowed navigations of American society, the letter forecasts *déclassé* adventures to the waiting tryst with writers and adventurers conducting dope- and sex-learning of culture and meaning. Cimino's specific comment about talking and "lingo" means to anoint the forms of drugged revelation as the Beat beginning, a beginning for Kerouac and Ginsberg, who explored a much greater range of substances and were slow to assemble the technique within their *forte*. Biographically, of course, questions of the Beat Generation's origin were fertile concerning drugs: Allen Ginsberg did not write to testify to smoking a joint on the rooftops of his Manhattan apartment until 1948 when he wrote "Kaddish." Cassady's narcotic emblem, or the vile diseases of alcoholism and crime during his youth, tested and overstated his celebrated conception of virtue. Poor living's perceived sickness and depression mediated agony into the spirit's destruction and its distorted ambitions in Neal as a child, recasting the soul's redemption through a professed sensualism. We might also say that drugs if they did not write the story, represent the drug addict's presumable condition and his worldview when handwritten into text. Resonant at all points is Cassady's persona, where other drug narratives shrink the personal angle to underscore drugged

---

[29] *Neal Cassady: Collected Letters*, 250.

depression and sickness, as in Kerouac's letters or Ginsberg's 1959 poem about LSD, "Lysergic Acid." In short, the Beats had initiated a psychedelic journey as writers, socialites, and traveling hoboes with many focal points to grow their discoveries, moving from Cassady's peculiar mythology as the progenitor to his attachment of the morphology of symbols and attitudes that would mature into that generation's literature. With readings of *The First Third* and Cassady's letters, *The Denver Years*, despite its contrived visual promulgations of fact and region, does much to propagate the contention that ideas and experiences came from Cassady's writings, not from those of Kerouac or Ginsberg. Our reading helps us retain psychedelic facts and the group's unstable learning curve. Findings and specific intellectual transformations, then, carve themselves away from the writer's immersion in the problem of drugs and, arguably, its rehabilitation of senses, body, and actions. The footage accurately prescribes Cassady's writing or the specific, thrusting imagination that pushed and molded it. With no specific examples of drug immersion, *The Denver Years* attributes the Beat contribution to literary and cultural modernism from the seeker's standpoint, mixing the vagrant and the rebel to conjoin moments into a resurfacing of psychedelic cultural interaction and self-development in the fast-changing world.

Chapter 10

Neal at the Wheel and Beatnik Adaptations of the Classic Form

At 74 minutes and encapsulating Neal Cassady's role as the Merry Pranksters' driver, *Neal at the Wheel* recontextualizes Beat-level ramblings. He adapts in form and materiality to the wind of changing times. Loosely put, Neal's acid-inflamed diatribe behind the wheel on June 25, 1964 on the New Jersey Turnpike headed to New York City to see the World's Fair found the older Cassady gorging his memories of race-car drivers, actors, and lay people in what was a peculiar, and potentially engaging and exciting, drug trip building on Cassady's flair for the road, machines, and lastly Beatnik social, physical, and historical expressions. When translating this provocative document, we should admit that Cassady's writing sought to cure and redirect biographical details, plus agonizing threads of poverty and sickness that LSD, in its moment, compares with Beat protégé Ken Kesey. As partygoers took the "red tabs," Cassady spun tale after tale to supplant the troupe's boredom and isolation among the thousands of drivers. As Kesey would, he projects popular culture's weight in spelling out a liminal, yet compunctious, adventure while tripping. One may easily pair Cassady with rehabilitation's special poetics through drugs. While appearing loud, dangerous, and excited, Cassady builds the Beat verbal *métier* to suggest life's exciting possibilities and its fabric of social and personal freedoms offsetting the glaring postmodern tedium that subordinated drug addicts. We get, as we would twelve years later through Jack Nicholson in *One Flew Over the Cuckoo's Nest*, the dint of popular culture's figures and practices, and the supple grist of liberation and the vocabulary of Beat transcendences telling us that LSD brought us freedom from the shackles of Victorian moral and sensual control.

The audio itself, with its sudden pauses, missteps of the road Cassady's frenetic jamming on his memories of race car drivers at the Le Mans Grand Prix during the 1920s and 30s. His tributes to movie actors, his sensory pulp fiction hearkening to Beat rejections of middle-class life, and his technique at reassembling a road journey by calling upon popular culture and film to drive successfully did much to compensate for the inaction of sitting on a bus for days riding cross-country. Cassady's idle passion for racing and gambling would not be spared in his wife's memoirs, and in 1955 she wrote:

Neal's obsession with the races continued to grow. He insisted now he was obligated to continue the system to atone for his guilt of having lost our savings and for Natalie's death. He turned a deaf ear to reason. Every evening with the newspaper race results, calculating every race and keeping exact scores with hieroglyphics in the margins.[1]

With such crippling accusations about what Carolyn saw as a wasteful pastime, we as audiences have to point out what constructive function Neal's tale-telling would ensure and what cognitive strength these flashy examples of self-presentation and evocation these tales actually could instill in us. Cassady's memories of the roadshow, as he had thought about it, are laced with pure Beat hipsterism, echoing poor addicts' aesthetic incomprehension. *Neal at The Wheel*, in this sense, extolls the classic legend of Beat and Road, with snapshots proving that Beat rhetorical multitudes could swarm and sweep the mind of its straight pretensions. Neal speaks his estimations of a "cool" road, praising the drug-taking group's imagination, and tells about magic adventures and popular TV formats to engage his complex, modern world. Before we engage this virtuous form's template, we allow Beat similitude to establish our legitimate tone, the certainty that experiences, places, memories, and comparable intellect at the helm of modern life could revive modern man, situating his dreams and ideas about the outside world from their sensory experiences and to remote places in their childish imagination. Neal's positive tone, too, illustrates confidence, maturity, and the sense that one could alter reality whenever necessary. For his part, Neal Cassady had written about his car travels, and Kerouac had also narrated Cassady as the driver in *On the Road* cross-country journeys. Though we cannot endorse carjacking as a form of psychedelic society's development and conjunction with Cassady's penitent sickness, it is also likely that modern man, as he grew accustomed to the prevalence of machine-product-environment developments, would distort his auditions and perceptions in a manic redevelopment of consciousness itself, to suit that immersion's peculiar needs. Cassady's memories are not dreams but live engagements on the road, building the lateral and timeless minutes of a technocratic existence in the addict's eye. In terms of Beat historiography, *Neal at the Wheel* shows Cassady rephrasing and executing Kerouac's abandonment of perspectives when he talks about his mescaline use in *Selected Letters*: we are led quickly to the question, what did Kerouac find when he was tripping and listening to jazz music in Mexico? Our answer did not satisfy, and Kerouac appended no transcendent fighting in his trip, giving no note as to what jazz and tripping could do other than to say that Shorty Rogers "blows entirely

---

[1] Cassady, Carolyn, *Off the Road*, 268.

different [from Miles Davis]" and that Bill [Burroughs] "got on a talking kick."² Cassady's rephrasing of verbal and mental anxieties in the Beat form and his frenetic delivery tell us the meaningful arrangement of ideas and scenes to tackle the vast, modern world and its technocratic indifference to our mind, Soul, and Spirit.

Through Cassady's adorned dialect, *Neal at the Wheel* passes through the entourage's voyeurism when viewing the open, wide highways of New Jersey, descending upon images, signs, and visible subjects:

> Now I got all the kiddies today—I guess we'll be good kiddies—it's a woman driver and goddam as fast as the first (…). C'mon around here, black car—shit, now you see what I mean! She doesn't have any concept, and her ass is full of beans.³

As the Pranksters and Cassady take LSD, Cassady's narrative grasp of the scene and his projected memoirs becomes fully Beat, building up his dialect's acrid swagger to project visions, histories, and superimpositions of the road's gravity as the Prankster's social messenger:

> Somebody like Cesar Romero, the man, laughing in the old way fluently like Campamani, good diddling right there—no, uh, then the next scene, ha ma pa, you know, but you gotta believe some eager had set fox and sear maniacal like Alexander, gotta believe, discover that's pretty here for Tom Edison wants someone like Tony Perkins—that's it! Somebody who is, who could be either way, but his cane, it's a definite erotic thing —he's obsessed with racing. I'd say Tony Perkins Cat, uh, not being approved of it all to the side, you'd have a mania for auto racing, even the like-seen Tony Perkins, wouldn't be good for football. Why this fellow can't race worth a damn; worse than the bunch.⁴

Several ideas would aggravate LSD's positive testament to the afflicted person's knowledge and perspectives. Cassady emphasizes his stress on movie actors, familiar Beat morphologies that are superb and recognized mythological hitches in the names and definitions, the pairing of ancient and modern, the climactic struggle between the intellect and brute force—and inevitably, his fangled Beat dialect dramatizing purpose and history upon tepid, redundant New Jersey urban lives sleeping in the void of their wealth and status. It should

---

² Kerouac, Jack, *Selected Letters*, 370.
³ Cassady, Neal, *Neal at the Wheel*.
⁴ Cassady, Neal, *Neal at the Wheel*.

be said that Kerouac, as early as 1950's *The Town and the City*, would write many such "master narratives."⁵ Superimpositions of post-jazz glory and depression upon San Francisco resulted from his Mount Hozomeen meditation in 1965's *Desolation Angels*.⁶ Ginsberg's journal entries in 1970 *Indian Journals*, too, breathe this narrative necessity—with street syntax's altering glare and in the urban media's romanticized unveiling and repository of surrogate glories at the century's beginning, too, Cassady would tell a history to glorify the bus participant's activities and general seriousness. But more succinctly, Cassady's rolling dialect was not just a superimposition—it replaced highway driving's true practicum: as a statement, we might see in LSD the outcome of imaginations that supposed meaning where none had existed. There, too, seems to be the tendency among Kesey's participants to invest scenes of lifelessness with the glory of ancient meaning. It is as if to say all journeys are meaningful, invigorating us with the memories and travails of modern man's post-urban struggles for ideas and redemption. The recurrence of inventor Thomas Edison and actor Tony Perkins states what Cassady had thought were their repressed emotions to love and to escape definition. They, too, constitute the LSD goodies of this experience. Cassady's returning comment about Perkins, "Yes, he was so young to go to war, switch that around, because he has to be younger father goes back to war,"⁷ turns the focus to America's wartime problems and to America's fragile youths who stared down life's challenges. Cassady descends upon his driving subject again, relaying the following:

> See, '26 or whenever it was—anyhow, he's pretty well emotionally, physically, any other thing he's tied up with, anything particular in the course but Le Mans. That's what he sees in. He vows like a sick cat, I meant, something like that, woman, you must work that yourself. But some were told, you liked that idea, is told. Mans, every year, one late thing, okay, so after the war, skip to other things.⁸

At this point, Cassady operates several instances of World War II reality for Americans—women working, men drowning in the unhappiness and misery of war, passive obsessions with pastimes like auto racing, and perhaps the tension between wartime and peacetime activities. Cassady runs these shards of daily experience together to weld a whole being, a guiding sense about where the American subject has been, stating modern man's timeless struggle against death, poverty, and his daily nihilism in the years after World War I. Cassady

---

⁵ Kerouac, Jack, *The Town and the City*.
⁶ Kerouac, Jack, *Desolation Angels*.
⁷ Cassady, Neal, *Neal at the Wheel*.
⁸ *Ibid.*

synthesizes America's argued-for imagination to enjoy the vectors of spirit and drama in sports as themes antithetical to war. Classical conditioning, then, reveals the LSD subject finding his alternative to war and against the destruction of talents in war through "the road" and supposes this is a heroic journey conceived out of bits and pieces of Cassady's imagination. We have situated biography's importance in re-entrenching spiritual and personal ambitions in *The Denver Years*. Behind the wheel in 1964, Cassady operates a much greater synthesis, originating from his Denver childhood but resplendently national and international when overstating the bus's symbolism during an authoritarian time. At its best, then, Cassady in *Neal at the Wheel* operates the pride of today's leisure culture, supposing a modern summit for the travelers therein. Cassady is clear and consistent in identifying sports such as auto racing as a timeless, recurring antidote to war and its carnage—the derived point is simple enough, saying that man's peacetime arts and passions marked a society where life was possible, and meaning could be found without killing an enemy. Of course, this attempts to herald patriotism, the subject of the Pranksters' journey. In these venues of the mind, Cassady creates a much broader circuit to express life while confined to the bus's vicinity while driving.

Acid Tabs and Beatnik Mysteries: How Neal Cassady Inspired Through LSD and Media

The specific tear-off of Cassady, with the Pranksters listening and participating in the festive atmosphere, starts with the pleasant feeling of "being optimistic" after looking at a damaged car surrounded by policemen.[9] The specific affair, where the Pranksters and Cassady had "wrong directions" and were trying to figure their way back onto the New Jersey Turnpike, builds the basic spontaneity and the touch of Beatnik revelry. There were, it appeared, many stories about "the road" conducive to Cassady's hallucinogenic tenor, or at least the spooling and casting of shards of jingoistic rhetoric steeped in airs of brilliant discovery. Lost and seeking the road to illustrate the adventure's success, Cassady is composed and sincere, speaking his basic trust in his videography and clarity when detailing community and characters in their happy, junked spirit:

> Here's a movie, see—1918, war zone—this is a street ridden by Cassady. Returning there, there's a rural bridge in town, the young, uh, balled been before, brothers, fathers, garage and all, feel the seas at big dawn and as a mother would say: I'm flying around a curve in an old Alfa

---

[9] *Ibid.*

> Romeo and lessee, all they know and you—hey son! And get to it all, the old man is an auto racer, and his brother [...][10]

Passages establishing the topic's personality, connected to visual and sensory metaphors connoting spirit, adventure, and mythology, are part of the entourage's essential problem of finding their correct route. Cassady, imaging shards of the popular racing culture and neighborhoods, touches the residents' lives with a familiar sensuality praising juvenile quests. LSD was then designed to supplant real geographies, to foreword heroic questing to the troupe itself. More importantly, it is a roadmap to learn vehicle driving that doctors and policemen would say they should *not* be taking. Cassady's specific manic-depressive tone insinuates this crucial bit of learning: that, namely, a tripper can function and can improve his performance in many areas, including building the walls of perception to state identity and responsibility.

As Cassady gets into the play of telling tales about the Le Mans Grand Prix—which started in the 1920s and continued up until World War II in 1939—Beat replays under LSD include swinging and rising pitch, loud statements and yelling, and the pure, spontaneous roll of ideas and concepts to state the triumph of sport. We may see, then, LSD as an invigorating force in the content of Beat syntax and writing to inspire the drug-taker to spirals of ascending glory and doubt. As Cassady sights a sign for Highway 55, "You recall the Le Mans, and he went racing after that,"[11] Cassady glowers into minutes of shouting form, contriving his ride to the form of a famous auto race match like the Grand Prix:

> You know, by some accident, at grab, some accident at the corner, he, now clutch, clutch fast, combinations it would tell—hit the sack and stop and sack and blow it! He's going about twice fast in the second gear, reaching for 40, blocks an accident and loses the race, you see.[12]

Cassady shouts and builds his voice because of his attunement to sports broadcasters, and the LSD allows him to tear off a spin on Beat Glories while changing gears with his bus and avoiding traffic as he makes lane changes. At this point, the superimposition of auto racing is complete. Cassady then tunes the drive to revive Beat glamor and the errant syntax with its pauses and side glances. Because of this similitude, a greater social being could be attained, plus the fantasy of experiencing a popular culture with volume, color, and psychic transfixion. It is worthy to say, then, that LSD allows Cassady to

---

[10] *Ibid.*
[11] *Ibid.*
[12] *Ibid.*

reconnect his memories and build psychic momentum through tales. This is not to say that other Beats or Cassady himself had learned to vocalize through LSD; that is, strictly speaking, not true, and no written examples exist except for Thomas Wolfe's depressive snapshot of the older Kerouac in *The Electric Kool-Aid Acid Test*. Still, *Neal at the Wheel* loudly demonstrates its verbal triumph, as Neal supplants youthful innocence and naiveté with reconstructions of his memories. We may easily call this "Cowboy Neal" at his moment of posthumous glory—there is confidence and real-time direction in his historical statement and its exciting find. Pop productions were certainly part of the Beat Generation's metric form; we ought to, at least, confirm that Cassady also searched popular culture to find invigorating examples that supply us with tripping's raw form and thus the mind's medic execution of its visual spheres. That, at least, confirms Cassady's continuing importance, bringing forth the physical man to the form of future psychiatric instances in the film where treatment's life-denying aspects are granted the most importance.

Inertia or Insight? What Neal Cassady Means to Counterculture Studies

Discovery's essential theme underscores the promotive tale-telling of reality in *Neal at the Wheel*. Still, it is a matter of fact that future historians re-valued this particularly rich piece of history about the Beat Generation writers. If anything, the audiotape heroically demonstrates the absorption of Beat vocabulary and forms in the medium of a new drug, LSD. This focus was not without aggravated bargaining: Leary gave Kerouac some mushrooms in 1961. Kerouac threatened the writers and wrote down "dozens of lines drawn haphazardly across the page."[13] Was the Beat technique, then, unable to construe form with "new" drugs that had gained the counterculture's interest? Though Kerouac would later write Leary about his trip and write: "some Golden Age dream of man, very nice,"[14] he is incapacitated *during transcription's moment*, and this meant the impotence of intoxication that shut drugs off from our scientific lens. I think that, in the bus trip's narrative and contemporary context, Neal's acid test on this bus demonstrates the Beat voice's vivacity and the true intellectual talent for using drugs to simulate identity and transcendence in the general populace. *Neal at the Wheel* ought to be considered valid as a document along with more familiar Beat geographies, nicely nesting the familiar, rich Beat concept of "place" but ascending through the spoken form into a new kind of modern belonging. Without the group's leader, Cassady made his literary struggle a daily one, surpassing the dynamic Beat literary minute itself.

---

[13] "Kerouac's Bad Trip," *Beatdom*, June 25, 2011.
[14] "Kerouac's Bad Trip," *Beatdom*, June 25, 2011.

Chapter 11

Hofmann's Potion: Canadian and American Connections in the Growth of Psychedelic Form and the Possible Legend of Psychiatry

We may surmise the key factor when examining works by the Swiss chemist and thinker Albert Hofmann. In the psychedelic group, he was the only true scientist who had worked in institutions throughout his life. Hofmann gets the credit for having synthesized LSD from ergot, joining the ranks of psychedelic thinkers around the world when he was encouraged to synthesize the mescaline derivative of the more common peyotl button found in North America. We then turn to the accuracy of his findings. To the import of his revelations connecting us with psychedelia's larger community of scientists, activists, and writers to ensure hallucinogenic drugs' popularity by continuing and expanding Hofmann's legendary experiments and, when possible, achievements—he was never the subject of any legal challenge, nor did anyone attempt to equate Hofmann with criminal activity. The son of a Swiss factory worker, Hofmann earned his doctorate in chemistry at the University of Basel in 1929 and was said to have synthesized a form of LSD as early as 1938. At a conference in 1996, he noted the following:

> Mystical experiences in childhood, in which Nature was altered in magical ways, had provoked questions concerning the essence of the external, material world, and chemistry was the scientific field that might afford insights into this.[1]

This statement's reasoning was clear enough: Hofmann believed that the scientific method and knowledge were accurate and universal enough to understand and thus project psychedelic drugs' importance, with no need for any official cultural basis other than science. His attenuation of romantic and

---

[1] Hofmann, Albert. "LSD: Completely Personal," From *Newsletter for the Association of Psychedelic Studies.*

literary forms in deducing this meaning meant to point out science's increasingly objective talent at understanding the brain, biochemistry, and cultural abstractions, telling us more about how drugs could be used in society to attain positive results. Part of the two chapters listed below underscores directions and opinions from doctors, chemists, thinkers, and liberal historians in psychedelia's conjugation as a discipline and its annexation of the psychedelic social movement as a challenging factor when it replicated knowledge. Films, then, judged Hofmann not only as a progenitor and thinker: they developed the studies' text, gaining ground to state the authority of Hofmann's private ruminations that did not evenly surface in psychedelic literature and its mass proselytization. Films do give a great deal of attention to documents, commentaries, and summarizations of researched forms. They, in short, paraphrase science's development and its necessity far from Leary's Millbrook mansion or from any specifics that came from the pages of Huxley, Kesey, or other writers who had taken up the challenge to popularize drugs as the meaningful antecedent to Western man's cultural and regional experiences. What becomes evident is the scientist's novel position. When faced with an increasingly diverse body of psychological research, but hitherto confined to detail the body's physiology and activities, a new chapter emerged, suiting the fashions of seekers who liked Hofmann's work and were apt to take up the expansion and direction of studies into those areas.

Kent Martin's 2002 amalgamation of interviews, unsolicited footage of Canadian hospitals, and general discussion of the "acid problem" during the 1950s and 1960s while scholars and pundits debated the future of hallucinogenic studies and, if possible, their relevance to modern societies, did not disappoint. It may be worthwhile to note concentrations of raw data and their interpolation suiting the goals of modernist studies because of the strong response from thinkers and chemists such as Hofmann, Humphrey Osmond, Stanislav Grof, Laura Huxley, Duncan Blewett, and Ralph Metzner. The 56-minute film, featuring the inundations and development of Hofmann's generalist proposal to the world that hallucinogenic drugs posed the sense's wide enlightenment and deeper stresses of memory and function in the lives of drug and alcohol addicts, was tunneled through a ten-year internship in Saskatchewan hospitals with doctors who tested Hofmann's discoveries, accenting the particular learning role in modern, socialist-dominated societies that had eschewed vision, fantasy, dreaming, and tripping to be the mark of non-functioning individuals. It provides viewers with tenable modern data suggesting the misgoverning of our minds and psychology and the very broad yet peculiar science that could draw modern humanity out of their professed sickness's tunnels. *Hofmann's Potion* is, in a word, optimistic when developing scientific data about drug use. The film records—amidst Hofmann's own idealistic, romantic sense that his discoveries would change the world—the objective picture and the case's certainty that doctors and thinkers made that LSD, mescaline, and psilocybin improved lives and restored the justice of living in a confused, post-rational world that denied man his spiritual communications.

Hofmann's Specific Literary Discovery and Boundless Inspiration

Strongly notable at the movie's beginning are Hofmann's comments: visibly excited and pointed about what he had discovered in the laboratory, Hofmann thoughtfully swept the form of socialist-rationalist discussions of matter, mind, and experience: "If you have open eyes, you may see the world differently. I mean, in the—you see it as it is. Wonderful."[2] Still, he is clear to disperse questions about the origins of LSD when touting his finding's sincerity: "Then we discovered that these compounds had already existed for thousands of years."[3] To state hallucinatory transcendentalism's broad history and the ultimate human challenge to understand meant to call up a wide swath of historical immersion and the relevance of that immersion. Turning this over to scientists and pundits meant that they would then examine how contemporary science and moralism had destroyed life, perceptions, humanism, and man's projected purpose. Hofmann's retold discovery, then, sweeps past time's annals, cleverly usurping centuries couched in rationalist-socialist thought that had suppressed the lives and functioning of hundreds of millions of people in their estimations of human action. Hofmann then summed up his abbreviations of life, experiences, and his global testament to learning himself:

> But under LSD, you see things that are not formed. And, hence, it's a different you, a different experience of our existence.[4]

Studies in Saskatchewan: The Task of Putting Acid to Psychiatric Truth

Videography and commentaries about English psychiatrist Dr. Humphry Osmond's supervision of alcoholics, people with schizophrenia, and drug addicts at Weyburn Mental Hospital are studied. They are resiliently determined to prove the validity of the doctor's studies. These studies examine the problem of managing LSD therapy, giving credence to the idea that methods and drug administration were and are credible ways of treating the mentally ill. Not all of Osmond's comments are aesthetic and romantic in their stewardship of alcoholics and schizophrenics: Abram Hoffer, the hospital's biochemist, gravely reported: "On the ground at night, it was always shrieking and crying, and

---

[2] *Hofmann's Potion.*
[3] *Ibid.*
[4] *Ibid.*

screaming. You could hear it all over the place."⁵ Osmond, who had also taken LSD as part of his experiments, abbreviates the dynamic tension between experience and place: "It was a long time, it would take many years, learning about it, learning how to behave, and then it changes, suddenly, dramatically, we may not like this."⁶ Still, he appoints specific avenues of perception and reflection into the tenets of modern man's corrugated responsibility:

> New chemicals aroused to our experience some of the unbelievably pleasant and sometimes quite terrifying mental agonies of schizophrenic patients—to some extent, to put ourselves in his shoes, for a few hours, these people have terrible experiences—that's why they're so tense. We know that seemingly small errors made in a caring form will cause that tension to rise.⁷

If we consider the quantum value of drug experiments, we tabulate the recording of perceptual and visual data without the benefit of true psychiatry. Still, Osmond was adamant when defending Hoffer's record: "I was able to prove many sound reputations."⁸ Osmond's statement at the movie beginning of the movie was to render justice to the renewed aestheticism's unveiling. It suggests controls and controlled environments that science had delineated to prepare people with an addiction, people with alcohol abuse addiction, and people with schizophrenia for a life of renewed meaning, and to state, years before President Johnson had tagged LSD to cause "slavery," the mind's integrity and sublimity amidst socialism-Victorianism that had shuttered discussions and format for the mind and the psyche. Osmond is firmly rooted in the film's excavation, found on tape in a lab coat discussing the study's purpose when examining psychiatry through doctrines of self-immersion to produce results. The footage and interviews imply, too, that many of Weyburn's doctors were taking LSD, and so compares and contrasts their experiences with those of the patients. Again, giving psychedelics a history, or a pre-eminent method that would be replicated and controlled the same way, lends the proceedings a tireless legitimacy. Osmond, for his part, recalls the experiments' "constancy": "We conducted hundreds of experiments using the different substances to produce schizophrenic-like symptoms in ourselves."⁹ Hoffer concurs: "We decided to use these drugs to see if we could get inside the skin of a schizophrenic, to see if this might give us a clue to how we might better treat

---

⁵ *Ibid.*
⁶ *Ibid.*
⁷ *Ibid.*
⁸ *Ibid.*
⁹ *Ibid.*

them."[10] Quite naturally, when we say that a schizophrenic possessed living and perceptual meaning, and of the kind that could help us understand ourselves better, we crush socialist-realist angles nixing content in human beings that value economic and political goals that widen the human spirit and its anti-rational deductions about time, color, place, and dreams. Osmond was, then, to change the social order, rebuilding human goals based upon anti-rational realities to foretell a greater human understanding. To use these drugs to get at the heart of schizophrenia clearly illustrates romantic possibilities for a human being possessed of a peculiar, deeply aestheticized reasoning that guarantees modern man their greater fulfillment in an organized, modern society. With its black-and-white films and unreleased outtakes of the hospital's goings-on during the experiments, *Hofmann's Potion* also posed sensory data consistent with Hofmann's persistent, wide-flung romantic tone. Color, nature, and dreams exposit the drugged experience's peculiar intensity and, perhaps, then, the schizophrenic's transcendence of objective reasoning in capitalist societies. The experiments maintain an open door, as different psychiatrists, thinkers, and chemists allude to the favored romanticist deduction that what was irrational or incompletely described constitutes the experience's lifeblood. Restated, the psychiatrists, doctors, and even psychedelic master Timothy Leary do not disagree about the uses of schizophrenic patients or specific indoctrinations common to LSD use. Instead, the film glorifies Osmond's valuable notion that the hospital had succeeded and that others could learn to manage mentally ill patients in controlled, scripted settings targeting dreams, emotions, and visions. All in all, the roundtable itself is convinced that conducting experiments meant using LSD as part of them. Blewett concurs: "You have to work with yourself, and you should put yourself forward. [Osmond] laid down the ground rules of research with LSD, and they were very sound. Compared with the research, Saskatchewan was miles ahead of the pack."[11] Implied, then, throughout the movie, is an adaptation of the medical establishment's sincerity and gradual scientific tones that could identify sickness's salient memory qualities and the tenability of Hofmann's recurrent thesis about the mind's enlightenment as the stepping stone to personal and social transformation. Treating patients with schizophrenia meant to practically state the problem to say that key attributes of a person's life and function might be recovered or rebuilt by using drugs such as LSD. This interface is continually documented, venturing a life that industrial-commercial dominance does not govern in its organizations of the brain, the spirit, or the mind. Weyburn Hospital, then, successfully manages a repository of repressed

---

[10] *Ibid.*
[11] *Ibid.*

and deranged subjects who could not register their specific reality in print or on tape. Hoffer stars the recorded fact's documentation summarily: "We became much more aware of what was happening to the schizophrenic patient."[12] He then underscores psychiatry's converse entity when he is interviewed on television: "Many of our people had not responded to the best treatment that we could give them. They are now sober and good people."[13] To say, then, that psychiatry had not helped addicts and patients with the "best" treatment was to say that modern man's organizations of brain and body were inadequate, and the human Spirit's storied visionary models would become the basis for developing modern humanity.

Osmond continues to occupy the moral high ground, speaking of modernism's possible fall from grace in the technologized, capitalized world. He refers to "the essential basis of man" as his antecedent to spelling out LSD's usefulness among the masses. He summarizes Hofmann: "[Albert] demonstrated a whole new way of using [knowledge] based on spiritual realization."[14] Hofmann's general technique would be created without exact written translations of patient experiences or specific ideational references to any previous mysticism. Such generalizations, then, about history, spirituality, and the mind cross-examine the Spirit's rational alienations as we turn the discussion over to drug-takers who, with no identity or class, vocalize their ideas and ambitions calmly and without precedent. Enough ethnography, nonetheless, was given to Hofmann, Osmond, and Leary's positive credentials as the basis to re-examine religious dogma and spiritual pathways—the gist of which, it appears, spell out modern conspiracies that deny humans their true relationality. It may not be enough to state that LSD's psychiatrists and thinkers voluntarily discarded class and identity privileges when donning these experiences along with their lab coats. It was more certain that the entourage's positive immersion allowed them to restrict what was, penitently, real regarding speech, vision, and memory.

Hofmann's Potion lends itself to the maturation of recorded experience over time. Seated in front of the camera and wearing a white lab coat, a young Osmond speaks to the camera: "These experiments have helped us to experience something of how these ill people perceive the world, its dimensions of time, space, and color."[15] Yet, when much older and relaxing as he sits on a couch and reflects upon the decades of study and collusion, Osmond recounts the tale's underwriting to attach skill and focus to the alcoholic's troubled daydream:

---

[12] *Ibid.*
[13] *Ibid.*
[14] *Ibid.*
[15] *Ibid.*

The great advantage with one of the hallucinogens is that you could make them very well aware of [their shortcomings]. It might also sometimes change their behavior. They might see it in a quite different light.[16]

Time, space, and color all accentuate the aesthetic hypothesis—namely, that persons acquainted with drugs consider this format the most reliable for telling what a drugged experience means. It organizes the principle of hallucination as an accompaniment to man's physical nature and to reason's peculiar cage, shutting out the mind's unfocused ramblings and ecstatic insights. But "shortcomings" target the addict's specific self-estimation: it, when made "different," liberates the rational mind, securing their ambitions, development, and cognitions: man can, then, *see his functionality in a better light*, without the manacle of science truncating and dissecting the politics of addiction's uncertainty when studied. Hofmann embraces the trend for speaking about drugged errata: "It's easier to formulate high ideas, but reasonably more difficult to discover how those ideals could be implemented."[17] Comments thus secure the scientist's gradual transformation of mind-body discussions, giving us ample light from which to study how psychedelic science, borne from modernism and judiciously annexing religions, Eastern mysticisms, and technological self-controls, could say that it was an objective structure. With Huxley's *Perennial Philosophy* published in 1944, around the time these studies commenced, Osmond and his entourage would recount the gradual accumulation of data and purposes behind Hofmann's discovery, subsuming mystic histories as a redoubtable and manifold form that spoke to the expansion of studies, and to the patient's exercise of them as meaning.

Hofmann's Potion traverses experimentation and study across continents: as Huxley had divined in *The Perennial Philosophy*, points of inspiration for dialogues of the mind and spirit were many, had been verified over time, and stood proudly and resonantly against Victorianism. The camera angle moves across continents, including Mexico, Canada, and Europe, essential grounds for crucial human examinations. Relatively, *Hofmann's Potion* does its best to acculturate the findings of Huxley and Leary to Hofmann's specific point of focus. Text involving these two thinkers ground the connection between disparate philosophical points of origin, with Huxley adding:

---

[16] *Ibid.*
[17] *Ibid.*

> Most of the time, it is not the ordinary experience but rather types of consciousness that have, empirically, an enormous value in having people live less self-centered, more charitable lives.[18]

The spoken admission's specific conduit, then, was not different from Hofmann's but followed his robust aesthetic of grandiose purpose to change society. From the unctuous cage of rationalism and mind-body separations, Huxley does as Hofmann did—propose a conscious expansion to suit the romantic´s urge to live, to understand it from within. *Hofmann's Potion* did, in relative sum, its best to situate the potential of countercultural studies. Though more political-minded and shorn of the chemist's private naivete, it confirms the brilliant aesthetic metaphor through a politicized emphasis. Wife and writer Laura Huxley gives us details of the breach as a basis for comparison: "The preparation for sessions was very, very careful for them—the day before, we didn't do anything, the day of the session was nothing except that, and even the day after."[19] Still, commentaries assure us of the peculiar gift of men like Hofmann and Osmond, to the point that we prescribe limits for understanding them. The film then goes to "Set and Setting: A Guide To the Proper Use of LSD," where the narrator recalls: "And then they were administered LSD, and we would mark them down on the cut, we put headphones on, and encouraged an internal journey."[20] Amidst the recollections of strobe lights, rose petals, and excursions into Mexican forests, *Hofmann's Potion*, despite its many notables, maintains the notion that Hofmann's discovery and his self-narration of experiences that came from it were genuine, original, and a persistent force underscoring the later psychedelics discoveries. Commentary from Myron Stolaroff and Stanislaus Grof assure us of the seriousness while demarcating a dour circumspection about "free" experimenters in the Leary generation. There is, however, much to be made of the connections implied within Leary's specific period. Notwithstanding the story's obvious reach, Leary did not study under Hofmann and found most of his published ideas separately; nonetheless, the separate academies breathe familiar respect for the inquiry, if opposed to the core ideas each one has chosen in psychiatry. With this in mind, it is safe to say that both Huxley and Leary professed and underwent some retreading of ideas that Hofmann had built into his studies.

---

[18] *Ibid.*
[19] *Ibid.*
[20] *Ibid.*

On Timothy Leary: Ideas and Possibilities for the Future of LSD

The film's recollection of Leary notes that the psychedelic thinker and Harvard professor envisioned and developed political languages and methods that change society rather than stick to pure psychiatry absorbed from institutions and practices. Osmond purported rosily: "Leary was a brilliant entrepreneur of notions. He did very, ah, but pretty good. Unfortunately, he didn't always get very good notions."[21] A thoughtful Stanislav Grof knocks out the legislation with curt appraisals of the thinker's training and ethics: "Tim Leary, from my perspective, created more problems than I think of having. He may have popularized LSD, but it all excited a lot of people to experiment. He did not get fair information for telling about LSD, you know."[22] He then ruefully surmises the legend to comprise the absence of psychic responsibility: LSD is "a substance that makes trillions of your cells singing the song of liberation."[23] To give drugs without being a patient and to take them with no thought-encoded supervision allows for the profile to be completely shuttered. Leary is introduced with no real advent from previous psychiatrists and states that he conducted many of his studies without planning. He believed in changing consciousness and conscious affiliations. Still, his departures from the academy and endless popularization as a thinking icon may submerge thought into waves of irresponsibility, improper understanding of physiology, and brain functioning. We may, of course, read Leary's treatises with some impact; still, problems arise when the specific ideologies are questioned, with many practices found to be indiscriminate, false, superficial, or subjective to deny positive transcendences and so causing the critical condition list at hospitals more trouble than an "idea" might be worth. "Did not tell" assumes a legitimate purpose, but one inconsistent with psychic diversities that could teach perspectives and social belonging. Grof then axes a specific mythology with psychiatric opinions that hallucinogenic drugs should not be used as casual intoxicants, nor could they produce the social change Leary might have intended. Leary, when on television in this film, said optimistically:

> You have to say that, uh, we're teaching people how to use their heads. The point is that your head has to go out of your Mind, out of the static waves of which you think.[24]

---

[21] *Ibid.*
[22] *Ibid.*
[23] *Ibid.*
[24] *Ibid.*

The innocuous comment, when paired with the assumption that "the mind" was Western, rational, technological, or socialist and Victorian, based upon controls and repression, did give advent to Eastern philosophies. What is not said, though, is how immersions could "teach" that. It is, in the depth of twentieth-century scholarship, possible to pair drugs like psilocybin with romantic expressions of mind and body. It is also true that when objective and contrived, modern consciousness shuts the brain's peculiar technology that depends more on vision than reason. Religious appraisals aside, the comment remains consistent with his stress on breaking out of "games," as found in the literature: Leary professed a need to change thought through immersions.

Psychedelia's Unlikely Associations: What Aldous Huxley Meant for Hofmann

Dr. Osmond's tone became especially colloquial when referring to Huxley, and he is listed in the narration as having administered Huxley's first dose of mescaline. He recalled, "I didn't want to end my career as a man who had written all that is mad, but [we] had a very pleasant time together. Also, I didn't think I made any great blunders, but Aldous liked the experience. It interested him, and he liked to think this was constantly something, scientific knowledge."[25] Huxley's evolutionary point might bring forth the obvious historical references at a cross between a new class of hallucinogens and Huxley's consummate studies of mysticism, narcotics, and expatriate journeys worldwide. Huxley had studied the Zen Buddhists, the pre-Columbian Indians of Mexico, and India's various cults and could use *The Perennial Philosophy* to tout the extra-sensory virtues of psilocybin and mescaline. Then, Osmond's credit furthers a direction Huxley was likely to pursue during the 40-year framework of his studies. Huxley directly wrote about Osmond's administering of the drug and that further LSD experiments were tuned to our written poetics as the means to write science, which is cross-examined from within the depth of Huxley's global, modernist studies: "Let us dream pragmatically."[26] Osmond did not alter the positive stature of Huxley's studies or the prolonged belief in a managed, controlling loop through drugs: it is more likely that his studies had, by this time, opened the door to refreshed media that illustrate tripping's general principles and prophecies common to the different hallucinogens during this time. Hofmann, too, had worked for Sandoz Corporation, which had shipped drugs around the world to doctors and psychiatrists. Huxley is, then, given a new leash to speak, pontificate, and theorize from beneath a traditionally modernist syntax that favors a managed approach to extra-

---

[25] *Ibid.*
[26] *Ibid.*

sensory or parapsychological governance of societies. Huxley's studies would be intricate, plus the authority to bury socialist realism in the medical profession.

Mysticism or Escapism? Al Hubbard and the Period of Drug Couriers

At the juncture of the Weyburn Hospital years with new psychedelic teams came opportunities to talk about drug runners in the business at the time, such as suspected CIA agent and smuggler Al Hubbard. According to writer and biochemist Myron Stolaroff, who took LSD under Hubbard's guidance, "I was just astounded at what I learned, and I felt enormously free than what I had before. We set up the [International] Foundation [For Advanced Study] in [Menlo Park]. We got a lot of help from Al, from the Sandoz Corporation."[27] Stolaroff appraises LSD circumspectly, putting forth a more organic vision closer to Transcendentalism and widely popular with hippies ready to "turn on":

> With a good LSD experience, what happens, is you resolve your inner conflicts and loads and the barriers that have developed, and you begin to reach down into the depths of your being, more and more levels of understanding.[28]

These fairly exact psychometrics, which appear to echo Transcendentalism when substituting hallucinogens into Nature's much more contentious, broad concept, suppose Stolaroff's positive reminiscence about an expanded, enhanced being fully aware of psychic possibilities and illustrative of a graded yet liberating curve of personal growth and mature self-appraisals. There was the evident, lurking stereotype—romanticism, in all of its forms, told of freedom and self-development through "natural" hallucinogens, or at least these drugs' pairing with Nature's aesthetics, principles, and intonations of brain-body resolutions. These themes paint Hubbard as an inspirational figure and a would-be mendicant with a religious veer in a cryptic unfolding of drugged dreaming. *Hofmann's Potion*, through its many notables, greatly democratizes and socializes self-discoveries through drugs such as mescaline and LSD, where Kerouac had applied the fault line of pure, incipient Orientalism to denature the foliage of perspectives and knowledge that it had produced. Though the film separates Leary's religious involvement from that of Hubbard, who "radiated an energy,"[29] Blewett supposes the rustic, déclassé tone of personal Being: "He lacked any credence because he didn't have the customary

---

[27] *Ibid.*
[28] *Ibid.*
[29] *Ibid.*

training. And, um, people thought he was a wild man."[30] Hubbard's role as an alternate *magus* is appreciated among the Huxleys, and Laura notes his use of a "CO2 apparatus" at a lunch with them. As an afterthought, Stolaroff notes: "I think Huxley enjoyed Hubbard. One of the things that [Hubbard and Stolaroff] planned was to reach a place where we could set up treatment centers worldwide. Eventually, Al set up a place in Vancouver, which was a place to, uh, give people LSD with a proper kind of setting."[31] Thus, several thinkers, including Huxley, lay the ground for the growth of institutions and consummate purpose, a chance to extend psychedelic immersions and indoctrinations into a braver, wider new medical world. The parable of the psychedelic man's unfinished history, plus the grit of his roughened, underclass politicians who were renegades that crossed legal and regional lines to pursue enlightenment and expanded new approaches to living and learning, gave psychiatry its welcome coloration. Studies and reports did not misrepresent the increasingly popular method of inundation, and medical and scientific technologies appraise a much greater institutional reach in the form of organizations and clinics with structured sensual re-development. As the paradigms of Leary, Huxley, and Osmond grew, they did so away from academic institutions, taking on communities and social interactions to spread popular science against the grain of psychiatry's hitherto limited axis.

With no template of written documents to codify and explain findings as scholarship, interviews, and solid narrative anchoring in *Hofmann's Potion* accomplishes the splendid and thoughtful diversity of opinions and the graded curve of ideas and studies that would build a formidable addition to today's psychiatry. The breach from the academy was not planned, but the scientists' guiding wisdom opined that greater study and success with those studies benefit change in sociology and psychology. Hofmann's self-conceived, broad-angle would be adapted and modified to suit general psychological needs; conjoined with this would be the success of theoreticians illustrating positive processes when rebuilding post-World War II societies and citizens. *Hofmann's Potion*, in its many voices, did accomplish modernism's literary and scientific tendencies in a thriving moment that was well-remembered and held within in it many expert shards of learning and experience that were more, not less, translatable onto the hordes of hippies during the 1960s.

---

[30] *Ibid.*
[31] *Ibid.*

Chapter 12

The True Multiplicity of Perspectives.
LSD: The Beyond Within

Jay Stevens profiled the experiments of 102-year-old Dr. Albert Hofmann, the creator of LSD and a frequent advocate and scientist concerning mescaline and psilocybin, in "A Bike Ride in Basle."[1] Stevens and Max Whitby, in the film *LSD: The Beyond Within*, exposited Hofmann's warm, affirmative tone when it came to experimenting with hallucinogens and documented the experiment's incomplete fortitude. Still, one must accept the psychedelic theorist's cautionary tale when Huxley says in the *Herald Examiner*:

All existing drugs are treacherous and harmful. The heaven into which they usher their victims soon turns into a hell of sickness and moral degradation. They kill, first, the soul, then, in a few years, the body [...] However the results of prohibition are not encouraging. Men and women feel such an urgent need to take occasional holidays from reality, that they will do almost anything to procure the means of escape.[2]

Rough guides to psychedelic theory gain objective ground quickly, and audiences find that Huxley's comments are plastic and unreasonable. They are, in context, political fiction to deflect controversies, instead assuming the conservative moral ground that shores up authority to state current perspectives as falsely ascendant in our modern imaginations. Still, Huxley's main thesis was that safe, effective drugs would be synthesized to advance the human condition. This supposition safeguarded research, study, and advancement of the author's techniques. What, then, was our composite assessment for LSD, mescaline, and psilocybin— "new" drugs that were popular throughout the twentieth century? Relying on objective data from experimenters, we will then internalize social and individual changes and perhaps the underscored strength of the general idea that drug addicts, sick people, and persons with disabilities could be helped through hallucinogenic drugs. Whitby's 83-minute *LSD: A Beyond Within*, with Peter France as the narrator, traces and forecasts the impact of Hofmann's discovery. While a Sandoz chemist twenty-five years

---

[1] Stevens, Jay, *Storming Heaven*, 3-12.
[2] *Ibid*, 10.

before LSD was outlawed in the United States in 1968. Conversely, it should be noted that the film did much to shore up objective angles for studying hallucinogenic drugs by recording the experimenter's experiences, tying Huxley's narrow dictation to contrast discoveries and intensities with pathology, and advancing critical psychological commentaries from leaders, professors, and lay participants concerning the positive and negative data found in trips during the 1960s. Hofmann grew from Huxley's narrowed thesis about social policy to position real examples that suggest growing human psychology to advance social change.

France explains at the film's outset: "The drug challenges our very conception of reality, and its turbulent history raises sharp questions, refining lines between private experience and public policy."[3] He adds the historical background: "Ergot is a fungus that grows on corn. For centuries, midwives have used it to stimulate the uterus in childbirth."[4] From this expansive beginning, where versions of ergot's historical use paraphrased its medicinal value, Whitby's film turns to Hofmann's spoken overtures considering, learning, and becoming used to hallucinogenic drugs as a means of engaging new or unfound realities. American writer Norman Mailer was adamant in stressing the point of knowledge that could destroy racist or unjust institutions or practices: "Man's nature, man's dignity, is that he lives, loves and finally destroys himself seeking to penetrate the mystery of existence, and unless we partake in some way, as some part of this human exploration then we are no more than the pimps of society and the betrayers of our Self."[5] Nonetheless, Hofmann duly exposed LSD's legality—and thus, Sandoz's legitimate role in helping patients—while presenting phenomena in a way that is easy for us to undertake. With no concentrated neurological or pathological examinations, Hofmann's comments made the study growth available, projecting self-examinations generating the emerging doctrine on man's spiritual attainments.

Albert Hofmann's Observations

What is excellently clear is that Hofmann's undertakings involve thoughtful, complex examinations of light, color, dreams, and perception. These emphasized expansions of studies and the cleverly wrought parable calling attention to centuries of exploration that socialist realism crushed to raise its modern morals above ground. Hofmann begins with his matter-of-fact statement of himself as subject: "I acquired a feeling of oneness with the world, a very strange experience which reminded me, [of] some experience I had in

---

[3] *LSD: The Beyond Within.*
[4] *Ibid.*
[5] Mailer, Norman, *Advertisements for Myself,* 325.

childhood."⁶ He then rosily documents his private sense of being: "Sometimes I almost see nature and forests and would have some kind of, I would say, mystical experiences."⁷ Hofmann, in short, is relaxed and confident, whereas Leary might have had trouble explaining LSD's relevance. He advances the drug's transcendentalism and modernism in a referential high point that religious followers and thought-minded citizens could access when exploring their everyday, conscious grasp. Saying of his first experience that "the external world was stranger and stranger,"⁸ Hofmann would join perceptual psychology with concept-object and color-body relationships, expanding Freud's thesis that our unconscious thought enriched our sense of Self:

> In the room, I was really astonished at how this room had changed. The room itself and the objects in this room were quite different. Different colors, different meanings, and objects like this chair had, most likely, it was a living object, moving from inside. It was so unusual that I got afraid and had to come inside.⁹

France continues, "LSD was perhaps a tea to unlock the unconscious mind,¹⁰" and that "research soon showed that LSD closely resembles powerful natural chemicals in the brain used to exchange nerve messages in brain cells."¹¹ When the film examined Huxley's influence on Hofmann's studies, it turned to mescaline's production and its basis in Native American lore, while a violin quartet plays a repetitive piece.¹² The notation in another music piece flanked with psychedelic colors is simple: "Sound, too, is strangely transformed; sights are swelled, and sounds are seen."¹³ Dr. Anthony Bruce then capped discussions about the drug's psychiatric uses: "treatment of chronic patients in hospitals for chronic status to develop a verbal formulation of the patient's basic conflicts." Open-ended discussions from the author, narrator, and field respondents confirm simple brain- and body-function developments, offsetting generations of psychological ignorance that force us to acknowledge our need for psychic development. Hofmann performs his mescaline trip in solitude thoughtfully, taking "4/10ᵗʰ of a gram dissolved in sulfate":

---

⁶ *LSD: The Beyond Within.*
⁷ *Ibid.*
⁸ *Ibid.*
⁹ *Ibid.*
¹⁰ *Ibid.*
¹¹ *Ibid.*
¹² *LSD: The Beyond Within.*
¹³ *Ibid.*

> Now, someone produced a photograph of a recording on the turntable. The voices were a kind of bridge back to the home. The uneven phrases were navigating a certain course, running so deep, and suddenly, I had an inkling of what it must be like to be mad. [...] None too soon, I began to return to that assurance. Finally, I was in a satisfactory state, known as Being-oneness, and then came back through the door. We're never quite the same as the mad have known.[14]

Suppose the goal is to intensify Hofmann's comment so that we may propose a logical and physical redemption of human beings through LSD. In that case, we must admit that "oneness" and "Being" were not concepts he invented. Mary Lutyens paraphrases Krishnamurti's coming into Being through his experiments during the 1920s in *The Years of Awakening*:

> I would ask you to look at my point of view; I would ask you to come and look through my window, which will show you my heaven, which will show you my garden and my abode. Then you will see that what matters is not what you do, what you need, what any person says you are or are not, but that you should have the intense desire to enter that abode where dwells Truth.[15]

Krishnamurti's anointed state, then, did not come from drug taking but rather from a consummate meditation of the various religions when focused upon an intense awareness of spiritual desire. Hofmann, by contrast, mixes modern and rustic perceptions, noting the superior sensations that come from negating or dissecting our modern Selves' minutes and spoken instances. Myths of transcendence, to be sure, grew from the living schism's intellectual engagement between what was rustic and modern: Hofmann, to be sure, spoke of realization's ecstasy, away from machines and technologies, or modern intellectual processing. But were modern instruments of technology, faith, and knowledge instrumental in building acid transcendences?

Without relaying the obvious detail—*The Beyond Within* staged classical music instead of rock—Hofmann's "trip," which impressed Huxley enough to try mescaline, operated four complete stages: language, sense-impressions, psychology, and self-realization. Hofmann did not stray from sympathies that call attention to Native American philosophy, which tends to de-literate human drug-takers when it situates what it calls "pure" consciousness. Nor are his remarks far from Hindu and Buddhist imaginations, which also historically

---

[14] *Ibid*.
[15] *The Years of Awakening*, 251.

The True Multiplicity of Perspectives 117

stress de-literalization when achieving states of consciousness and spiritual inclusion. Hofmann was unsure to speak, transforming mescaline into a new consciousness but broadly commenting on their phenomena to delineate abstract states of psychic, inner awareness. Contrasts with Beat Generation authors of the period could not be starker, with Kerouac's peyote trip in Mexico in 1952 giving audiences a purely romanticist syntactic puzzle:

> I went out and walked around feebly in the moonlight of the park with no coat wanting to sit in the grass and stay near the ground all night by moonlight, with the lights of the show and the houses all flashing, flashing in my eyeballs, not in technicolor riot but in a great flapping of light that clapped over my eyes in intervals, as if. I knew the light was a throb and is.[16]

Kerouac's easy graduations into Being may be a garbled tale that begets consumption. Still, the effect of it was wide open: to situate Being while transcending madness, which in part stresses human separation and isolation from social Being. Mescaline's narratives do not become more stylistically refined or maintain unified structures of Being. In 1971's *A Separate Reality*, Don Juan admonishes Castaneda, telling him that Mescalito had taught a convulsive, dancing young tripper "a song."[17] In short, Kerouac's memoir does not explain any phenomenology and transposes words without reasoned materiality—the body and mind's exclamations are sacred even though we cannot describe *why*. Prose, in short, never was "clean" or "reasoned," and the countercultural pundit enjoyed a wide subjectivity when composing thoughts and experiences that critics thought had no meaning.

Still, Hofmann's identifications of body and spirit re-assemble philosophical engagements of our awareness: command, belief, and language all attach themselves to the consummate Oneness. Lastly, we welcome Hofmann's first experiment with the drug without prior knowledge of his drug habits or their format to again suggest free transcription of content and individual annexation of the drug's properties. No cautionary remark from other Harvard professors like Richard Alpert (Ram Dass) colors the picture. In context, Hofmann's pure discovery was complete enough to replicate twentieth-century mythology. This was not without adverse risings, and in the 1970s, a scornful Don Juan consistently stressed Mescalito's leadership of drug experiments.[18] Still, to say that an enhanced consciousness could be reached with no indoctrination

---

[16] Kerouac, Jack, *Selected Letters*, 1940-1956, 370.
[17] Castaneda, Carlos, *A Separate Reality*, 102.
[18] *The Teachings of Don Juan: A Yaqui Way of Knowledge*, 61.

promised man his intuitive directions and the success of his conditioned experiments. In its free translation of ideas and contexts, much-ballyhooed romanticism duplicates and furthers the drug's necessity and meaningful interface with modern consciousness, shuttering spiritual inquiry. This effect appears when we problematize those impulses and render their artistry imperfect spiritual structures that, when complicated, raise consciousness instead of directing and suppressing it. Hofmann's last statement about madness suggests learning's necessary transition—there is no mind-body distinction, and emotions and thoughts enjoy their interdependence.

Conclusion: Hofmann's Later Reflections

LSD: The Beyond Within develops strong engagements of drug use's praise and criticism: there are numerous accounts of persons affiliated with the drug that point to LSD's social dangers and physical dangers. One professor aptly recorded a tripper's belief that he could "fly" when taking the drug. Still, comments from British politicians such as Lord Christopher Mayhew recall some of his positive horror:

> The psychiatrist afterward said this is nonsense. You couldn't have had these experiences because, as the film shows, there's no time. And the psychiatrist would speak, and I've accepted this, and I was showing the symptoms of what they called the disintegration of the ego. I accept that, too.[19]

Mayhew, in this segment, operates a straight pathology that interrogates the decline of the human subject: the comment tears LSD down to destroy human function. It takes away the basis for his reason. Still, despite Mayhew's obligatory resistance to LSD, he records an outcome in favor of psychic transformations to project a non-realist portrayal that extends the arms of belonging and being:

> Now, after thirty years, when I remember that after the experience, I remember that afternoon, not as so many minutes, but in my drawing room, interrupted by these strange experiences, but as years and years of heavenly bliss interrupted by short periods in my drawing room. When I recorded and when I recall the various other symptoms, I think

---

[19] *LSD: The Beyond Within.*

the simplest explanation is that I had these experiences, and they were real and that they took place outside time.[20]

Carefully melding philosophical and psychological shards of awareness, Mayhew arrives upon a transcendence of time that situates bliss and God-like inclusion that is warmly romantic, taking advantage of anti-reason to forecast human functioning outside of time—dispelling Immanuel Kant's statement of time and space as primary functional anchors for human existence. He reiterates the religious parable, where different comprehensions that do not comprise a quantum of Being dependent upon man's daily reasoning power had figured our memory to be strange and therefore tied to the individuated memory as its message-bearer. LSD's positive democratizations of experience and temporal, recorded memory bore witness to the presence of psychic powers that escape scientism. This finding fosters a shield of greater meaning in the technological-military consciousness that mends its excesses through materialism, time, and space. A greater, less defined functioning for the brain that appends to Western magic and non-Western histories operated. Criticism aside, we own up to the fact that, as with Huxley, many LSD prophets were reluctant to endorse the drug because they doubted it could be understood and controlled. Still, religious realms were given agency, presenting a different functionality to audiences and a beginning step for dramatizations of a greater mind and the sweep of its contents as image-referents of something private, nuanced, and imperfect, escaping quantification. Interestingly enough, Mayhew's experience did not depart the form of Dean Moriarty's experience smoking "green, uncured marijuana" in *On the Road*[21]. The historical frame tale recurs during time's absence to restate doctrines of Being, bearing its selfless attachment to the subject identity and the Ego's surrender to avenues of Truth beyond our rational Selves.

Expanded hallucinogenic contexts, then, fight with the body's more straight pathologies to convey the dynamic messenger within the addict's moment of difficulty. In these ways, too, *The Beyond Within* included several examples calling our attention to a new sense of parapsychology without investigating doctrines of the spirit and soul that often deny our perceptions their meaning. The conflagration of perspectives suggests a greater referencing centered upon a divine Self beyond time and so upon trips and excursions that could widen critical responses to existing neuropathology. Of course, Freud cautiously spoke to the persistence of ideas and memories holding no reason, professing that unconscious driving desires compensated man for his moral ills. These

---

[20] *Ibid.*
[21] Kerouac, *Jack, On the Road*, 184.

ideas had not, however, been analyzed concerning time, and so remained the beginnings of the twentieth-century spirit's persistence.

Hofmann's dictation of LSD and mescaline trips was not, in short, meditated through aesthetic or moral theories, as Huxley was friendly with. Instead, he conjoined objective data to assume an ethical theory resonant with a more analytic theorization of the nature of human experiences. The studied waves of acid's prolegomena attributed Freud's broader front to necessitating conscious change and institutional change. Sandoz had freed his inquiry of the necessary political activism, stating that virtue was directly pulled from perceptions. The medical angle was thus broadly suggested: there is abundant text narrowing our focus onto people with an addiction and mental health patients to resurface noble neurology that might reconnect souls that generations of addiction and poor health destroyed or neutralized. Cross-examinations, too, tell us that Hofmann was a separate entity from the counterculture, contrived as distinct forces furthering a different lineage. Still, the friendly, penitent gaze approximates future studies and those studies' innocence, free of any political reagent.

Hofmann's redoubt is done without examining his published work, including 1970's *Plants of the Gods*, in any detail. With the focus on Hofmann's discovery, not his prose, we finally allow the scientist-thinker to pose his essential questions at the movie's beginning. Our relaying of spoken text may cause us to relay some better parts of specific theoretical and analytical ideas that he would espouse. Still, we are spared terminologies and theories for most of this film. It may be worthwhile to count these as a beginning to understanding how modernist theory elicited convincing responses about what psychedelic theory is, without monikers or trite sayings, connoting the emergent counterculture's key values. Still, the weight of Hofmann's comments exudes the same seriousness that was true of Freud, with aesthetic tropes promising discoveries and their impact upon contemporary cultures. Studied commentaries, by contrast, told us of the experiments' success and their careful, nurtured eye while studying the afflicted. *Hofmann's Potion* internationalizes perspectives and affords us a rooted scholarly tradition when tackling modern life's most aggravating problems by making Canada our essential conduit.

Chapter 13

Dr. Timothy Leary and the Popularization of Psychedelic Forms

Dr. Timothy Leary, long wanted by the FBI as a criminal and an enduring advocate of drug tripping during his life, bears the form of considerable scholastic immersion and involvement that includes his organization of hippies and professionals to "Tune In, Turn On, Drop Out." Dreams of literary and scholastic transcendence can easily be found in the secondary criticism about Leary, including the following from biographer Robert Greenfield: "As he lies awake in bed, the boy dreams of heroes. Huck Finn smokes a corncob pipe with Jim as they float down the Mississippi River. Horatio at the bridge. Lancelot setting off to find the Holy Grail."[1] A cursory note finds the general format of watching a psychedelic film. Many actors in the unfolding psychedelic maze, scholars, and laypeople convolute its evolving forms found in published research. What was evident, too, was that Leary's frequent travels were meant to spread awareness, and he had thought about how his indoctrinations played out when talking about modern man's realization through drugs. At the same time, we obtain the obvious seed of difference: Leary was not a man of letters, and though he published research in many journals and presses, he did not write and think from within the same modernist cage as Huxley. I noted in *Seeing the Beat Generation* that Leary envied the group's "bohemian" status and ability to "report back." Clearly, at the onset of Federal Prison, there was writing anxiety and the anxiety of knowledge translation.[2] Therefore, his life and outlook were narrowed to the point of taking parapsychology to its root forms to state the text's authority rather than its adaptation. All this did not detract from his finding a true stance about the many-faced 1960s counterculture. Still, it is more likely that Leary's studies, unlike those of Huxley, would necessarily be welded to the epitaph of Eastern philosophies and their composed archetypes of transcendence. Leary's work, therefore, stubbed out the pattern of mysticism's Western inventions, bearing no synthesis between East and West, and thus operates a more concentrated transition and self-

---

[1] Greenfield, Robert. *Timothy Leary: A Biography*, 3.
[2] Chandarlapaty, Raj, *Seeing the Beat Generation*, 109.

realization through his amalgamation of visual and aural texts from the pages of an Eastern typology and its referenced indoctrinations.

Therefore, readings of *The Tibetan Book of the Dead* are perhaps the most useful to understand the collage of perspectives from interviews, hearings, and speeches where Leary promotes the idea that LSD can improve social consciousness and paint new forays into conscious evolutions. It is very likely that when he appraised Huxley, Hofmann, and Dass, Leary decided to present in tandem the details of his immersion rather than generalize about the stream of findings pouring in throughout Western history. It was not without equal grounding in the well-educated, prolific Huxley, who, in *The Perennial Philosophy*, wrote about Vedanta practices: "The original Mind is to be recognized along with the working of the sense and thoughts—only it does not belong to them, nor yet is it independent of them."[3] Statements that stress positive links between neurology and philosophy might, then, vocalize mysticism's continuing re-invention through drugs or enlarged claims to psychic legitimacy when referencing ancient mysticism as the guide to hallucinations. Lest we call Leary's scholarship any less referential, we may nurture the claim that the two men came upon many ideas and states of being simultaneously, with liberalism giving way to the studies' materialist realism. Of course, Michael Horowitz carried out the main breach in the direction of perspectives in his book, *Moksha: Aldous Huxley's Classic Writings on Psychedelics*: "It seemed to me a fundamental potential of this chemical agent had not yet been sufficiently considered or recognized, namely its ability to produce visionary experiences."[4] We will also attempt to recognize Leary's specific insights and those of his supporters and how these findings complement the work of Huxley and Hofmann, two men who had taken both LSD and mescaline and written about the drugs' modern interfaces.

At a Glance: Leary and the Specific Minute of Realization, Captured in his Studies

To try to understand Leary's specific discoveries found in the film, I thought it might be useful to provide the personal context—namely, a time when I took LSD at a Grateful Dead concert in 1993 in Oakland, California. In interviews and public speeches, Krishnamurti argued that LSD and marijuana "destroy the brain"[5] and that drugs such as these provide a preconceived notion of brain function that is not spontaneous, nor do they consider the living world.[6] In *You*

---

[3] *The Perennial Philosophy*, 59.
[4] Horowitz, Michael, *Moksha*, preface.
[5] Krishnamurti, Jiddu, *Awakening of Intelligence*, Part IX.
[6] "Jiddu Krishnamurti on Psychedelics," *Dipitum Magazine*.

are The World, he provided a generalist notation: "The Christian, when taking drugs or seeking some great experience through different ways, will see something colored by his conditioning."[7] Visual instances coincide with this; visually, my concert experience *was entirely* preconceived as I looked out into the crowd and saw a vision of me as a paranoid boy with an older girl holding him. In terms of the sound and feel of the music itself, however, this experience *was not preconceived*, and rhythm and sound had produced a peculiar set of harmonies interacting with graded, colored light in the building. Because of this perceptual angle, the experience's power was enough to pressure me to leave the building and hear the remainder of the concert from the parking lot. "Energy" could come from sound and spoken words rather than from one's hallucinations. I believe that, too, with Leary, Huxley, and Hofmann, one might consider the auditory experience's originality and the mix of perceptions rising above the eye's perceptions. One may, then, discard stereotypes that say that psychedelic visuals are our main instance of tripping, re-appraising Huxley's deathbed experience, and molding together spoken words, sounds, and feelings derived from those media. When answering Krishnamurti, it became clear that my elder had grimly appraised the redundancy of LSD-induced visual metaphors: "[drug users] have no sense of responsibility, they think they can do anything they like, many, many hospitals are full of these people who mentally are unbalanced through drugs."[8] When covering Leary, the guided prism was less efficient to the task of the idea's proliferation than it was to the other senses. Should experiences be stereotypical, we argue that they reduce brain functions. Still, when they are not, we are summoned to find out how much brain psychology Leary knew and how useful his techniques for self-discovery were. In retrospect, Krishnamurti's commentaries forced the onus of proof upon Leary's profound, ingenious populism when speaking about LSD. It is certain, given earlier psychedelic thinkers' ambivalence about the social standard gained by drug use and the treatment of drug addicts, that the film's evidence states the factual norm that may, in principle, set up the experiences' positive success, introducing humankind's specific consciousness that prepares the way for adaptive psychology.

As a subset of the natural sympathies and conscious discoveries that LSD enhances, it is necessary to demonstrate, as in any psychological study, how the drug elicits positive or meaningful responses when watching films devoted to their theoretical exercise. In his analysis of *The Psychedelic Experience*, Leary wrote about the impact of phenomena to generalize about tripping's importance:

---

[7] Krishnamurti, *You are The World*, 133.
[8] Krishnamurti, Jiddu, *Awakening of Intelligence, Part IX*.

Of course, the drug does not produce the transcendent experience. It merely acts as a chemical key—it opens the mind and frees the nervous system of its ordinary patterns and structures. Set denotes the preparation of the individual, including his personality structure and mood at the time. The setting is physical—the weather, the room's atmosphere; social—feelings of persons present towards one another; and cultural—prevailing views of what is real.[9]

Leary then unveils his specific *praxis* to understand drug experiments from the advice of "manuals":

If the manual is read several times before a session is attempted, and if a trusted person is there to remind and refresh the memory of the voyager during the experience, the consciousness will be freed from the games, which comprise "personality" and from positive-negative hallucinations, which often accompany states of expanded awareness.[10]

Leary, in short, weds his academic studies of Buddhism to the precise method to elicit states of awareness that dismantle the subject's personality—in context, the social and moral controls, and thus our speech and visual codes, repeat Victorian moral dominance and its organization of individuals. In doing so, he counteracts Huxley's more pluralist development of conscious ideas, stating for readers modern man's absence of perspectives or conditioned states when he isolates and romanticizes the Buddhist *oeuvre*. De-Christianization is, then, bound to nagging questions about Leary's spiritual aestheticism—a truly romantic conception must come from illogic, not logic, and so engendering personality to spell out the unconscious as part and instance of a greater, more navigable psychology. "Voyage," of course, envisages the mind's transcendence, but "cultural—prevailing views as to what is real" re-opens cultural paradigms, advancing the chance at a myriad of spiritual experiences that could redirect our psychic state against normality's subordination of it to class, status, education, and wealth to stage the problems of drug addicts and neurodivergent patients.

Without attempting objective neurology and with no quantum evidence to form this part of this work, Leary generalizes that indoctrinations are sympathetic to the brain's re-awakening and self-realization of content as a kind of awareness. He issues no straight rendition of the patient's practical realization or of specific emotions or states of being. Instead, it uses the drug's therapeutic powers to reorganize outlook and meaning away from realist

---

[9] Leary, Timothy, *The Psychedelic Experience*, 3.
[10] *Ibid*, 3-4.

fetishisms and fiction. From this angle, he tends to Buddhist organizations of indoctrination, ignoring other religions but admitting that other cultures around the world could assign reality from their standpoints. Leary's Pavlovian impulse to proselytize, then, creates new outcomes for the resultant case studies' proliferation, wiping away Being's fetishism with a fairly open chart of what might come next. Once again, we must allow that Leary's studies were embryonic and, while thought to project objective trends, were different in that the spirit's liberation contrasts with Huxley's unspecified doctrine of control. The two men concur on education's leading hand but differ when considering higher consciousness's democratized stream of synapses, increasing a wide range of practices, media, and sources to suggest Kesey's grand psychedelic re-opening of meaning broadly. When questioned, Leary spoke less about drug use's metaphysics as a positive science but instead transposed government-military conspiracies onto the ordering of human principles. We shall, then, turn to the films to deduce Leary's success at mitigating his ideas, to even suggest that there were legitimate psychological contributions. Huxley's warning about jazz in *Brave New World* reflected a new responsibility for Leary since not all practices were liberating, nor could anyone philosophy give us genuine results about man's psychic rejuvenation. Close readings of Leary's text and instances in film, then, tell us more about specific techniques and studies that give life to the psychedelic form in psychology studies that, from Freud's time, were and are normative, making us realize that Leary did not think that capitalist-military organizations offset the states of awareness, nor the subject's inclusion in today's world.

Leary's Studies of Buddhism

Leary reaches a narrowed point concerning vision in his readings of *Bardo Thadol*. In the analogy of drug taking to Tibetan knowledge, he wrote:

> Thus, in the Tibetan *Thadol*, after the seven peaceful deities, there come seven visions of wrathful deities, fifty-eight in number, male and female, "flame-enhaloed, wrathful, blood-drinking." [...] Instead of many-headed fierce mythological demons, they are more likely to be engulfed and ground by impersonal machinery, manipulated by scientific, torturing control devices, and other space-fiction horrors.[11]

Leary's reading of Tibetan Buddhism through drugs, then, restates Huxley's identifications of material-industrial sickness and technological destructions

---

[11] Leary, *The Psychedelic Experience*, 54.

to situate Krishnamurti's ringing denunciation of "ego-loss,"[12] stating that "none of the higher phenomena will appear" because participants could not *recognize* the visions occurring in these experiences."[13] Finally, Leary proposes "re-entry" into the egoistic mind "on one of six levels, or as one of six personality types."[14] Leary matches the subject's depersonalization with enhanced physical and mental self-perception: "The voyager may also feel that he possesses supernormal powers of perception and movement."[15] What must be uncovered, then, is not the clarity of one's visions. After all, critics had already closed discussions about drug use's visible pathology, and Krishnamurti and Huxley scolded the subject's moral destruction through drugs. Leary's imagistic parable, where bliss and feeling met modern man's terrors that spawned the loss of personality and awareness, unveiled a tenacious subject who could take modern existence's horrors and deteriorations, linking them to the larger culture, not to the counterculture. Leary's indoctrinations stand wholly intact, severed from monotheistic religions' positioning of Heaven and Hell. Visions and hallucinations, then, lay within indoctrination's positive annexes, not only to be studied and pontificated about. One aspect of our study of Leary in film must address illusions of positive psychic transformation, gaining cultural and language ground to testify to the learning paradigm—and to the didactic angle, as many writers and thinkers had overrun this point with infantile, irreverent positioning of these key states of consciousness. Restated, what did Leary inspire in his followers, if anything? Was this key point ever cross-examined to produce capitalist culture technologies, or could such a pattern be established in the growing number of drug-takers? Modern man's decisive moment, too, should be studied carefully concerning this point—LSD rapidly declined in popularity after 1970, and key avenues of the wild, fertile tale of prophecies and hallucinations gave way to less systemic evaluations of the body and mind. Leary's addendum to future countercultures must be considered in light of *Brave New World*'s adorned social hierarchy splitting and interrelating Being's instances.

Lastly, when we moor Leary's findings and discoveries to his much-adorned prophecies, we envision the practitioners' collision and the seriousness implied to constitute Leary's genesis as a thinker who reflected upon his times. Films featured interviews with Leary while on trial and in a Federal Penitentiary, contrasting discovery's innocence with the movement's stance in mobilizing youth. At the outset, it should be said that films did not always delve into

---

[12] *Ibid*, 55.
[13] *Ibid*, 55.
[14] *Ibid*, 63.
[15] *Ibid*, 60.

scientific findings but rather paired them with relentless videography and pictography that ensnare moments of *praxis* contradicting and counteracting Huxley's more rigid thesis about hallucinogens and their indoctrinating powers or resolve them into unrepentant idealism so that we may crown a practical science. It should be noted, too, that Leary is, in film, more a thinker than a researcher, and the scientist's research base was retroactively investigated. Published works accord the thinker's seriousness, but Leary's comments about others simultaneously dispense our positive ire and awe. Getting closer to the front of psychedelic journeys and excursions telling the coming 1960s counterculture, too, may force us beyond the heel of case studies and prophetic teardowns of the contemporary order. In their insouciance and penitent devotions, they pave the way for social transformations that are more intricate than those Huxley devised in *Brave New World*. Another useful point of comparison owes itself to the internal dissection of details about Leary's 1996 death.

Simply put, why was the author's death useful to our grasp of psychedelic studies? What key points in Leary's self-reflection spoke of a legitimate perspective about him or his theories? Biographical questions also urge the full sweep of Leary's life and times, though it should be said that many psychedelic films include overlapping content. Is the film's rhetoric strong and deep enough to increase humanities studies that advance a sustained point about the durability of findings and mores gained from taking drugs? It should be noted that, concerning drugs, not all films engender the same depth of visual and spoken presentation. We might then assume all materials should remain tied to the primary works. This is a false assumption, and the film gives us an internal look at how ideas and concepts were formed and what, potentially, they meant. We now turn to Leary's presumed anxieties as a thinker and purveyor of reason.

Chapter 14

The Collective Body of Interpretation of Leary's Life, Work and Times, and its Relevance to Trends in Psychedelic Film and Literature

Collections of interviews, news articles, and stories in the Timothy Leary Collection at Harry Ransom Center loudly told of the author's non-furtive glance and administrative skill when organizing psychedelic immersions and street-level revolt. Paired with the writer's brilliance and telescopic focus on drugs are accounts of abuses in Federal prisons and the progressive formats for tripping, telling us firsthand accounts of the live teaching of the subject caught in the developing framework. I think the time is reasonable to state what we may expect from films related to Leary's efforts in building psychedelic humanities and *praxis*. He, like Huxley, was an organized and controlled social and personal event, and he believed that psychedelic science was exact, enjoying its proponent influence in the worlds of knowledge, academia, and politics when they favored institutional and cultural change.

Biography

Dr. Timothy Leary was born to an Irish Catholic family in Springfield, Massachusetts, on October 22, 1920. After a stint at West Point and then with the US Army, he studied psychology at the University of California, earning his Ph.D. in Psychology in 1950. While a lecturer at Harvard, Dr. Leary composed his first accounts of his research on LSD and later psilocybin. President Richard Nixon called him "America's Most Dangerous Criminal," and Leary was sentenced to 10 years in a federal prison and was re-sentenced in 1973 after he fled the United States only to be captured in Afghanistan. In most studies of the 1960s documenting Leary's travels, studies, and public appearances, Leary was more dogmatic about psychedelic drug-taking's positive values, easily more forward-leaning than the thoughtful, discretionary, and aesthetic Huxley. He was also efficient in the integration of psychedelic science with undefined instances of positive drug therapies and their role in re-conditioning the human subject. Leary, though not more objective from all disciplinary angles, was the most objectively directed of the psychedelic authors, focused on changing psychology with no political examples of modern reality.

Accounts from the Timothy Leary Collection include several news entries concerning Leary's arrest, trial, and incarceration, starring the stiff-handling judge and police who handle Leary's drug case and convicting him. Our focus should not be upon Leary's issue of social justice alone but should give credence to his meditations' experimental nature and what those might mean for our studies. Sitting in jail, Leary opts for the following transference of psychedelic grandeur upon the prison's decrepit, cold expanse:

> The prison cell is my home in Space. It's enforced meditation. In time, you will find me in Benares, the dirtiest city in the solar system. The smell gets stronger, like a monstrous fart stinking like wet earth. It's nice. Pilgrims stream in, pray, wash, meditate, and cut out with added merit, each adding to the aroma of burning flesh and open gutter sewers. Hindus who die in Benares go directly to heaven, a sort of baksheesh from Shiva chuckling in the purple throat and pulling up bunches of Hindus by their tales like mandrakes. India is free, like psychedelic drugs.[1]

A few pages earlier, Leary exposed the journalist's talent when interviewing him and the occult glories of the generative news empire in the 1970s:

> Tom Lynn is a twenty-year old weak blond Aries. He sits next to me in the TV room, telling tales of Vietnam, marijuana, Tokyo opium, acid love rituals in Army hospitals, hashish concubines in Bangkok, and shooting horses in the ladies' rooms in filling stations where he worked. At night, he stands outside my cell pretending to sweep, leaning on a broom, babbling me hip tales until the bull bellows him back to his cell.[2]

Besides deriving instances of the prisoners' peculiar fellowship in dire times, news clippings in confinement confirm the dope traveler's literary inheritance when he examines books and mantras from far-off cultures. Meaning's transposition, though distorted and unsure, to large audiences committed Leary to expanded notions of consciousness and the interplay of metaphors extolling psychedelic brilliance. Leary's options were not new and had been the subject of more accurate dialogues about otherness from James S. Lee and Allen Ginsberg.[3] Still, his professed dreams, or the transposition of his remote

---

[1] "Leary, Escapade, 5," From Timothy Leary Collection, Box 1.9.
[2] *Ibid*, 3.
[3] Lee, James S. *The Underworld of the East*, 45-50.

details and nebulous religious psychoses from the Hindu religion, pair our lack of legitimate scholarship with the drug-addled scheme of positive redemption. It would be said, too, that adherence to the intellectual principle survived the test of jail and that cold ruminations could still lend life to people searching for belief and consumption in the "new" world of drugs. At the end of "Escapade," and after numerous dope tales spelling out addiction's cruelty and its improvised formats, Leary exclaims:

> The Earth has orbited halfway around the sun since i was first arrested, and my chemistry is working at speeds conditioned by being locked in a cell for over six months.[4]

In the broader context, "Escapade" spills out the author's more infantile ramblings, the pain and perils of jail, and the depression and anxiety common to ruined addicts in transition. Leary's writings took on an embryonic form and vastly incomplete psychedelic science, borrowing its content from hippie Orientalists interested in the exotic novel and its translation of form onto American readership. Burroughs, who had avoided jail while *Naked Lunch* was on trial, could easily prime the obvious criticism: Leary held no meaningful impetus nor any experiences within his grasp, making the pages of his journals necessary.[5] There was no measured learning or the basis for studying drugs anymore. Moreover, Leary had no legal precedent to continue his studies, so his comments and meditations are empty and fractured, with no guiding necessity.

Techniques of adaptation and prefocusing of one's intellectual pretensions were not new. Leary didn't invent their narration: they were most concentrated and dutiful in Arthur Koestler's 1940 novel *Darkness at Noon*, with its powerful yet impotent communist diaries and monologues, and in Alexander Solzhenitsyn's 1962 novel, *A Day in The Life of Ivan Denisovich*, where the socialist's survival skills are tested. In their deep certitude, these works count modern man's repressed archaeology as instances of living, producing abstractions of context to identify with idealism's followers. It is certain from "Escapade," a 42-page story, that Leary did not drop the movement and was searching for some medium of expression to recount the knowledge he had gained. Leary, like Malcolm X, turned to reading and thinking when a prisoner: it would, in part, offset the severing of drug addiction. Should we add Leary's infantile recess of thinking, we would demand that films and writings express the counterculture's essential themes and exposit from them. Distillations of

---

[4] Leary, Timothy, "Escapade," 18. From *The Timothy Leary Collection*, Box 1, Folder 9.
[5] Burroughs, William, *Naked Lunch*.

knowledge and perspectives might underscore the template for man's actual learning and historical meaning.

Leary, Christianity, and Literary Communities

Newspaper articles, too, anchor sustained biographical and political formats for examining Leary's ideas and histories when they conformed to the reasoned bubble of psychedelic speculation and then to the peculiar ground for man's re-engagement of these ideas. Joe O'Sullivan interviews Leary in *Ave Maria* magazine, where Leary's Catholicism is examined in some detail. Leary begins: "In celebrations about the death and resurrection of Jesus Christ, the aim is to re-state the power and ancient meaning of the Catholic Mass."[6] He also notes, "Within fifty or a hundred years, the Catholic Church will be using LSD as a sacrament."[7] These ambitious statements, unfortunately, failed to integrate specific histories telling us whether Christian Europe had ever used sacraments. They obfuscated the local, Mexican angle of the Don Juan-created spirit Mescalito, a favored subject in Mexican Catholicism. Still, Leary's Catholic predictions and suppositions professed a resurgent political confidence and a proselytizing focus that could amalgamate and project critical detail counteracting 'expatriatism' from Huxley. He would take on the indeterminate histories in visions and altered sensory minutes, setting temporal goals for their progress and re-integrating key spiritual and psychic meditations. This fact did not mean that Leary's claim was factual. Still, they window his self-perception of a greater mode of Being offsetting the West's military-capitalist history that diminished modern history's imagistic and spiritual ruminations.

Readings of Leary's published scholarship may afford us the technique for situating hard facts and historical inferences about experiences and conditioning: these point to the group's success and culminations of the writer-thinker's achievement in changing psychology. We might, then, ask ourselves if psychedelic films spoke about the trend of accomplishments when reading the author's life, times, and travails. "Religious Implications of Consciousness Expanding Drugs," published in 1960 and part of a Harvard University psilocybin experiment with 400 participants, specifically targets criminals and drug addicts to cure their sickness and adjust their behavior. The obvious spoke to Leary's grasp of psychology as a modern science: Leary noted that "66 percent of the respondents found the experience pleasant and would be willing

---

[6] Sullivan, Joe O', "Interview," *Ave Maria*. From The Timothy Leary Collection, Box 1.12.
[7] *Ibid.*

to try it again"[8] and that prison inmates had also taken the drug. Still, Leary points to the experiment's basic problem:

> Were these insightful, life-changing, conversion-type reactions simply transient intoxications, or could they be made to stick? If the psilocybin experience were built into a systematic rehabilitation program, could we demonstrate enduring and measurable changes?[9]

After recalling several "highs" derived from music and the relaxing of memory, including a jazz listener who records "the deepest aesthetic experience in his life," Leary recalls:

> This illumination, when shared with other group members, becomes a powerful instrument for maintaining philosophic expansion.[10]

Leary, too, staged "enlightenment" versus "ego defensiveness," operating man's potential freedom from "games." These metaphors are decisive in saying that Leary had proven his point and corrected psychic imbalances through psilocybin. We might, then, strip psychedelic film of its abundance of positive stereotypes common to psychedelic organization and indoctrinations. Mentioning jazz, too, repairs drug archaeology to suggest a greater ethical minute of self-development that is anti-racial and might consider the participants' specific memory to be psychoactive. These, when paired with the long history of shamanic and occult cultures around the world, signal psychological change and diversification. Estimations of truth ought to be simple enough to gauge psychology's evolution and the simplicity of ideas and abstractions that constitute wellness and obedience. "Ego-defensiveness" and "games" spell out the counterculture's opposition to capitalist norms, which define product-object relationships as building blocks to one's Being: from this, Leary's ideology was clear and consistent with the thread he would develop, and that escaped his guiding hand. We would, in short, like to identify the counterculture's consistency to state the validity of Leary's teachings.

As we turn our focus to Leary's complex and conflicting myriad of experiences and imagism found in film, we would appraise ourselves of the fact that his work, though unique, spoke to a common herald and interfaced with many of the ideas that were found among literary greats during the twentieth century, forcing forward the illustration of scientific details against the perceived

---

[8] "Religious Implications of Consciousness Expanding Drugs," Box 1.10.
[9] *Ibid.*
[10] *Ibid.*

opulent romanticism and Orientalism characteristic of Western man's initial period of study. Though we may not, in short, gather purely objective ideas from Leary's studies, we are likely to confirm the basic scientific principle, after proving its hypothesis, that Leary had developed a set of cultural values common to its maintenance.

Chapter 15

A Shared Spotlight and the Messenger's Return: O.B. Babbs' *Timothy Leary's Last Trip* and Timothy Leary's Long Journey

O.B. Babbs's role as the omniscient narrator of the 55-minute film *Timothy Leary's Last Trip* accomplished the key themes of a documentary film in several ways. Firstly, what transpires in this film dilutes our notion that Leary was an accomplished psychedelic thinker: examples are few, and printed newspaper articles noted LSD's criticism instead of its praise. The young Babbs, Merry Prankster Ken Babbs's son and a star character in movies such as *Stand By Me* (1989) and *Psycho* (1998), narrates at the film's beginning, sifting together complete, unadorned stereotypes concerning Leary, LSD, or the 1960s. Introductory commentaries by fellow LSD-influenced writer and producer Ken Kesey are superficial in tone, including a cameo with a skeleton telling of the possibility of ergot's role in medieval societies during famines.[1] Worse, there is no true excavation of Leary's many writings, nor even a hint that his studies themselves breathed any impact in today's criticism. The sole example of LSD scholarship is a newspaper clipping assuring readers that LSD patients exhibit the characteristics of paranoia, sickness, and craziness.[2] Lastly, I believe that the superficial tactic previewing Leary's terminal prostate cancer and his attempt to connect with the details of his death is cronyism, loosely bringing together his positive *hubris* through the interpretations of a warm, receptive Kesey who, having put aside his differences with his elder, secures for Leary the positive legacy that history routinely denied him.

At a Glance: The Film as a Partial History of the 1960s

This movie would seem unsatisfying and dull from a scholar's glance were it not for the conversational angle. Through visual and spoken anchors and with Grateful Dead music in the background, this film examined reflective angles, featuring an all-star cast in which Kesey, Leary, Neal Cassady, O. B. Babbs, Wavy Gravy, and others put together shards of Leary's LSD puzzle, and stars the 1960s

---

[1] *Timothy Leary's Last Trip.*
[2] *Ibid.*

explosive political scene and facets of discovery's diaphanous frame. The film describes and visualizes the melting pot of travels, notables, and colorful comments to tailor what could be called Leary's positive wisdom. The film's shared enthusiasm, too, rebuilds context and perspectives against Leary's peculiarity and controversy in his thoughts and diversions when ideas had appeared crucial. We are, then, led into a rich fabric of travels, thoughts, and images vaunting the collaborative tale against dogmatic statements about Leary as an LSD *magus*. The rich biographical tale of Ken Kesey, the Merry Pranksters, and the Grateful Dead, too, appear to frame the positive didactic angle for populist readings. Loudly sequestered within songs, images, interviews, and Super 8 films was the tale's ambivalence and recorded positive growth.

As a general exposition, *Timothy Leary's Last Trip* truncates and delimits scholarship, and it must be admitted that more could have been said to secure Leary's place in the popular imagination. He was America's Most Wanted Criminal during Richard Milhous Nixon's Presidency, and his published titles re-invented psychedelic studies above the vanguards of surrealism, futurism, and modernism. There is no adherence to any remittance of opinion gained from Leary's elders, Aldous Huxley and Albert Hofmann: Leary's thoughts were decisive. The film, too, greatly limited psychedelic inferences from Grateful Dead guitarist Jerry Garcia: all of this is condensed under the guise of Kesey's verbal comments to attribute a literary, instead of oral, beginning for LSD's study. Also missing and probably needed in great detail were academic comments that criticized LSD. Instead, we are pointed to newspaper articles over 30 years. We may ask: what constituted a legitimate psychedelic study in this film? Why were so many key public examples doffed in favor of narrowly defined, often humorous introductions to the positive talent for expositing the drug's significance?

Babbs's introduction of the 1960s as a period of social revolution, too, ignored the Vietnam War, the Civil Rights Movement, and the Women's Movement, leaving behind many scenes and snapshots of the period that could point to the movement as a benchmark of political realism. Instead, the Pranksters' bus rolls through a street of stunned New Yorkers while young men and women dance in the darkened venues, taping the music and recording findings about behavior, feelings, and their conscious minutes.[3] The Dead's LSD legend and rock and roll's rise were truncated to avoid comparisons or complications from this biographical tale. There was, of course, a short introduction to the guise of the Beat Generation, including a cowboy-hatted Neal Cassady; Babbs states questionably that Cassady's fame was all about his stint as the Pranksters' bus driver, not the storied years of discoveries and writing: he is limited to one row

---

[3] *Ibid.*

with reporters, to which he innocently replies: "why did you guys show up?"[4] Poet Allen Ginsberg, who wrote provocative instances of LSD's naturalism and terror that included the 1959 poem "Lysergic Acid" and 1966's "Wales Visitation,"[5] was not covered. Novelist Jack Kerouac was also largely left out of this picture: this is a key flaw in the film's outtake, as Kerouac had taken mescaline as early as 1951 while in Mexico.[6] By contrast, Kesey is narrated as an educated writer and thinker, and grit is given to his meaningful leering and ruminations about what it all meant.

However, the many windows of interpretation and conversations revived the notion that something important and broadly relevant was happening, even if it was more likely to document the discovery's unanswered questions and shore up political conspiracies in American life. Simplistic or grandiose statements of LSD's power annex the idea's positive mystery. At the same time, it pushes past any historical study to suppose that drug experiments offer us new visitations of life rather than a utopia. Therefore, our first question tends to be about the film's form for expressing what social revolution meant and not from individual prophecies. Again, textual paucity gave credence to the idea that LSD was active and popular, not scholarly or contrived. The film's generous, rich trailer of visual examples includes teen youths taking LSD trips, bridging both Leary's and Kesey's rise to stardom.

Videography and spoken interviews from Leary and Kesey filled the wide gap between scholarship and pretense as it was outlined in the media. What should be understood is the proven dynamic when taking into account the public's increasing interest in hallucinogens. When we contrast Leary's positive hubris when in a maximum-security prison in 1973 on the subject:

> LSD is the most powerful substance humans have ever developed for the mind in compression of nuclear energy or fissional material. I think that, in the right hands, scientific or disciplined people will bring about changes.[7]

The following news article supposed the sobering fact of administering it to patients in hospitals:

---

[4] *Ibid.*
[5] Ginsberg, Allen, *Collected Poems* 1947-1980.
[6] *Jack Kerouac: Selected Letters* 1940-1956, 370.
[7] *Timothy Leary's Last Trip.*

Patients who have difficulty tend to be emotionally labile after hysterical or paranoid personalities.[8]

The drug's effect on patients and explorers during the countercultural period was not describable, and the parties and tune-ins graduated hordes of unfocused addicts. We would, in tighter estimations of video footage and spoken commentary, say that the Merry Pranksters, their antics, and their visual and occult practices could expand human conditioning, illustrating a new science that could build its practice in the panorama of divergent modern scenes, growing the drug's popularity and its inferential meaning. Leary's serious comments and abstractions of states of awareness then inhere his reflections on the growing and meaningful experience: he turns over the visual presentation to countless examples of carefully set-up trips and loose adaptations of the shamanic cultural arts hinted at in his diaries and treatises. While lying on a bed, Wavy Gravy robustly attributes Leary's potential spectacle: "Tune in, turn on, drop out was, you know, major, major headlines everywhere."[9]

Leary's Relationship with Ken Kesey and the Increasing Anxiety

Sources and interviews, however, circumvented scholarship's pale, with the narrator boasting alongside a *Playboy* interview with three photos of Leary, "the news of Leary's radical research had already spread to all corners of the world."[10] *Timothy Leary's Last Trip* did not, in short, favor intellectual transmission of research: evidence of the author's notoriety, his private thoughts, and the reduction of these in his old age replaced broad scholarly examples found in journals. Abstracting Leary's importance through Ken Kesey, Neal Cassady, and Jerry Garcia developed an extended narrative with the help of Super 8 films that trailed the Merry Pranksters and the Grateful Dead. Photos of Millbrook, by contrast, limit themselves to the portrait of painted eyes on the mansion's walls. Much attention and videography covers the Pranksters' rise and their colorful, triumphant tour of the United States. Overall, they contrast with the stiffened commercial angle of shops and residents in the city streets. When projecting the Acid Tests, Babbs assumes the practicum to build LSD culture through its sonic avenues and numerous formats that tried to capture sound, light, color, and contrasts that present successful making:

---

[8] *Ibid.*
[9] *Ibid.*
[10] *Ibid.*

What the Merry Pranksters were doing was making a movie about it. They packed their projections, microphones, wires, and instruments onto the bus, went to a rented hall to set up, and waited for the audience. But the audience soon learned they weren't there to watch the show. They were the show.[11]

As the tale unfolds, *Electric Kool-Aid Acid Test* author Tom Wolfe relates the details of Kesey's ill-fated row with Leary, who refused to let the Pranksters into his Millbrook house in upstate New York:

> Word came down that Leary was upstairs at the mansion, conducting a very serious experiment, a day trip, and could not be disturbed. Kesey wasn't angry, but he was very disappointed and hurt.[12]

An irascible, older Leary attributes the meeting's unfortunate end to the makings of his depression: "It was revealed that I couldn't party much. I came down, took photographic evidence, and submitted my ass out. After that, I was on the run."[13] The adage about the meeting was relayed to us as college students while smoking marijuana and taking mushrooms. According to my friends in college, Leary didn't want to share participation or notoriety with Kesey. By then, he was a Stanford graduate and a writer of his impact. We are not given indications in the film as to why Leary attributed the meeting to his instability and legal troubles, and no footage is devoted to Leary's escape and arrest. "New" examples aren't covered, without much elucidation of Leary's later affinity for virtual reality games—a friend had once said the games themselves were "like taking acid." I found Leary on television two years later, hunched over a shopping cart and extolling the virtual reality games he had bought at a store.[14] Still, the opined message from teen rockers during that time was that Leary was a prick who opposed democratization, with songs like the Moody Blues' "Legend of a Mind" a repeated part of rock radio.[15] Still, the rift between the two men is an excuse to shore up those bonds later in the movie, and at the annual "Hog Farm" event in 1995, hosted by Wavy Gravy, Grateful Dead bassist Phil Lesh appears, and both men shake hands.[16] Scholarly viewpoints aside, we then peruse the rift between scholars and performers and the idea's indirect transference onto improvised experiences from those who

---

[11] *Ibid.*
[12] *Ibid.*
[13] *Ibid.*
[14] Rushkoff, Douglass. "Most VR is Total Bullshit," August 26, 2019, *Medium.*
[15] Moody Blues, *In Search of the Lost Chord.*
[16] *Timothy Leary's Last Trip.*

had learned enough about how to stage trips for large audiences. Still, partying and frolicking were not the marks of a thinker, and more could be learned through study without expanding the realm of trips through their popularization. A strong component of the film's later scenes, too, featured Grateful Dead guitarist Jerry Garcia. Unfortunately, this was not a fair comparison since Garcia did not write down ideas and concepts, instead building his sound to interface many genres of music and sonic intensities to replicate the psychedelic experience without written instances of dreams, hallucinations, or states of awareness. Garcia's peculiar style, it can be said, built many LSD states of awareness into segments of playing, welding modern rock sounds and styles into a chaos of emotions and self-transformations that beguile Hofmann's picture of "oneness" that was such a garbled tale.

I think that examples such as those in the movie's beginning also cause us to estimate what commentaries may tell us and why Leary's reunion with Kesey after the former found that he had prostate cancer in 1995 matters. Again, *Timothy Leary's Last Trip* extols Leary's radical aspects without connecting Babbs' reading of the 1960s to any political conflict that demonstrated the counterculture's will, nor did it consider truth's obvious and feigned perfection. Leary, when courting Buddhism, developed much of his written impulse and brought to light some of the necessary occult studies through, as Huxley had, his estimations of the value of these traditions. Through Babbs as the narrator, Kesey redefined his peculiar pupil status while he was a college student:

> I came out of the University of Oregon, the prettiest little boy I'd ever seen, and, uh, I went to Stanford on a fellowship, and while at Stanford, I was given the opportunity to go to Stanford Hospital and, uh, take part in the LSD experiments.[17]

Babbs then identifies the crux of the two men's narrative tension with no pretense: "But Kesey wanted a media more powerful than the written word."[18] Though Babbs overstates the film's beginning and oversteps many key parts of the counterculture's dissemination, this comment is active, calling our attention to psychedelic-friendly techniques and media stating the counterculture's authority when presenting psychedelic drugs. Babbs also identified controversy among the Pranksters, with Leary also contesting the word "prankster": at one point, Kesey exclaims, "Ay, it's the intrepid traveler here! Reading from the West Coast, we're known as IS IS, that's The Intrepid Search for Inner Space."[19]

---

[17] *Timothy Leary's Last Trip*.
[18] *Timothy Leary's Last Trip*.
[19] *Timothy Leary's Last Trip*.

Countercultural jingoism's chant attests to ambitions, casual interpretations of fact, and nebulous futurism to unshackle consciousness from writing. Leary's protest, by contrast, was also meaningful, and what could be learned must have the right concept-object development, serious enough to merit indoctrinations and their meanings. Neal Cassady rounds out the extended discussion about the Acid Tests. Nonchalant and beneath a cowboy hat, Cassady evokes the popular form with neither hesitation nor any of the reporters' nagging queries at his much-told stardom speculation:

> It's joining the reality, ceremony, and commencement exercise, essentially with the heads. And the people who would like to know what they're doing.[20]

Cassady's cool, composed statement of countercultural fact—that they were there to learn, not to pontificate—is the breadth of countercultural theorems that invest necessity and organic purpose to state control and the identity of that control. We might, then, suppose tripping possibilities away from the author's didactic theorems to say that knowledge belonged to everyone and that these psychological forms were guides to ample pathways of self-growth. Cassady's non-cameo appearance in a cowboy hat, in his turn, confirms the generation's relevance to older generations who had traveled the worlds of drugs with no formal organization or stated purpose. This introduction may tell us of the torch's passing, and one's surrender to new gods and politicians. It was not without controversy: Tom Wolfe had cut down Kerouac in *The Electric Kool-Aid Acid Test* by saying that Kerouac was "the old star."[21] But Cassady's political adherence would foreword discoveries characterizing Beat poets such as Ginsberg, a conspicuous and photographed visitor to Grateful Dead concerts in 1967. As a way to state a rejuvenated effort, Cassady's statements complicate the counterculture's set of prophecies, at one point, turning to his spoken format while driving FURTHUR: "we're we're sadistic crime, we we will get their ears and make some fun."[22] To state the counterculture to be criminal and pleasurable continues the Beats' positive front and those of liberal writers such as Orwell, who in *1984* unveiled a leader that encouraged rebels to distribute drugs and commit crimes. Liberalism's criminal *ethos*, as found in literature, was to be continued, and it even adopted Kerouac's 1955 call to "be a crazy dumb saint of the mind."[23] Thus, counterculture's re-invigoration through Leary and Kesey de-intellectualized much of its process, courting verbal

---

[20] *Timothy Leary's Last Trip.*
[21] Wolfe, Thomas, *The Electric Kool-Aid Acid Test*, 102.
[22] *Timothy Leary's Last Trip.*
[23] *Jack Kerouac: Selected Letters*, 1940-1956, 487.

derangements and public humor to build the focus of its leader's noble, ascetic possibility. The etymology of Kesey's "Prankster" enshrines humor, fun, and mischief to circumcise its notation of the new Being: it is consistent with humorous renditions of modern perspective, deranging and rebuilding the human psyche through its travels.

Facing Prostrate Cancer: Leary's Second Heralding of Truth

Leary's coming death and his erstwhile reunion with Kesey would be celebrated at the Hog Farm with costumed Dead Heads, a cannon shooting, and an invigorated Leary who proudly proclaims, "I'm on the outside looking in."[24] Yet accounts of the two men coming together are not accompanied with a splash of renewed learning: we are given no real examples of how Leary's learning and discoveries match newfound concepts of death and are instead palliated with a joking Kesey praising Leary's Irish identity and his love for drinking whiskey. Festival participants retold their basic knowledge of Leary and his role in the LSD revolution. Beneath spacey eyes and intoxicated heads, their praise hangs on elemental forms of teaching that were not expounded. In the film, few Buddhist references corroborate what Leary's pretense seems to be saying. The film shows us several meetings, but they are crony-like excursions into the author's habits, tastes, and participation in mainstream life, dry of any serious inquiry into hallucinogens. Still, an interviewed piece showcases the generation's robust confidence in their discoveries, even when postdated:

> Kesey: You know, we talked about this nearly thirty years ago. Everybody could believe everybody here. Leary: I remember. It seemed like wild dreams then. It's just happening so fast.[25]

Leary's synopsis of knowledge's acceleration and Kesey's relaxed broad statement of its positive inclusion point to the proliferation of perspectives and their critical mass. They also signal Leary's surrendering of purpose to new combinations and doctrines, advancing counterculture as a living force that could change human beings. That change is "happening fast" spoke smack in the wind of the War on Drugs, and here was a generation unfazed amidst the 1990s' suppression of subjects and experiences, breathing confidence that the experiments had been successful. Babbs does not ignore criticism of this point: Garcia had died of a heroin overdose in 1995, and the Grateful Dead disbanded. "Happening fast," then, presumes that intellectual technologies and cosmic experiences would indeed redraw the human psyche and belong to that society,

---

[24] *Timothy Leary's Last Trip.*
[25] *Ibid.*

even after the destruction of its proponents. The point begs further study: after Garcia died in 1995 and the passing of William S. Burroughs in 1997, LSD factories were busted, and the drug's production declined. Still, Leary holds out his pins for a greater discovery on the horizon beyond, with greater satisfaction gained from the counterculture's three generations.

Filled with Super Eight films and interview spots with the generation's elders, *Timothy Leary's Last Trip* did more to illustrate the counterculture's controversies, telling of generational change and changes in creativity. With occasional detail, the tripping graphic held a greater momentum than dry, airbrushed comments about the studies. Still, the tenacity of the tribes is relayed by minimizing the authorial point and nixing the pages of Leary's formidable studies, instead giving us details about the organizations' root intentions and filling the pages of the American experience with color, humor, and confidence that consciousness was changing. The deliberate suspension of key instances of Leary's life and works engages our senses and sense-inspired history coloring to comprise the ongoing experiment with growing institutional variables.

Chapter 16

The Studied Portrait and the Looking Glass at Life's End: Dr. Timothy Leary's Special Relationship with Ram Dass in *Dying to Know*

Perhaps Gay Dillingham's 99-minute retrospective, *Dying To Know*, will give us more insight as to what scientific and procedural knowledge might be gained from the study of psychedelics. Firstly, the framed tale duplicated the screenplay from films such as *Timothy Leary's Last Trip*, re-confirming Leary's death as a crucial step in the process found in what they were studying. Still, we should admit that the film, as it offered more rigorous biographies of both Leary and Dass and more solidly forecasts their path to knowledge and reason, did not answer all the questions about death and instead was more of remembrance about what constituted psychedelic knowledge. The film's sustained biographies of the two men also document their travels and run-ins with the law. As with *Timothy Leary's Last Trip*, I would say that this film also shares the spotlight between two men, cross-referencing Leary's wisdom and dedicated studies with those of his compatriot, the man who organized and directed Leary's seasons of trips. Grudgingly, it seems, Leary's death involves an account from the two men about how to experience one's death in terms derived from the Tibetan scriptures. Throughout this film, Leary tells us why life and death are part of man's psychic attainment of knowledge as one exits the world of Being.

The film, produced in 2009 and including a dual portrait of Leary and Dass, was richer in scholarly interpretations of psychedelic drugs and their positive therapies: more effort was given to examining the drugs' usefulness in treating people with an addiction and in changing people's mental attitudes. This film also took advantage of the modern political angle, discussing the controversy of Leary's taking drugs and administering them to students as a lecturer at Harvard University. The narrator notes that Dass's career (birth name: Richard Alpert) appeared more promising and prestigious than Leary's. He finds Dass expositing Leary's character and testing his commitment to psychedelic studies. Moreover, the film examines newspaper and letter examples of the studies themselves, giving insight into precisely what Leary may have thought about possibilities when taking drugs such as LSD, psilocybin, and mescaline. Renowned movie star Robert Redford marks the presentation of videography and commentary with a personal division of Leary's epistemological responsibility, as images of Hindu god Siva, goddess Durga, Leary himself, and the brain sit in the background, and as confetti rained down a street:

> Caught between the Catholic desire to please and a rebellious nature that ran deep, Tim spent his life walking the edge between conformity and chaos.[1]

Staging Hindu cosmologies to be rebellious operates a historic academic struggle, and the abiding dictum that Eastern abstractions of truth predominated counteracts Leary's Catholic sensibilities that, when natural or romantic, promised happiness as the modern Western man might understand it. It was not to say that Leary did not operate a dense Eastern mythology or series of inferences: it was more true that several writers emphasized this trend, hoping to divine truths and states of being that Christian inquiries had closed to uphold reason. Quoted researched entities in the film gradually gain their factual density, culminating in Leary's discoveries concerning mescaline in 1963:

> [the prism] literally means mind-manifesting. After their sessions, many repeated common perceptions, barriers dissolved, and everything seemed alive, even inanimate objects. They felt an oneness with everything. Colors and solid patterns are transfixing and more mesmerizing. The experience seemed to come in waves.[2]

As the screen turns to pictures of Native Americans in the desert, rolling clouds, and psychedelic patterns, the narrator states: "Leary now saw the research as connected to the centuries-long use of psychotropic plants."[3] Leary's trip, as it references many ideas found in those of Swiss psychologist Albert Hofmann, operates a dynamic graduation away from European models stressing dream sequences rather than naturalistic or cosmic points of focus. Leary's expanded model, in short, would be useful to hippies and shamans from the 1960s onward. This novel and special relationship with Hofmann at Sandoz, Incorporated is traced to give us notions of transcendence as spawning the rise of American realism and immersions that could rebuild post-analytic philosophy through psychotropic drugs. Dass explores Leary's Catholic origins in several instances and the learning pretense of Leary's elders, giving the nod

---

[1] *Dying To Know*.
[2] *Dying To Know*.
[3] *Dying To Know*.

to the professor's wit, honesty, and profound commitment. It might daunt to admit that not all Catholic thinkers espoused conformity with contemporary mores. It was more likely that Dass chronicles, in the beginning, Leary's relentless impulse to change knowledge and to manifest greater inundation with primitive or medieval models to resurface man's truly natural impulse for living.

Did this Mean Anything? Mortality and Leary's Second Coming in front of the Camera

What, then, ought to be made about Leary's diagnosis of terminal prostate cancer in 1995? How are we supposed to learn anything from one's death that illustrates the value of psychedelic inquiries, borrowing the assumption, of course, that drugs were meant to be taken to enrich life or to abstract from us perceptions that correspond to the living organism? There are several interpretive translations from *The Tibetan Book of the Dead*, a major engine of thought and idea production in the documented research of psychedelic researchers that included Leary. Mark Griffin's translation emphasizes man's increased conscious grasp, deriving the ascent above ordinary reality and the totality of our conditioned senses:

> It is the totality of the ocean of consciousness, the Great Light, the infinite expression of mind in its completely unconditioned nature, and all of the mechanics of the individual existence. We understand our conditioned nature to be hinged on the assembly of memory that is assembled around the operation of the sense, organized by the intellect, and apprehended by the reflex of consciousness that we call ego. This is the underlying support of the egocentric identity.[4]

Griffin then ties the specific phenomenon of death to the ego's erasure and, thereby, the continuity of what conditioned memory has produced during one's life and meditations:

> Once struck by death, the very swift and irresistible force of the separation of the elements of your mind from your body and the absorption of your individual being back into the ocean does not wait. It's almost like a machine.[5]

---

[4] Griffin, Mark, *Bardo Thadol*. 3.
[5] *Ibid*. 6.

Staging the ego's demise as an irresistible, mechanistic force attributes the human mechanism to the powers of memory and the intellectual development of human and social contexts that problematize being, and so the memory's compassion for remembering and applying the principles of reason for one's self-production. Hallucinations and visions constituted the ego's fruition and the enduring legacy of creation in the body through languages, cultures, and physical beings. Dass in *Dying To Know* enhances the compassionate angle and, in doing so, offers re-constructions of the soul and the mind and their humanistic redemption in the face of the real biography that recalls Leary's expulsion from college, arrest and long-standing status as a Federal criminal wanted for LSD manufacture. Repairing at least the human being's tacit virtues, or at least their freedom to move between rational and hyper-rational collisions and common virtues that could arise from manipulating or redirecting one's perceptions, ought to rebuild at least one's capacity to "go on" from life, perfecting visions of truth while subordinating them to the greater, more infinite process of death. Dass's collaborative point was not to say that Leary could master death through his studies or that death was the consequence of taking drugs. His effort is to make it meaningful, a necessary step in the living process, and a necessary outcome for Leary's ostensibly broad studies.

Remembering the Harvard Years: Ram Dass

Dass's warm, conversational tone establishes the basis for Leary's biography and the sensitivity to learning found within such an undertaking: it could be said, sourly enough, that Leary ought to have written and published something regarding dying to preserve his thoughts. The conversational avenue, with Leary drinking beers and talking with an older Dass, is clear enough in restating countercultural valor from within modern epistemological worlds:

> Dass: I saw you were laughing at the system, and I had no sense of humor whatsoever.
> Leary: Man, I saw supposed to laugh at Harvard.
>
> Dass: I began to see what a visionary was. Timothy could see outside of the systems.[6]

At another point, Dass offers his spindle on the tryst with psychedelic destiny: "I was like Mr. Power Player in academia. Timothy was way outside of that. Of all the colleagues around me, he frightened me because he was so free."[7] The

---

[6] *Dying To Know*.
[7] *Dying To Know*.

collective steam of comments from Dass establishes the ability to put together, dissolve, subvert, and go beyond modern man's complex intellectual terminology and topography. It was not a small accomplishment, and we as audiences ought to figure in the truly awesome tale of modern man's amalgamation of living consciousness through "systems." It was at least possible, then, to interdict the breath of a revolutionary pulse. Knowledge and truth were beyond our quantum control through theories and their specific aspect of text-idea production. There were neurological and cerebral reasons locked inside a cortex that was not Kantian and thus could not be abbreviated with versions and vindications of Victorian realism. Leary, in short, could synthesize one's greater ideas and knowledge's more subjective locations. He could dissolve, it would seem, reason through the positive stress of freedom. The thinker's notation included letters from Leary and Dass to Sandoz, from Harvard at the time of the experiments, and comments about previous thinkers such as Huxley. Leary reports: "I had a good conversation with him. He told me that, you know, he thought these drugs were the most interesting things he had ever found. The potential was enormous. He didn't see any downside to them."[8]

Shedding the contemporary angle may tell us that many parts of Leary's ambitions and research goals had never been studied: mired in avenues of government-military conspiracy, he had not been given his due, nor his body of specific ideas and findings that would not make it into print. More importantly, the dissection of themes and ideas in Leary's life may take off from the advantageous rendezvous with other authors exchanging ideas free of the political fiction of published productions. It also documented that many authors worldwide had discovered psilocybin and mescaline simultaneously and had often come up with the same body of conclusions about hyper-rational or anti-rationalist connections in the brain.

Dass, balding, with a mustache, sometimes dotingly recounts the Leary family tale to shore up his elder's prophecies. Erstwhile, the biographical sketch illuminated the bright light of vision and brought us nearer to compelling tales about his personal growth. He surmises the following at the movie's outset:

> He took birth into such an interesting tension in terms of his mother, a very conservative Irish Catholic. Very tight, held in tight, very judgmental. His father was a dentist, but from the Learys, a kind of wild, Irish drinking, divorcing, going off and running away type of family.[9]

---

[8] *Ibid.*
[9] *Ibid.*

Fructive, swaggering portraits of the family engender maternity as a basic form of the author's moralism. These paths may pull us closer to the portrait of what drug interactions mean and how this contrasts with the identity of a scholar and thinker. In *Seeing the Beat Generation*, I have noted the evident form of Burroughs' indoctrination. He was haunted and terrified by his dreams, and it was this alternate minute of self-conception that drew him so strongly to taking and writing about them. Leary, however, was not terrified, enjoining legitimate scholarship from many angles of participation and the idealism of those perceptions and actions. The narrator continues:

> Timothy's paternal grandfather advised him to find your way to be one of a kind. He acted on that guidance, questioning authority.[10]

Of course, the narrator intones the more obvious frame of mind: "Following in his father's footsteps, Leary was a genuine hellraiser as a young man."[11] The positive antinomy between family members, too, spells out the specific intellectual pretension to change human minds and shatter, in some form or other, working philosophical instances of truth and social Being. Whereas Burroughs, then, commiserated and eviscerated his challenges, Leary was robust, ribald, and promiscuous. Literary inundations, however, may not be as simple, and by extension, Leary retold his envy about some of the Beat Generation writers and said he was envious of twentieth-century literature's sympathies and visionary brilliance. Still, Leary's Roman Catholic beginning cloaked his learning quests in the positive tunic for having pleasure. This fission between male and female role models strengthens working models of inquiry and popularizations of psychedelic theory and art as their partial focus.

All this is not to say that *Dying To Know* did not aggressively target fact-based studies to get at the crux of what Leary was researching and preaching to millions of Americans. Leary and Metzner set up a "Psychedelic Session" to "produce a psychedelic or ecstatic experience without using drugs."[12] Psilocybin was administered, however, and findings based on setting concluded that 18% of the respondents reported 'mostly perceptual' findings, 38% found them "very pleasant," and 38% of them were 'very eager' to take the drug.[13] At the level of mescaline, Leary drew out questions of dosage—"5,000 to 10,000 micrograms were required to produce effects"[14] similar to those of

---

[10] *Ibid.*
[11] *Ibid.*
[12] *Ibid.*
[13] *Ibid.*
[14] *Ibid.*

LSD. Specific studies annex Leary's role in promoting drug properties, giving their interactions a specific impact on psychology studies. Clear, simple renditions of drug interactions were found in American literature with the 1953 publication of Burroughs's novel, *Junky*: it might be said, then, that anti-narcotics groups and the United States government suppressed whole bodies of research. Still, specific research angles measured the possibility of learning and conditioning. Not far from the research findings of Hofmann and Huxley, they suggested wider dissemination and a more positive basis for the study.

When facing death's penitent gaze, friend and researcher Dr. Huston Smith completes the living parable: "But like a good Irishman, he just pulled tricks out of a bag."[15] Questions as to why Leary's Irish identity may mix with the picture of other Irish thinkers and writers: it was frequent that these men configured ethnic origins of other races to suit their quest for learning. "Tricks" may signal deception but also cleverness when sporting new ideas or the humanities of distant, remote societies. They may also proscribe their content to shore up and popularize basic findings. At a glance, Leary's biography is meant to be detailed to the point of shedding wisdom as well as a factual basis to re-examine research and historicity: it was said, as often, that Jack Kerouac's French-Canadian identity and his father's role as a publisher, built many of the stakes of the author's ambitions and intellectual foci. *Dying To Know* takes as its chart the expansive societal grasp required to build ideas in the twentieth-century world.

---

[15] *Ibid.*

Chapter 17

Understanding Ken Kesey

Ken Kesey's novels, travels, and organization of trip-takers gave him the right to be represented in general psychedelic studies. His two novels included 1962's *Over the Cuckoo's Nest,* and 1964's *Sometimes a Great Notion,* and both were critically well-received accounts remembered for their intense humanitarian meditations. Lest we give too much ground to counterculture's godfathers, we should briefly remember that academia was real for Kesey and his complex and deep modernist engagement as he rose to the fore after his studies. Kesey, who graduated from Stanford University in 1960 with a Master's degree in creative writing, was motivated and deeply convinced about modernism's tearing down during the early 1960s. He sought answers beyond the literary pale while working as a hospital volunteer among drug addicts who would report their LSD and psilocybin trips. Kesey's frequent imbibing may have loosened his grasp of essential materials. Still, it was more certain that Kesey gave us an entirely new historiography funneling change into metaphors for mental abstractions and free travels through the world of drugs. I taught *Sometimes a Great Notion* to my students at Memphis State University in 1997: students equated Kesey with "pot-smoking rednecks," and I was left unsatisfied about his literary forms that, when veiled and censored, did not tell us of an engaging author that minted conspiracy, irreverence, and collaboration with various thinkers and pundits.

At a Glance: Ken Kesey's Beatnik Origins

Studies of Ken Kesey's letters, housed at the Pennsylvania State University Library, could forewarn us of the dangers of the special modernist aptitude: Kesey's writing style and his smorgasbord-like agenda, and the sort of unglued schizophrenia it guided was not stylistically different from Beat Generation fiction and poetry. A 1963 letter to Gus Blaisdell demonstrates his form's unique infancy and the correlative sameness with authors like Kerouac, Ginsberg, and Burroughs, who published poems and stories in magazines like *Yugen*:

> The receiver replaced by a fat hand with glistening red hair and a ruby ring. Hand slides from phone to polished mahogany table top (...) creeps slowly backward over the table edge (...) settles over brass drawer handle (...) opens drawer to reveal a scuttling throng of bright red crayfish

(...) and stiffens in horror. "Wha-!! That crazy bid!! He must've knocked me out and flown that airplane himself!"[1]

We are given the same dictations when we read about Kesey's life and written works: could we find urban romanticism's more pervasive examples and then attach literature's accompaniment to hallucinogen-related transcendence? We might then figure out how film adaptations of the first-run movies accentuate the author's guiding theory about mental illness and its growing cultural reconfigurations. Plugging in the most informative body of data—Milos Forman's 1975 movie, *One Flew Over the Cuckoo's Nest*, reflexively targets the psychiatric hospital as the bearer of modern man's destruction, as he gives away his instincts, freedoms, and subjective attunements to the outside world. It is a primer for psychedelic studies in that Forman generously affords us visual and conversational detail, corroborating the destruction of man's psyche and, in the end, suggesting avenues of freedom and involvement operating from psychedelic drugs and that, more importantly, Victorian precursors to treatment did not activate or develop the body and its instinct to live a meaningful life. Shock therapy in this film streamlines demands to allow drug experimentation as a means to cure addiction, psychosis, and dementia. Lastly, Kesey's riddle was inscribed in Forman's movie through Randle McMurphy (Jack Nicholson): the author had learned the secrets of psychedelic connection while in a hospital, paying attention to conversations with patients, surroundings, images, ideas, and conditioned responses.

The Ambivalence of Study in the 1950s

One Flew Over the Cuckoo's Nest features Kesey's strong immersion in critical theory during his collegiate studies and his suppositions as a non-degree-seeking graduate student at Stanford University. The introduction featured the theories, due in part to socialist realism's advent, from Hungarian psychoanalyst Thomas Szasz, who in 1959 wrote in his book, *The Myth of Mental Illness*: "The idea of psychiatric illness is scientifically worthless and socially harmful."[2] Although it is documented that Szasz supported the legalization of drugs and was a noted, published researcher on the subject, one could glean the psychedelic thinkers' penitent ideas. At the same time, overtures to persons such as McMurphy were deliberately panned and shut out of the academic world. Our implied meaning, of course, curtly shuttered discussions around

---

[1] Kesey, Ken, "Letter to Gus Blaisdell, 1963", from *The Ken Kesey Collection*, Penn State Libraries.
[2] Kesey, Ken, *One Flew Over the Cuckoo's Nest*, xv.

treatment, remanding them to the ever-present moralism in the 1950s. Kesey himself deduced the living parable, noting the following:

> Therapy meant learning to internalize the moral codes of a particular society, not treatment of an illness.[3]

Kesey's introduction to the psychiatric hospital, signaling his private emotions and the anxiety for one's learning of disciplines and knowledge, summarized in part, guiding Victorian opinions that result in modern man's psychic destruction and misdirection. Moral perspectives, it must be said, were shared with several authors, including William S. Burroughs. Kesey's main point stemmed from Burroughs's routine inspections of treatment centers around the time of *Junky*'s 1953 publication, and moral perspectives were, in fact, counterproductive, not considering the subject outside of strict, rigorous moral codes likely to destroy the patient's normal function. Should we get closer to the idea of "normal," we would find that Kesey unearthed a great deal of imaginative detail that would result in the positive sketching of his patients in *Cuckoo's Nest*. As an instance of this tendency, Kesey directly builds into form philosopher Michel Foucault's broad, far-reaching studies about the asylum: "he began to consider whether madness meant the common practice conforming to a mindless system or the attempt to escape from such a system altogether."[4] Kesey, in short, performed the expert twist of situating the psychedelist's findings and enthusiasm to posit our recognition that psychiatry was a very limited science and could not develop our objective understanding of patients and that, in its current form was tied to moral repressions inhibiting personal and cerebral growth necessary for the living organism during modern times. Insofar as Forman's movie, which pleased Kesey despite his objections to character roles, professed neutralization and materialist suppression of the subject's instincts, memories, and ambitions as modern humans, as the current scheme to be found in the hospitals, we ought to at least grasp the scientific indifference keeping patients crippled and nonfunctioning. Then, we must spell out how drugs might change that, or at least how the mid-twentieth century's peculiar legacy uses character, conflict, and place to build a new psychiatry based upon personal freedoms and drug interactions that would grow sensibility in complex modern times. It is necessary to admit the foreword, as Kesey espoused many ideas from the critical tradition or its place in his times. At the same time, modernism's output dwindled, and ideas began to be constructed from stereotypes instead of real experiences. He continues

---

[3] Kesey, *One Flew Over the Cuckoo's Nest*, xvi.
[4] *Ibid*, xvii.

literature's deconstruction and re-direction of that content, as ideas from the world's far corners were suddenly real, essential, and interactive. Letters and unpublished materials illustrated our pretension to build knowledge; however, a great deal comes from *Cuckoo's Nest*'s foreword, which states the rising staff of knowledge and the peculiar moral fiction pervading institutions in our world. Films expressing biography and documentary will ultimately state the science's legitimate configuration and the characters' wielding of this grasp to build circuits that could live in the countercultural minute. In doing so, Kesey might change how people thought, acted, and spoke.

Chapter 18

Milos Forman's *One Flew Over the Cuckoo's Nest*: Countercultural Objectives

It should be noted that Milos Forman's film version of the literary novel Ken Kesey's *One Flew over the Cuckoo's Nest* carried forth the counterculture's basic objectives when defining and conceptualizing Victorian structures of power, both ideological and practical, muddling experiences as we might know them. Though Forman did not take the operative chance to suggest that drugs were antidotes to the Victorian ward and the psychic, verbal, and practical controls found in Nurse Ratched (Louise Fletcher), it is generally agreed that actor Jack Nicholson, as Randle McMurphy welds together many aspects of the liberated parable, to target psychoactive-leaning popular cultures such as the Beat Generation during that time. While it is clear from the movie's beginning that Victorian models stage psychic and intellectual control, it is a misnomer how authoritarian models deactivate the subject rather than bring them back into the social milieu. Abundantly, and in the film's countless scenes, normative, mainstream society uses a narrowly purported reduction of body, mind, and soul to demarcate its institutional control.

Plot

Forman performs this eclipse of romantic sentimentality at the film's beginning; in several scenes, three black orderlies enter the hospital to take charge of the patients and execute Nurse Ratched's orders.[1] The pairing of Negro orderlies with psychiatric administration replayed Victorian assignments of race. So, the level of knowledge—with force and with minorities as willing subjects, white men and women built their institutional and intellectual dominance, favoring conservative models of justice in human realms.[2] Still, one might question Forman's adherence to text in some sequences. Reductions of Billy Bibbit (Brad Dourlf), a neurodivergent patient, may force us to restate the question: do drugs rebuild patient attributes? After all, Bibbit possessed in his exclamations several novels, vision-related ideas that drugs supposedly activated and are connected to visionary perspectives. McMurphy's eventual

---

[1] Forman, Milos, *One Flew Over the Cuckoo's Nest.*
[2] *One Flew Over the Cuckoo's Nest.*

murder at the hands of Chief Bromden (Will Sampson) is staged in the light of a Native American concept of virtue and belonging, claiming victory in death and then walking free.[3] Of course, no attention is paid to drugs as an activating force, and Bromden, though purported to give us the pinnacled point of Native American shamanism and doctrines of personal freedom through drug use, did not trip and is silent for most of the movie. Gradually, Forman moves us away from these introductory social points to signal the greater world's growth within the web of drugged visions and their inferences. Further, when McMurphy finds two prostitutes for the male patients to drink with, there is no pertinent suggestion to bring into focus a different life. Energies in this film truncate its possible directions in thought, building totalitarian models that could obscure new dialogues of study permeating psychiatric evolutions during the 1950s.

The theater adaptation of the novel, which appeared in 1963, starred rave reviews, and these praises conferred on the novel's topic and characters alike continue to the present day. Critic Vanessa Cate notes, "McMurphy quickly uses his charm and audacity to assert himself as the alpha male and shakes up the routine in the hospital, breaking the rules and pushing buttons as he pleases."[4] She adds concerning the cast: "It's less a face-off between McMurphy and Ratched than an ensemble show. And the ensemble does shine brightly as a ragtag group of misfit crazies."[5] To advance the equality of characters and elucidate perspectives and personas beguiles the text's production from Kesey. Characterizations set up the novel's illustrative point that there were souls painfully neutralized and oppressed. In this context, did Forman's film attend to the characters' legitimate development in the story? A second, more guided question concerned Kesey's text: when accurate, did the screenplay exhibit the potential for psychedelic change? Certainly, Nicholson, in his main part, exudes personal freedom, exercise in one's contemporary social world, and humanity's repressed ambitions concerning sex and libation. McMurphy also routinely questions and outrides Nurse Ratched's repressive control. Was there a greater suggestion in the film to outpace Victorian models, and could any deducible truth be drawn from Nicholson's performance?

I think it is plain enough to say that the uses of electroshock therapy, though not new, served to demonstrate the falsity of Victorian sciences and suggest broad changes in how patients were treated. The example of Ratched's rationing of medicine and cigarettes serves as a gainful ploy: patients are not given rights. They cannot stage a vote to establish control of necessary items. These specific controls meant that suppression of the patients' rights carried

---

[3] Ibid.
[4] Stage Raw, "One Flew Over the Cuckoo's Nest," 2014.
[5] Ibid.

with it guaranteed non-interaction and non-adaptation to the rigors of the world around them. McMurphy's role, of course, was dual, carefully considering what his record and rape charges would mean for the re-drawing of 1960s institutional reality. Of course, sex offenders use society to procure needs and circulate their morality and outgoing beliefs about what activates humanity and physical sympathies through violence. But Nicholson builds a strong interaction with the other patients, including Bibbit, who is suffering the most brain damage, and rebuilding speaking and acting components spawns Bibbit's attempt at a breakout in an alienating protest of restrictive conditions. This idea was difficult to navigate: twelve years later, Dustin Hoffman, in 1988's *Rain Man*, is abducted and does not learn anything from his condition.[6] Still, Nicholson's role is endearing, and he practically becomes the inmates' leader. His repeated challenges of Ratched's authority, while coming with electric shocks, pursue the idea that a psychiatric ward should be run differently.

Kesey's Recurring Observations about the Afflicted: McMurphy's Accentuated Case

As Nurse Ratched arrives, most patients are silent and docile in the grim taking of medicine. Nicholson was led into the ward in handcuffs and wearing a loose beanie, quickly matching his comic oeuvre to the inmates' tune while they were seen smoking and playing cards. What is noteworthy is that Nicholson's wacky, frisky persona tunes up the emotions of the inmates rapidly: he pulls a good card for the card game, laughing noticeably, and mocks Chief Bromden, howling a derogatory caricature of Native American chanting.[7] Also visible is Nicholson's giddy nature at being incarcerated. For the first time, there was a disabled or dangerous patient who was happy, apparently at the change in the psychiatric profession and the instance of its change being unofficially present.[8] The laughing persona and Nicholson's transformation of daily events in the passive similitude of institutional domination of the subject advances Kesey's perspective that humor, follies, and verbal and physical freedom carried from three generations of American pop culture could change one's disabled status. It also nicely points to Kesey's evolution as a Prankster: McMurphy is very much like a Prankster, revitalizing the tradition of verbally, facially, and tentatively lampooning the modern tedium. Critics may also deduce the portrait of confined powers as if to say that treatment uplifted human emotions and feelings about life. Bibbit, sour and vagrant while holding his cigarette, instantly likes McMurphy. The affair, being born, situates the

---

[6] Levinson, Barry, *Rain Man*.
[7] Forman, *One Flew Over the Cuckoo's Nest*.
[8] *Ibid.*

revival of brain impulses from the viewpoint of an observer confident that life will change soon. This is not to say, despite obvious parallels with Beat Generation writer Jack Kerouac, that a session was one with Pranksters and that the conditioning of hallucinogens was nigh. More, it was to note criminal arrivals in the psychiatric prison, in a stark and revealing contrast to Burroughs's somber, pitiful portraits of drugged destruction in the Lexington hospital in 1953's *Junky*. A new era had come, with it a range of cultural and criminal formulas and auras situating a newfound Being that had roots in things the young could innately trust. Race theories aside, we are given a glimpse at the new generation and, with Nicholson, its rise to reject authoritarian dictations. Ideas that popular culture could cure illness were common to twentieth-century American culture: they also state the modernist subject's successful weaning away from Victorian social and moral codes. What did Nurse Ratched represent according to Kesey and the Victorian model of science and psychiatry?

It is necessary to investigate philosopher Michel Foucault's dual concept of Victorian repression, one that measured the human condition and sought to punish and repress certain aspects of the projected social being of the patient. Foucault's thesis that madness operated a parallel structure in the positive world, meriting status, governance, and personality might excuse us from viewing inpatient commitments as mobile racism without true governance. We would, of course, find that repressive techniques had been reified and purified to focus on the debilitations of the spirit and the mind as per the structure of dysfunction. Foucault ties these concepts down to language and the subject's expression:

> On the one hand, the man of reason delegates the physician to madness, thereby authorizing a relation only through the abstract universality of disease; on the other, the man of madness communicates with society only by the intermediary of an equally abstract reason, which is order, physical and moral constraint, the anonymous pressure of the group, the requirements of conformity.[9]

Critics agree that Nurse Ratched uses the repressive model to acquire power and objective control of an institution; she, too, uses mannerisms and obedience as primary anchors in that control. Silence and submission and the striking of tongues build the arm of purport for this axis of post-Nazi power. Nurse Ratched observes and scolds profanity, sexuality, and alcoholism as monikers that require the ward's necessary guidance. A vote is staged for the

---

[9] Foucault, Michel, *Madness and Civilization*, xii.

giving out of cigarette rations, then closed before the inmates are aware of the potential change: Ratched then manipulates time and the ordering of events to deny patient rights.[10] In that sense, Ratched's dominance is challengeable because the patient's needs are preferentially ignored.

Meanwhile, the patients take their medicines silently amidst the gloomy, dimly lit ward halls. It was clear that directions could lead either way, bracing us for shock treatments that crushed the inmates' rebellious spirit.[11] Still, Kesey did not operate shock treatments in a vacuum, and other writers such as Paul Bowles had tied them to punishing drug addicts in works such as 1962's *A Hundred Camels in the Courtyard*.[12] Shock therapy's grounding of context existed for some time: Kesey, with his descriptive material psychology, focuses on treatment's denigrating spectacle as it existed during his times.

Why Foucault Matters to the Psychiatric Generation

Foucault's morality, however, was not limited to any one mode of control and could be manipulated and extended since this was the twentieth, not the nineteenth century. McMurphy's presence, too, confirmed the rise of psychedelic thought and its potential legitimacy. Abstractions from Jack Kerouac's main character, Dean Moriarty, may tell us what was waiting inside a population waiting to learn, eager for change, and intrinsically pleased that the ideas they held would become meaningful. Familiarity from Nicholson shores up Kesey's general point that the emotions and favorite pastimes were and are meaningful to building the subject's esteem and neural adaptation: they project a waiting minute where freedom, borrowed from McMurphy's criminality, changed the sequence and intent of the inmates' living purpose.

Screenings of Forman's version of this novel do more to accentuate basic transpositions of fact: the hospital or psychiatric ward, rather than rebuilding and re-acclimatizing neurodivergent patients, aggravated their condition's sickness and did more to debilitate them than rehabilitate them. The initial staging, grey and behind locked doors, finds McMurphy in handcuffs, loudly and wildly celebrating his newfound incarceration. McMurphy then takes on Dr. Spivey to claim that Rocky Marciano had earned veneration for punching men out.[13] Scenes are accustomed to the 1970s, not the 1950s, and it could be said that Nicholson's gregarious, swaggering persona is more punctuated by the surroundings and uses of color TV when staging the story. Medicines are given with a classical music accompaniment, so Forman elucidates the patients' sour

---

[10] *One Flew Over the Cuckoo's Nest*.
[11] *Ibid*.
[12] Bowles, Paul, *A Hundred Camels in the Courtyard*, 30.
[13] *One Flew Over the Cuckoo's Nest*.

faces and toneless appraisal of the medicines.[14] A meeting of the patients with Nurse Ratched presiding leads to a loud, violent scuffle over the matter of one patient's violence against his wife: the debacle between Dale Harding (senile), Max Taber (schizophrenic), Charles Cheswick (manic-depressive), and McMurphy (rapist), demonstrates the depth of Harding's problem. Ratched quickly outflanks McMurphy, who is painfully afraid of treatment, and the meeting melts down into a loud fight over Harding's use of the word "peculiar."[15] Forman rebuilds Kesey's point that Victorian models of health sought to justify incarceration and challenge patients to find reasons against their governance. Ratched manipulates illusions of a democratic process: further, Nicholson learns the same morning about the extreme difficulty of managing people with a mental health condition and so stimulates his quest. It is evident that Nicholson saw the hospital as an opportunity to develop new identities: it is also certain from the scenes that Victorian notions of care, punishment, society, and action were more likely to produce disease rather than help with it. Also clear is the electroshock's waiting portal; patients dare not speak out lest they be remanded. As a person with schizophrenia stares at a window and argues with it, Nicholson sits with the patients, pulling a "Queen" card for Martini (Danny DeVito).[16]

Nurse Ratched: The Case Against Victorian Hospitals

Ratched, for her part, took advantage of Victorian ideas concerning confession as a means of establishing a case history: she, for example, raises the audience's interest in histories of spousal abuse and the propensity to use repression and shock therapy to prevent it. Spreading the types of mental disease through a meeting is thoughtfully arranged to build a toxic din in the meeting room. Incarceration seems ineffective at building case histories or communicating any learning or reforming of those involved. Of course, Nurse Ratched solidifies doctrines of female control by challenging the male patients' identity. Therefore, the circuit of small, intellectualized patients and occasional criminals retell the recurring fellowship with male underclass subjects that could not evade the law. Tracking the variety of patients makes us more conscious of the hospital as a prison, confining and treating people for their political rather than physical or mental characteristics. This misconception, or rather Victorian science's penultimate misconception that recurred in Foucault's *The History of Sexuality* a year later builds a loop of wide dysfunction.

---

[14] *Ibid.*
[15] *Ibid.*
[16] *Ibid.*

Shock therapy would continue to be a popular focus in Kesey's active writing period; Paul Bowles used it in "He of the Assembly" to describe how *kif* (cannabis) smokers were handled by police in Morocco in 1960[17] . Anthony Burgess employed it in the character of Alex, a convicted murderer, as part of an experiment to control crime by managing the offender's desires in 1962.[18] There was a popular concept emblematic of mental health punishment during Kesey's heyday, and it is employed to destroy brain-body impulses. In truth, Kesey and Forman are both using the electric chair to illustrate mental rehabilitation's poverty and the protective idea that patient participation and expression were key identifying factors when treating mental illness. Naturally, the idea of asylum revolt is accentuated, and so many viewers find a narrative about control and actions. Still, the disparity between well-adjusted, leonine nurses and anxious, troubled, and terrified patients aptly demonstrates the Victorian apparatus's power and points to Nicholson's innocent, uncontrived role in changing psychiatry.

Perhaps the most telling impulse of this film, with its several patient meetings and the tapping of McMurphy's mercurial, street-savvy presentation, is the attention given to patient care and the outlook for the patients, many of whom have no opportunity to live a free life as a citizen. Nicholson's aggressive takeover of the ward's patients balances an emphasis upon criminal estimations of mental health justice—with requests and efforts to play sports, hook up with girls, and enjoy the benefit of recreational lives—against more piecemeal issues of justice that may expose the fastened, impassive indifference of the patient's lives. McMurphy, for example, unsuccessfully tries to teach Bromden how to throw a basketball, coaxing and pushing him to play.[19] He also unsuccessfully tries to convince Ratched to allow the patients to watch the World Series, grudgingly getting a positive vote out of a closed vote but unable to convince Ratched.[20] By contrast, patient activities are limited to card playing and puzzle making, and so situate the patient's lives as passive. The film's videography includes many older patients, senile and sad in their self-conduction—the didactic strategy was not far from Burroughs's narration of arrested addicts in *Junky*, nominally cleaner but firmly a passive snapshot of neutralized patients. When McMurphy is required to take his medication, he complains that he has no idea what medicine is being given or even *why* he is required to take it.[21] Of course, the medication's meaningless, automatic administering presumes our

---

[17] Bowles, Paul, *A Hundred Camels in the Courtyard*.
[18] Burgess, Anthony, *A Clockwork Orange*.
[19] *One Flew Over the Cuckoo's Nest*.
[20] *Ibid*.
[21] *Ibid*.

indifference to specific patient conditions, to suppose the administering of justice without any real psychiatric reason—a moral reason, a uniform sign of the patient's admitted offense. Continued emphasis on sports and girls bravely play into contemporary rehabilitation theories to stimulate and develop the body and offset the disease.

But McMurphy's refusal to take the pill and his attempt to stir up opposition to Ratched's control of daily content forces us to ask what psychiatry was for and allows us to deduce that decisions made with the patient's lives were arbitrary and supposed that science itself could not diagnose or treat patients at all. Ratched calmly rebuilds stereotypical reasoning when defending her management of the patients. She refers hospital ward issues to the older patients, who "have nothing" but the circumstances of the patient's life.[22] Through McMurphy's volatile, erratic, and sometimes controlling protests against hospital authorities, Forman illustrates criminal savvy and persuasiveness among patients. Themes of hope and self-realization are knocked out of the picture by Ratched's cold, pointed evaluations. Though McMurphy has no chemical medium to offer the patients—drinking is included, with two call girls administering the drinks—Forman nicely suits the hospital's narration as a monolith of negative, not positive, control, suppressing daily content and directing the patients to forms of passive obedience to government-mandated social norms. Nicholson, in short, took down ethical notions through the passive model's exposition, wherein patients will not recover, take on responsibilities, or even have a useful memory of their records. A manic-depressive and pained by any quarrel, Cheswick composes himself with the help of Nicholson, countering Ratched:

> You know what, I don't understand this, Miss Ratched, because Mr. McMurphy said something yesterday about the World Series baseball game. I've never been to a baseball game. I'd like to see one.[23]

It is important to state the film's obvious tryst with social meaning. Cheswick has never been to a baseball game. Thus, the normative development of a human's interests and ambitions has not been addressed this way, and he cannot see himself as a normal person who could enjoy the country's favorite pastime. Cheswick's example suggests Forman's concept that neurodivergent patients have not had the chance to understand life as a normal person would nor enjoy the full benefit of robust, interactive psychology. Cheswick exudes the suppression of content, and maybe permanently so. But Cheswick, reduced to

---

[22] *Ibid.*
[23] *Ibid.*

crying in Harding's scuffle, is composed in this exchange, speaking for his ostensible rights. At this moment, where patients were not functionally destroyed, and their speech and elocution were intact, we may see for our benefit that Ratched has no real intention to recover human life and that the mental hospital may have regressed from the time of Burroughs's incarceration at the Lexington Hospital in 1953.[24] The depersonalization spoke about suppressing memories and experiences and, more poignantly, the problem of building community relationships. By the time Eddie Murphy, as Ray, reads letters to jail inmates aloud in 1999's Life, the film's parable is completely void of the concept of rehabilitation as no one wants to "learn" anything. Nicholson projected the patient's casual transformation from the justice system's passive, neutralized receptacle to one growing and developing from media proliferation and the stirring of one's emotions, body, and senses. Neurotherapy, and the therapy of the human body, communications, and living senses that were not cerebral, told us through Beatnik-like executions and confrontations that the coming psychedelic medicine could re-attach our senses and our dialogues to the repairing of one's Being.

Chief Bromden's murder of McMurphy in the movie's last scene and his escape by throwing a control panel out the window were accompanied by Bromden's instruction to him that death is a form of liberation. It also suggests that Bromden could speak, understand, and think about all McMurphy's moves and insurgent instructions in silence. Of course, the obvious was also imminent—Bromden is a Native American, and so supersedes American reasoning about one's mental health and what a vision may mean for healing—well in line with Native American psychology concerning drugs. As a centerpiece in Cuckoo's Nest, McMurphy suggested an anti-racialism that criminals had courted and drawn forth into literature for years. In retrospect, motifs of silence and craziness in Forman's movie spelled out race and class warfare, so the transposition of "new" learning was designed to activate the mind and body.

---

[24] *Ibid.*

Chapter 19

The Merry Pranksters' *Tripping*, Kesey as Prophet and Countercultural Leader, and Pop Perspectives

With continuous footage of the FURTHR bus, city streets, Prankster sessions, dancing, nudity, and people along the stirred countercultural ways, *Tripping* valued Kesey as a countercultural progenitor, prophet, and caretaker. Unfortunately, the pairing of Kesey with rock and punk notables such as Jarvis Cocker, Malcolm McLaren, Ken Babbs, Marianne Faithfull, Fatboy Slim, and Norman Cook was uncommon, so it should be said that their thoughts operated very different social and intellectual threads while the engaged, mature, and thoughtful Kesey paid tribute to his journeys and his development of spirit and God through the bus's adventures and beyond. Video footage accomplished the goal of glamorizing "the Bus" and its super-American adventures. Still, LSD testimonies did not advance the picture, even though Kesey defended his stance that acid-heads exercised a greater social functioning, a transcendence that was incomparable and accurate. Vikram Jayanti's film built vestiges of Prankster glory by stating its objectives as equivalent to God. Commentators, however, interject missions of popular simplicity, tuning us to the lifestyle choices and persistent gangsterism that had annihilated countercultural political pretensions. Kesey's intellectual spheres, though filled with emblems of the entourage's living spirit and their cartoonish redrawing of America, God, cities, people, and historical change, situated the group and its novelty against pale, lumbering colors of the American façade as it stood in the 1960s—its commercial grandeur, and its simple inhabitants who took an interest in the bus as it rolled through the streets. Footage accomplished Kesey's multiple intentions—though clearly in time to Kesey's written works, the humorous combination of a bus decorated with slogans, popular symbols, and dancing men and women atop its stairs, at times waving to the goers-by in the streets, told us what Cocker warns us of—the absence of visible instruction to tell an acid-head what s/he has actually "learned," or its value when negotiating existence in this world. In truth, *Tripping* took the angle of advantage that countercultural history, mythologies, and practices were not that pervasive or detailed in describing drugs. There, too, was a void-like mismatch between the two, meaning that LSD's purpose was bargained for in the material-industrial world and held no parallel conceptions. The gainful question of "why" would be answered through elder notables that included 1970s writer Hunter Thompson; the meditative portrait, where an engaged, reflective Kesey unpacks his collective thoughts and actions for the idea of modernist transcendence, depends on Thompson's solid meditations to bring into focus what FURTHUR's travels meant for the 1960s, America, and the world.

An Ambitious, Gleeful Journey: Hunter Thompson on LSD's Compassionate Origins

In a dark shroud and wearing a cowboy hat and glasses, Thompson recalls his times with Kesey and the Pranksters and what might operate in our tradition for evaluating the seriousness of "cultural adventures" to establish the political values of LSD in America's hamlets and cities. Within the low-toned, comprised intellect of one of America's greatest popular writers, Thompson meditates on the potential for specific archaeology: "I never believed in LSD, but I understood the power of it. It was more than the Holy Ghost, more than Jesus, and even more than the Federal Government. Yeah, it was a powerful source. A little bit like witchcraft, maybe."[1]

Conversely, the writings did not document Kesey's responses concerning religious or mystical attentions. There was no specific mythology of traditions and symbols he deemed necessary to experience tripping's spiritual uplift. Thompson, who wrote 1972's *Fear and Loathing in Las Vegas* and who was popular because he wrote about drugs, pushes acid past Christianity and America to unveil a supernatural power wider and greater than America's symbolic and metaphysical traditions, transforming us to the point of destruction. Then, Thompson lent this undrawn, endless phenomenon to engulf tiny American Christian steps toward what could be called a "real" morphology. He says, then, that LSD surpassed America's cultural moment, to re-christen it with a limitless, beautiful mystery as our beginning for life. Thompson performs this tactful summarization of contexts without referencing Eastern philosophical threads about a "void" and a "beyond" that engulfs us. Kesey did not need to appoint a religious tradition to vent his attention to super-consciousness. Thompson, of course, confined these tendencies to awareness, not suggesting any piecemeal transformation of authority. He puts forth tripping's physical power as an antecedent to American, Christian, urban existence, telling us of the greater history and its transcendent certainty during our time.

---

[1] *Tripping.*

Thompson continues deliberating when asked about his meeting and partying with Kesey's entourage: "I didn't know Kesey at the time, but there was a shared perception. I wrote that, uh, it's a war from now on; those swine have murdered the myth of American democracy. Yeah, it was clear that the game had changed."[2] The comment comes after explanations of JFK's assassination about the changing thought in America. Thompson coldly enunciated the messenger's power without growling or boasting when relaying telepathy's clash with American intentions and foundations: the thought that topological *meaning* could be lost negotiates our modern history, ideas, and actions. It meant the destruction of symbols and their significance in the American social-moral idea. It also called for the renewal of the human spirit and its self-conception. Thompson's accounts of drugs were grimmer and comically pointed away from the reflections or ideation of one's intoxication. They tell us, then, that Thompson gave a certain amount of ground to Kesey, consistent with his ideas that could move us towards the fiction's exact dictations. America's psychedelic notables push forth the train of ideas and suppositions that could support drug-taking countercultures.

For his part, Kesey earns points of twentieth-century wisdom when surpassing the actual width and maturity of pre-Industrial American transformations:

> It's been around forever. You have to move out of consciousness to be able to see beyond the doorway of the cave. There's nothing new about that. The fact that there could be a pill, a little tiny pill that could give anybody that experience without spending thirty years in a monastery.[3]

Kesey's formal idea—namely, that American Christianity could and should be transcended, strips bare the perceptual moment to say that possibilities and thought existed far beyond the scope of American institutions in their current place, laying the ground for future histories that hearkened a much greater revolution of concepts, ideas, and responsibility about human experience. At this moment, Kesey is modernistic—there speaks a "tradition" beyond the annals of recorded cultures in America, and there is a connection to an endless and procreative spirituality indiscriminate of religion and doctrine. Then, the positive moment of sheer megalomania brightly told us that America and its medical appurtenances concerning expressions and feelings will change. The point is solidly grounded: Kerouac and Cassady had traveled across America and Mexico to internationalize Spirit further. At other times, Kesey is adamant

---

[2] *Ibid.*
[3] *Ibid.*

about the point about God and LSD: "You better be damn sure."[4] The stark move, too, escaped dictations of authorial responsibility that had come from previous psychedelics—hallucinogenic drugs could be referenced in society with no culture to guide them, within the spirit of positive invention erasing boundaries around one's perceptions, memories, and resolutions of experience. This is intellection, which is considered the possibility of one's freedom from culture when engaging in things considered as spiritual or magical. Still, critics are likely to press this point harshly: Rock band Pulp's singer Jarvis Cocker muses somewhat coolly: "If you decide to go off the well-worn path, I know this will be easy to get lost. You haven't got that many examples to follow."[5] This statement, borne of the senses from which ideas and experiences came from tradition, causes us to exhume enough details to gather the spiritual secret without telling us the details about its points of origin. It states the dilemma of American experiences that were "new" and thus uncharted. "Getting lost" offset drug use bearing no standard tradition within American life. With few examples and distant memories of even those, counterculture developed the necessary details of its morphology, indoctrination, and method, suiting changing times while holding within itself adventures and mysteries that quelled its ambition to override the experiences. America's beauty, too, would be re-examined without humanism and with the sublimity of internal meanings spawning an uncast culture that, in penitent terms, rejects American conservatism as its model and instead would propose unkempt and untethered themes such as Soul, Spirit, Fun, Power, Life, and Mind—with no attachments, and only positive regard for the endless evolution of those themes in the newest universe, which may then be redrawn to suit the ideas rather than the people. Dialogues about the spirit were not inscribed in *Tripping*; there, too, appears to be no eschatology to speak of. At one point, a gusto-high Kesey proposes ritual art's declassification when taking LSD. The key idea that meaning could be thus individualized to produce histories and transcendences was also again to strip bare the façade of the American public life, soaked and hewn in its Christian and European institutions.

Careful to reference Aldous Huxley and Timothy Leary and their role in shaping 1960s counterculture, *Tripping* did, at least, forge an intellectual hierarchy that could project guiding themes and at least some history when telling the psychedelic tale: the intellectual focus, when paired against the leonine approval for Beat muse and writer Neal Cassady, would successfully anchor the impact of Kesey's thoughts and suggestions. Commentary from Fatboy Slim (Norman Cook) eschews the connection to the younger

---

[4] *Ibid.*
[5] *Ibid.*

generation's pleasant point of similitude with the ideas of older generations and maybe their ambitions' advent during their times:

> Neal Cassady, I think he was kind of an inspiration. But he didn't have the business or organizational belief in social skills to kind of be an ambassador and take any further. I think he was kind of the previous Beat Generation and like a kind of link to the psychedelic generation.[6]

Cassady's output in *Tripping* was limited to driving the bus and cavorting with dancing women; nonetheless, the basic idea by which drug tripping could grow from a familiar root is conceived to echo "the road" and the FURTHUR bus to enjoin 1960s cultural traditions. Still, Slim operates from his prejudice, as his adventure was not pragmatic or politically directed towards any stable of the American conundrum, and capitalist-funneled excess might tell us that we were still within the steam of escapism and old histories that had not targeted "the system" as precedent to liberation. Rock testimonies are refurbished when an English singer and actress recalls her stint dating Rolling Stones lead singer Mick Jagger and her LSD trip: "It was wonderful to have. Wonderful."[7] To state tripping independently without the guidance of Kesey or his predecessors ensured free transmissions. A British woman's perspective gives credence to rock forms that could elucidate the drug's properties and rock's inclusion into spiritual and supernatural discussions. *Tripping* is an instance of rock revolution and stirs greater notoriety than that which could be derived from either Cassady or scientist-thinkers, including Huxley and Leary. We would see not only a culture's formation but also that of a system of human development in rebellion against capitalism. Still, Jayanti is clear to stalk the instances of underground and liberal developments with those of the government. Said and done, the FBI realized Huxley's nightmare when LSD is used to weaken enemy combatants. An official document reads sourly: "Testing arrangements in further of this mission should be operationally realistic and yet as controllable as possible."[8] The narrator enshrined Huxley's aesthetic intention, seeking " a realm of pure sensation."[9] To tell it briefly, *Tripping* did not use nearly as much footage of the FURTHUR bus as would 2011's *Magic Trip*: it was clear, however, that the psychedelic equation had grown its focus and could tell more stories about the participants. Despite the limited transcription, traditional references

---

[6] *Ibid.*
[7] *Ibid.*
[8] *Ibid.*
[9] *Ibid.*

to the history and authors allow us to see enough examples of the rock n' roll participants to set up Kesey's potential legacy.

However, internal comparisons between the videography and commentaries by notables and the narrator were most focused when the film turns to Kesey's "acid tests" featuring the Grateful Dead. As the narrator coincides, "no one had ever seen anything like them before. The late show, the cacophony, the creative chaos, everybody tripping on free LSD,"[10] the screen's seconds include a woman in a gown, singing, several dance-goers on the floor, including men with Joker-shaped face paint and wearing American flag-like stars on their backs, the DJ shouting and getting into the music, and the Dead playing amidst the tumult and strobe-patterns of light.[11] As the lights turn blue, a DJ shouts above the audience: "The mission will go on."[12] Interestingly enough, this was not the most compelling sequence of the film's videography, and comparisons with President Johnson's 1964 election campaign commercial could do as much to symbolize the government's learning and translation of hippie ideals advancing love, God, and community. As a girl blows against a cocklebur, the atom bomb goes off, and Johnson's voice returns: "We must either love each other, or we must die."[13] An ominous, grave-colored voice begins in darkness: "The stakes are too high for you to stay at home."[14] While it is important not to hide the obvious marker of popular American culture—the US Government had not banned LSD and was studying it in some instances—we should also allow Kesey and his entourage to be close at hand, waving the American flag proudly against Goldwater. Virtues of love, society, and God were, then, transposed from the Pranksters' vision of human ultimacy to the government's belated prophecies. Kesey thus gains a revolutionary consciousness consistent with American capitalism-authoritarianism's frequent rhetoric that absorbed the fluid concepts of liberal aestheticism and romanticism. Johnson's mandate to make a world "in which all of God's children can live"[15] directly absorbed hippie naturalism. Johnson would later come out against LSD in context and fight the Vietnam War. Still, for the time being, he had vaulted his political message above that of the counterculture—to promote, for example, his Great Society that included minorities in the general milieu. Kesey's bus trip, then, had entered the moral outlook of his country and was considered to be part of the perspective of the country's leader. Johnson was also waging a campaign

---

[10] *Ibid.*
[11] *Ibid.*
[12] *Ibid.*
[13] *Ibid.*
[14] *Ibid.*
[15] *Ibid.*

promise not to wage a nuclear war and would adhere to that: "all God's children" supposes, however, the protection of South Vietnam as well. *Tripping* did not appeal to Johnson's clever manipulation of the LSD story: it was more likely that his media exploited the message of racial equality to answer the reels of popular discontent raised with Kennedy's assassination to build interest in the Great Society.

I believe that potentially, the strongest threads in this work, by comparison with the much longer *Magic Trip*, benefitted literary notables and showcased the printed imagination's weight as rock had acceded to its peculiar system of thoughts and teachings to the outside world. Thompson established this continued thread in his drugged inquiries, and rock and punk stars attribute meaning to the evolutions of the counterculture. What "could be learned" was ably nested in Kesey's prophecies. What is heard in this documentary, then, is that the counterculture *built* a kind of tunneled history to attribute LSD to be a social history, with a political purpose and a license to preach the gospel of tripping through tripping exercises on a series of tours that were quite different from those of music acts at the time. When considering the film's visual examples, the political and social angle is quite extended to suggest culture itself being changed: this was not, characteristically, the form of the rock generation until the middle of the 1960s. Learning was not applied to the form of specific trips, and the count of personal mediations on fictitious psychedelic themes was not objective. He must be materially studied to encode the dimensions of thoughts or memories. However, the meaning was and is not encoded in any system of determinations. Kesey's learning curve with LSD ought to be replicated with a minimum of doctrinal prompts and statements. Cursory painting of FURTHUR and raising of the American flag to contradict Senator Barry Goldwater's famous 1964 speech is simple polity. Still, we are likely to drag away some respect for Kesey's concept of his first LSD trips in a "room" and then support the idea that future trips might build the vocabulary of symbols that could derive geographies of meaning that build the romantic emotions and sentiments that could bring us back to timeless-sounding threads of ideation. The formative apparatus of LSD is, of course, never touched in this movie, nor is Kesey's hospital stay as an acting reagent in the mind. Little or no attention is given to Kesey's later published works; nonetheless, Kesey's meditations guarantee the counterculture's moment, implementing the individuation of one's meanings. Commentaries, in short, re-entrench the dynamic inquiry into counterculture's pasts without suggesting anything that is not superficially set in the times. Still, *Tripping* certainly re-dredged American exceptionalism to express what a "trip" might be valid in finally expressing. The renegade journey's democratic impulses, with one's ideals in some cases constituting the visible helm, may cause us to re-value the system of techniques that inform LSD use.

A Starring Success: Kesey on the Kool-Aid Acid Tests

Kesey also enshrines the breadth of his technique and the ferment of psychedelic be-ins such as the Kool-Aid Acid Test and Graduation, saying the following:

> You could feel what everybody was feel—feel the electronic resonate with everybody else. Everybody feel the dark, back and forth—pong! But you feel it. And you're actually adding to that the Grateful Dead and the light shows, ecstatic dancing, strange costumes, and so right there in front of everybody was everybody.[16]

Yippie co-founder Paul Krassner confirms the sentiment that the acid tests were successful, without finding more specific bits of data, as the women dance with men with painted costume fixtures on their faces:

> Looking down, seeing what might've been the Grateful Dead playing and bowlsof punch, electric and plain, and this audience swirling around, and I thought: wow, if I were a cop, I wouldn't know where to begin.[17]

What the videography did, at this stage, was present the human multitude—to the point at which, when Kesey is interviewed as to the content of the tests and graduation, the Grateful Dead was performing on top of his bus. Our immersion was to be continuous, imperfectly displaying the tendency for music and dance to orchestrate psychedelic transformations, community, and the depth of those experiences when they are commonly held. Kesey did not have a scholarly or psychiatric tone for the experiments but arranged meaning's collective finding around immersions with music—this demonstrated the Dead's fluidity and their musical form and the tendency to derive hallucination and internalized devotion to peace and to belong by building a relatively new art form that could grow and individualize psychiatric experiences. In doing so, Kesey appointed the peculiar naturalist metamorphosis, Sufi-like dancing, and immersions in light, color, and sound to be our collective Being, with room for individual explorations that may be said to be less scientific and more conjoined with modern man's generational history of romanticist attentions. Thompson, though mercurial, jubilantly attaches the group's success by saying: "There was no doubt the train was leaving the station and people wanted to be on it."[18] Faces in the videography connote optimism and pleasure. Still, no specific references for the acid tests "came from" or any physical antecedent in world

---

[16] *Ibid.*
[17] *Ibid.*
[18] *Ibid.*

archaeology. Loosely told, the parties and trips help us visualize iconographic and human naturalism, romanticism, and freely drawn hallucinatory realism that might pair the mind with happiness and belonging instead of crucial introspection. Thus, Kesey transformed our ethic for taking hallucinogens: somewhere, a free, broad universe pleasantly attuned to the Earth's glories supplanted the didactic intellectualism of earlier countercultural thinkers. Kesey adds the tone of Eastern introspection by reminding a reporter, "You start by saying, 'Never trust a Prankster.'" The inscription was not his—a common Buddhist saying goes, "If you meet the Buddha, kill the Buddha." In this moment of robust glory, Kesey added the dictum of freed experiences, freedom from instruction, and the democratization of deist self-inference. *Tripping*, for its part in the videography and commentaries, maintained its separation from parapsychology worldwide, which had required a specific indoctrination but absorbed many of their root experiences and ideas. The point appears novel—by saying these experiences and subjective conscious roots were "new," we project a new functionalism to them, a kind of freedom from the structure of language and word that could document the rise of repressed social imaginations as the tablet of scriptural and physical truth.

Specific concepts and aberrations from commentators may accomplish what many in the counterculture had opined was their real intention—to pose drugs as part of "new" consciousness and the newness of experience when guided by the peculiar, post-Beat intellect of Kesey and his followers. *Tripping*, in his form, does advocate Huxley's hypothesis that drugs could operate a controlled conscious mechanism. Still, the stereotypical narration of Kesey's life and times and his experiments establish a new science form that, though popular and relatively uncontrived, had stressed enough scholarly virtues and humanism to guide collective, rather than individual, responses. No clue of the failure of drugs to promote self-liberation is accounted for in this film: the robust, grand telling of the tale measures the innocence, fruition, and mass appeal of a greater, wider mode of expression, giving time to document where key Beat ideas were trapped and then propelled to the world stage. *Tripping* recurs to the abundance of Beat metaphors but situated Kesey to be the controlling force, a direction not favored by some, and what we would inevitably call psychiatry's positive and populist explosion onto Victorian-modeled America. Thus, it documents the 1960s counterculture and its visual development to transpose psychiatry's idiomatic instance that transformed lives and political, social, and personal exercises shadowing the many-faced American realm, boosting a final period of modernist realization.

Chapter 20

"We're We're Sadistic Crime": Neal Cassady Driving the Bus in *Magic Trip*, Re-Casting Beatnik Glories of the Road

Alison Elwood and Alex Gibney's 1 hour and 47-minute anthology of trips, travels, and critical commentaries by Kesey, Paula Sundsten (Gretchen Fetchin), Zonker, and Chloe Scott in *Magic Trip*, at length, re-calculated and forecasted the ambitious, many-faceted ideas about "the road" as it may have been conceived by Jack Kerouac when the 1957 novel, *On the Road*, was published and enjoyed its wild, sweeping success among America's mainstream. The film, in tune with Kesey's maverick journey across America, bravely attempted to assemble footage across America and so documented the drug trips' pure experimentalism and the group's free interchanges with America's beguiling, sprawling realities as the melting pot of cultures, institutions, and uncertainty in 1964. The omniscient narrator attempts to pose the depth of the film's problem, which was to explain the ferment of trips during this excursion and the tour's improvisatory nature:

> For forty years, Kesey and his friends edited the film, forgetting what they would, and then it was tucked away, forgotten. Now, they're going back to the vaults, using film and audio interviews of Ken and his friends to write the story back to life.[1]

Overall, the film documents a series of drug trips and pens the pure experimentalism of forms and practice to project a newer, wilder America focused on the persistence of vision and the humanity of those visions. It also positively documents the traveler's lack of experience, their embryonic focus, and the indoctrinations' relaxed nature that may or may not steam the pot of memories and footage to comprise any deducible pattern to the escape found in trips and their re-forecasting of modern man's consciousness. To be sure, the bus trip, where the FURTHUR bus drives from California to New York to take in the World Fair's activities and exhibits, was pulled off without disasters or

---

[1] *Magic Trip*.

noticeable adversity: like *On the Road* and *Visions of Cody*, it documented Cassady's manic-depressive control, or rather his crazed set of indoctrinations beguiling the participants' trips and endeavors. Part of the dredging up of this crucial anthology, and even of the robust, colorful footage that documented fashions, wit, and cultural explorations, meant to show us how Kesey and the Merry Pranksters reconstruct tripping's fictional anxieties and how Kerouac's novels decisively impacted Kesey to form his visions of the psychedelic experience.

Introduction: Kerouac and Cassady

It should be noted, at the outset, that drug tripping was positively and meticulously documented in Kerouac's popular novels and that Cassady had operated as a teacher, shaman, and acolyte who was willing to absorb and build drug-taking possibilities. Again, some impact is breathed from commentaries in Babbs's *Timothy Leary's Last Trip* and statements that Cassady was more effective and influential as the bus driver than a writer, thinker, and anthropologist. Considerable footage is devoted to Cassady as the counterculture's rhetorical, cosmic, and romantic adventurer: even more time is given to illustrate the specific drug trips' experimentalism and to expose the cast's communications as they navigate the group's sexual and social ambitions while traveling. Of course, *Magic Trip* is, like *On the Road*, a passive attempt to redraw the American experience through travels and drugs. We will, in short, note prophecy's absence and the relaxed, easygoing development of ideas to confidently bridge modernist anxieties with an unwritten tendency to shed indoctrination to savor life's positive momentum. A movie that tells us tales about the emerging, *pathos*-less rock and roll generation, *Magic Trip* featured and replayed Kesey's authorial dictations and reflections. These archaeological findings were, to be sure, important because Kesey embraced modernist forms and their rhetorical sympathies with drug tripping. He had borrowed, as did Burroughs, the modernist syntactical inspiration. He read but noticeably affixes sympathy for FURTHUR's experimentalism and the impromptu arrangement of idea choices when driving and exploring.

From the authorial side, we are likely to track LSD tripping through models favoring unconditioned, relaxed applications of consciousness that hold no true scholarship or psychological conditioning as our erstwhile guide. On November 15, 1950, Cassady wrote Allen Ginsberg while in San Francisco:

> The heightened sensibility that one experiences after a good bomber (joint) is so delightful that it is absolutely imperative for one to really take it slow. The actual process of placing the feet, swinging the arms, and otherwise maintaining balance so as to float thru a crowded RR car was my concern. I slid into my seat without the usual sign of recognition

to this sharpie beside me. It's not only a flying mind that's characteristic of fine t; the whole body responds with exertion—eventually—eliminates that type of kick. Again, too, the opportunity to 'go' seldom presents itself often in the manner one wishes: fuck and blow.[2]

Cassady's reminiscence painted marijuana tripping with few logical constraints: it is not tied to any one conditioned philosophy nor to religious literature that could identify for us the value or truths to be found in visions. Taken in context, the vast archeology of goofy, improvised partying on Kesey's bus indicates a depoliticized taping of offstage partying through laughter, color, sex, and humor. Being a "Prankster," then, was to be a foil of non-literate transcendences compatible with the group's revived naturalism, a new configuration of experience that was, in its ambivalent series of moments, *free*. Still, we are certainly incorrect to shed authorial groundings, as Kesey's mind focuses on transcendence, holding within his prose several models that identify psychic destruction from standpoints very close in their sentiment and emotions to those of Kerouac. The cross-country journey is filled with wide avenues of color, finding the entourage smoking joints, dropping pills, having sex, dancing and playing with colors and nature, and hosting partiers on the bus's rails without shirts: clearly, *Magic Trip* proudly featured modern man's freedom from Victorian social and moral orderings of the body, experience, idea-creation, and their relevance as our basis for learning and experiencing. Humanism was given its positive account when Cassady mires the bus into a mud bog; participants then take LSD "soaked in a jar of orange juice," musing about the Arizona meadow's positive features and then sporting strips of paint on a T-shirt as the new "tye-dye."[3]

Commentaries from Kesey and the bus participants easily established the footage's modernist tone and freely advertised the trip's social dilemmas in the aftermath of JFK's assassination. Kesey states thoughtfully: "Shakespeare, writing today, I don't think he would use a scroll pen. So I started going out and taping recorders to see if people talk like they do in novels—they don't."[4] Philosophy professor and bus traveler Jane Burton operates modernism's primary trick to state societal diffusion as the basis for knowledge: "It got to be a kind of party, how do I describe it? It was a bunch of lunatics running around and trying to get to the East Coast somehow."[5] Innocence was also foregrounded: when Zonker, the self-described "sleeper," describes his attraction to Stark

---

[2] Cassady, Carolyn. *Neal Cassady: Collected Letters, 1944-1967*, 199.
[3] *Magic Trip*.
[4] *Ibid*.
[5] *Ibid*.

Naked, he quips, "She's just so strange."[6] Overall, however, *Magic Trip* broadly defines the troupe's humor, follies, and specific actions countering the political realities of the 1960s to surmise its casual redrawing and easy re-conceptions of American democracy through LSD and perhaps the air of indifference to ideas and principles soaked in the mantle of responsibility that was Pax Americana. We are given the added note of JFK's death as an event necessitating Kesey's transformation: of course, with the free world's leader dead, FURTHUR's impetus to learn, to grasp new forms of knowledge, and to spread happiness and fulfillment, were natural overtures to the coming LSD generation who partied amidst the stain of the agrarian idea that our feelings, perceptions, and abstractions gained from free culture would build anew the American *topos*. Of Cassady, Sundsten warmly offers the following:

> When he opened his mouth, he said about forty words. And all of a sudden, everything and it was and is alright, and beautiful and funny and meaningful, all at the same time.[7]

Examining the stroboscopic nature of Cassady's conversing tongue, which said itself to be massive, megalomanic, liberating, and crazy, helped to establish certain boundaries when we applied Beat formulas and themes to modern thought. This concept was important because we are trained to view the Beat meditation as irrational and incomplete, a misstep rather than an ascending step in high modernism's prolonged moment.

Neal Cassady's "Trip" and Beat Generation Writings

As an extension of what is truly "modern," psychology bears that responsibility—namely, how language construes the subject and what pattern of psychosocial development rose from this. Any signs of fighting or disintegration are left out of the proceedings, except in the form of lady wanderer Stark Naked. Kesey's leadership of the entourage is never challenged, and the trips were wildly successful at activating the trippers' positive enthusiasm for drugs such as marijuana, mescaline, psilocybin, and LSD. I think, therefore, it is apt to stage the obvious textual beginning of Dean Moriarty's smoking "green, uncured marijuana" in 1957's *On the Road*. Beat studies comprise an introductory, unpublished form of rancor about America's Drug War.

Conversely, its properties and drug interactions comprise some of our methodologies and anoint the much more powerful LSD pill with its wider

---

[6] *Ibid.*
[7] *Ibid.*

transcendence onto the mind and the spirit. "Getting high," *a la* Cassady, meant several transformations of our brain to accentuate harmony and growth in thought- and sense patterns or to dispel their rancorous impulses and resulting actions. Cassady is given a virtual kingship of the entourage in *Magic Trip*, with several reels where he is seen dancing, shirt off, face angling comedic-like, or driving the bus, sermonizing to himself in the depths of his wild, atheistic camp. Fetching points out, too, that the party-goers stayed up all night listening to the uptick of Cassady's Beatnik-tuned rambles. *Magic Trip* lent considerable democracy to developing ideas and the re-constructed mind, as we would understand it in its peculiar translation: modernism would initiate counterculturalism. As the journey from California to New York goes on, the film assembled a series of drug trips, with interactions with the 1960s world, including Arizona, Texas, and Louisiana during what was seen as relatively tough times for drug tourism—America's seemingly peaceful, innocent background stood in contrast to charged racist outcomes in the region from hippie excursions like *Easy Rider* or Grateful Dead Road tours. Kesey reads an example about Nurse Ratched in *One Flew over the Cuckoo's Nest*: dialogue, in short, annexes the author's history towards the generation of humanity's alternatives to psychic self-destruction under the axes of institutional and moral control. As FURTHUR goes through New Orleans, Cassady introduces the hippies to the jazz scene, observing a piano player.[8]

Commentaries and interviews established the surrogate tone that Kesey took responsibility for the experiments, believing that they would confirm his ideals about LSD. At an early moment in the trip, Kesey wrote the 1962 novel *One Flew over the Cuckoo's Nest*. Kesey did not hesitate when interviewed: "Being crazy is painful."[9] In the immediate context, we may wonder why this novel is paired with the troupe's jubilant adventure or what such a condemning work could tell us about alternative therapies reviving and rebuilding human psychology. Still, Kesey operated on this point to tender a minute of the issue's justice and the serious nature of improving adult lives in the late twentieth century. As the entourage nears New Orleans, Kesey reads from the pages of the book, zeroing in on Nurse Ratched as his partial subject as a literary author:

> I know it's the Big Nurse, carrying from a thousand parts she used today. Needles that gleam like porcelain. Bold copper wire. Big Nurse tends to

---

[8] *Ibid.*
[9] *Ibid.*

get real put out if something keeps her out of her morning conversation with her machine, which she calls Adjusted.[10]

Kesey then reads from the novel's end, where Chief Bromden destroys a window and breaks free, recontextualizing deeply entrenched modernist avenues of confinement and suppression in one's soul:

> I took a deep breath, bent over, I heaved my legs under the weight tearing out of the floor, I was able to get an arm around it and my other hand under it and let go, and carry the panel through the screen and a ripping crash. I put my hand on the sill, and bolted over the pass. I ran across the grounds. I felt like I was flying.[11]

In short, the text's illustration of readings paired the mentally ill's abject condition and their dramatic liberation to comprise a historic virtue, redeveloping of Beat and modernist rhetorical patterns governing the spirit and also the written form's retextualization of mental illness. Freedom dynamically engages the patient's senses, watching him grow and mature, tracking several mental and physical engagement metaphors. Remotely located and "far" from the Pranksters, this example touts the author's triumph as a modernist thinker. Without engaging specific psychological states, we might give added attention to the film's form for building experimental patterns of color, insight, engagement of reality, and sound to mean more than intended.

Gretchin Fetchin and the Women of LSD Trips

Entries by Paula Sundsten, Chloe Scott, Tom Wolfe, and Ken Babbs promulgate the viewer's feelings of the general population and the democratization of conditioning and meaning to state the Pranksters were collaborators, urging their contributions to the trip's intended psychological mission. Sundsten (known as Gretchen Fetchin) calmly establishes the pacing of racial overtones when the entourage reaches Lake Ponchatrain in Louisiana: "You have to remember, this is 1964, and right when the Civil Rights movement came, it was a White- and Black-only consciousness, really prevalent in the South."[12] However, Sundsten carefully appraises the trip's meaning and exposes the ballooning anxiety: "Ken was trying to run this whole thing and be philosophical. He was caught up in a million different trips."[13] Chloe Scott relates the more

---

[10] *Ibid.*
[11] *Ibid.*
[12] *Ibid.*
[13] *Ibid.*

adventurous and romantic details of reconnection with the group's apparent heritage with literary heroes such as Beat Generation authors Kerouac and Ginsberg to note positively what authors such as Tom Wolfe had assured us were solemn and had produced a schism. She proudly notes the equipment's transference to Kerouac's New York City apartment, then recalls:

> And that night was fan-TASTIC, that sorta got out of hand, doormen kept coming up saying, 'Everyone's complaining, so, and everyone's excited that Kerouac was there and has been moved on end.[14]

Kesey returned to the form's special punch when contrasting literature to paint the narcotic form's dramatic impact: "(Ginsberg) was kinda like a folk signer to me, a poet."[15] To paint the special details of a reunion between Kerouac, Ginsberg, and Cassady, under the auspices of Kesey's grandiose plans, stirred the wind of literary transferences that may breathe life into an enhanced American drug addict, to say that romanticist continuity accentuated Kesey's predictions, and so his adventures' nationalization. To say, categorically, the event was a success flapped in the face of everything we were taught: counterculture fractured, and those fractures impeded their dynamic form during the 1960s. Still, Sundsten proudly intones what Kesey took longer to say: namely, that the speedball of ideas swelled over the trip and could have produced more intellectual repercussions had they used the footage. Kerouac, to be sure, held at waste his agenda by 1964, repeatedly shutting the door on hippie examinations of his concepts on TV broadcasts like *Firing Line with William F. Buckley* during the 1960s and in *Desolation Angels*' positive ellipsis, which meant to keep his dialogue internal and freed of the counterculture's bubble of re-examinations of his content. *In its late foreshadowing, Magic Trip* documents the revival of thought and directions through their meetings with emissaries from the 1950s beatnik past in an attempt to re-ride its history, cinematography, and genealogies. Ginsberg's re-introduction was crucial, as he, too, was given the impulse to speak about his poems, as the film runs a reel of his reading of "Howl," situating the damaged soul's rebirth. Crucial re-absorptions did not stop with the film's makings—Ginsberg would attend and enjoy a Grateful Dead concert in 1967. It is worth noting that Sundsten and Kesey stage the "second coming" and a second coming for the generation's ideas that were clearly in tow by this time.

A considerable effort was invested into extending portraits of the troupe's sexual exploits, which were consistent with both Pranksterism and the foliage

---

[14] *Ibid.*
[15] *Ibid.*

of rock tales caught on the microphone in rockumentaries. Zonker introduces the peculiar tendril of exposition when examining Stark Naked: "I'm attracted, there's no question of it. She's just so strange."[16] Naked does her part for the troupe's glory, cavorting without clothes on the bus's outside. Still, the troupe's most delicious memory would come from Sundsten, who tripped on acid in the bog where the bus had floundered:

> Once I hit the pond, I understood I was high. The water opened itself up to me and a new dimension. There was no murkiness; there are real crystals so I felt they grew from each other (...). I could find the algae was talking. It was welcoming me into its own existence. It was like the Nature Spirit saying, "Finally, we were in contact with a human being" Trying to get through to you guys for a while. They were happy, and I was happy.[17]

Sundsten's series of transcendences upstage much of the billing for Kesey's adventurous quest—a woman, possessed of herself as a spirit of Nature, re-states Being's rhapsodic sensing of Being and responsibility with no cameras and only her private sentiment that taking drugs illuminates cosmic agency. Sundsten's pretense, then, compliments Kesey's open-ended form, broadly casting the newfound promise to relate to the Earth and its life forms. The goings-on include considerable commentary and scenes highlighting women's experiences: this reality was, it must be said, less true for the Beat Generation. Women are free to explore in such a way that the collective experience stars them in the prolonged whirlwind of self-discoveries. Of course, shattering Victorian themes of status and separateness were duly rendered, and what appears to be the main thrust of this lengthy excursion was to distend gender controls to suit a newfound sympathy between the sexes. It was not as though *Magic Trip* sequenced only tales of progeny and the hold of that instance as perspective. It was more likely that the door to self-examinations and prolonged hallucinatory feelings about the world was now graciously open and could re-write the enshrined studies of their elders without logical ordination.

Conclusion: Kesey's Possibilities After the World's Fair

In its final estimation, Magic Trip ruefully admits that the excursion failed, leaving the participants with nothing except brain content in their trips. These ideas and experiences failed to soothe the entourage's seething ambition for change when abstracted into written form. Of the World's Fair itself, Sundsten

---

[16] *Ibid.*
[17] *Ibid.*

notes aptly the bus participants' decelerating tense: "Well, nobody kept together, and there was nothing to feel, and it was so dispersed."[18] Of the bus's subsequent trip to Millbrook, it is noted, classically speaking and in tune with Beat's ramblings, that Ginsberg arranged for the meeting of Leary with Kesey. Instead, we find a depressed exclamation about Leary's friend, Ram Dass: "This reading scared the shit out of me."[19] The point, in the form of this depressive introduction, was fair enough. Curiously, much of the text of *Magic Trip* captured the irony that participants were not that well-informed about psychedelic science and that their partying and planning had not considered the abstract velocity and depth of Tibetan and psychiatric studies that much. Also suggested was that the confluence of Kesey and Cassady as troupe leaders did not mold the group into a dynamic learning force that could go farther than their trips. Youthful insouciance, dallying in the unguided world, produced points of realization and depression. Commentator Robert Stone, amidst the deluge of future cities, singing accompaniments, and crowds milling around the fairgrounds: "We didn't know the World's Fair was a thing of the past."[20] But commentary about Millbrook was more neatly paired to expressions of youthful misunderstanding, and indeed the fracture that spun endless liberations of the formative tense for examining and using hallucinogenic drugs, with Sundsten stating, "We were explorers, and they were scientists."[21]

Magic Trip's remainder advances a defeated journey. Instead, it seeks to consecrate the series of visions and Kesey's author-public figure role in raising interest in the counterculture through Kesey's interactions with the music scene, Haight-Ashbury, and government conspiracies that reached his ears while facing marijuana charges in 1965. At this point, Kesey's narration and positive quips tell us that he did not understand the outlay of popularity guaranteed by the counterculture and that he might never fully understand because of his legal status. At this point, it is noteworthy to detail the fact that Kesey's transcendence and organization of social resistance allow for a positive momentum consistent with liberal political theories, raising his Beat influences above ground.

Notes from Kesey's "jail journal," at the first instance, tailor beatnik responses to the foliage of new findings and trip-related excursions:

> Got my shirt off, belly to the afternoon sun, listening to Bud Shank jap flute music shift into the Redwoods (...) painstakingly darning socks

---

[18] *Ibid.*
[19] *Ibid.*
[20] *Ibid.*
[21] *Ibid.*

pulled over a light bulb (…) mellowed by a little bit of the ball of opium Ramrod and Gazgirl smuggled in the other night (…) listening, stitching, doing good Oriental job on each sock.[22]

Kesey is then confronted by a narcotics officer, Mr. Molinari, and ejects the following: "Mr. Molinari," I answered, ceremoniously adjusting my shades, "Allow me to make one thing clear before we continue our conversation. I'll lie to you."[23]

Kesey's positive ejection of hallucinogenic fact is not far from the absentminded syntax and cultural escapism in Jack Kerouac's 1965 novel *Desolation Angels*. The Orient's use of declassed syntax positively coincided with Kerouac's trips, so it does not represent any breakthrough that had not been attempted before. Kesey's statement, however, that he would "lie" replicates Orwell's dictation of rebel agency in *1984*, showing us a greater positive commitment to the counterculture than Leary, who could not assemble as strong opposition to government control and brainwashing. We may at least sanction the counterculture as an active force and one bearing a tradition that had materially thought about the odds of fighting America's parent culture.

Tackling the generation's naïve innocence, impervious lack of scholarly training, and the depressive wind exhaust emanating from the heels of their broad-schemed journey across the continent may expose the experimental form's glaring weaknesses as an entourage. It might signal the generation's lack of cognitive direction and their willingness to ignore it in favor of templates of sound, light, and humor as bellwether points of magic inundation into the depths of what cannot be explained, cannot be captured, and could not be related to the much more high-managed modern trends. The World's Fair and Millbrook told us about the group's loss of connection, a connection that could not be tied to the wisdom of modern man's everyday imagination. The Pranksters hang around, flutes playing, bathing in the creek, waiting for a benediction that did not happen because of the two camps' vast differences.

Kesey's positive anxiety, or the anxiety of a man uncertain of his purpose and in some way determined to preserve some fashion of it, is duly exposed because of his 1965 arrest for marijuana possession. His bluster is derivable from the first series of reporter interviews: "I feel like, I've seen this movie once. You're blowing your ticket if you don't get something rewarding."[24] A dour reporter curtly and solemnly faces the TV audience: "In the meantime, he will tell the

---

[22] *Ibid.*
[23] *Ibid.*
[24] *Ibid.*

teenage world of the evils of drugs."[25] The sustained impact would produce indifference, depression, and apathy in Kesey, complicating his outlook but projecting his legal status onto the lives of LSD takers: "This is not the thing that is happening anymore."[26] But what *Magic Trip* demonstrates positively is the wide swath of ignorance surrounding the LSD pandemic, the effeminate languor of pro-acid devotees to the "cause" of the drug, and the uncertainty with Kesey's message, captured in Tom Wolfe's *The Electric Kool-Aid Acid Test*, to "go beyond LSD." Arrangements and staged events also elicit the period's ambiguity, giving us less insight into what a "graduation" means and allowing a funny Garcia to exclaim, "hallelujah!" to the form of Kesey's stated withdrawal from experimentation with the drug.[27] At other points, Kesey appeared defiant: "Once Pandora's box is open, you can't, um, regulate and mix to use the stuff that flies out of it,"[28] while a thinned interpretation states the drug's dangers: "powerful new drug keeps producing weird and dangerous new hallucinations."[29] Kesey's arrest was followed by commercials, news reports, and clamors to "put people back on the ground." The section is illustrative of the surprising lack of knowledge and indoctrination and the weak government appraisals spelling out the drug's dangers and the threat to society. At other points, a girl on a bad trip struggles on the hospital bed, pleading for her life—again, to demonstrate the dangers, but with no evidence showing the trip's real experience inside the mind or within the experience's context. Preternaturally, the left's response was narrow and shallow, with girls and boys attesting to LSD's impact on understanding life and protest signs that merely state, "DOWN WITH FUZZ."[30] Still, a defiant Kesey arranges for the "graduation" trip party and pontificates loudly the resurgence of the culture and the lack of a need to change it as "enough people" have signed on to the scene for taking drugs. If anything, Kesey's moves during this time raise Jerry Garcia and his band, the Grateful Dead, to be heirs to the LSD equation: the parties, with hippies dancing and enjoying themselves, do not spell out any specific criteria for having passed, nor are there indications from Kesey as to what his criteria were.

I think the videography of *Magic Trip*, plus the interviews and stories housed in archives, tell us much about how social and intellectual change in America could offset the military-industrial complex. Authorially, responses among students and young people are short and believable, and life's paradigm was

---

[25] *Ibid.*
[26] "Plans For Acid Ceremony," *San Francisco Chronicle*, October 6, 1966.
[27] *Magic Trip.*
[28] *Ibid.*
[29] *Ibid.*
[30] *Ibid.*

short enough to propose government-military conspiracy in thoughts that were complex, not nature-derived, and not pleasurable. Parading the "bus" is matched by a sour Kesey's interview in front of the bus: he, illustrating the depressive tone about the survival of drugs (probably, with him not part of it), allows the experiments and participants greater acuity in saying why LSD could contribute to understanding life, spawning a moral perspective that Huxley was reluctant to form into any single moment of *praxis*. Of course, music culture would benefit tremendously: it was likely that Garcia, free to evolve form and the syntax of notes, could come forth with a much more personally rewarding equation for Being and belonging. Kesey exhibits emotions that concur with having been busted: he is no longer allowed to consummate the entourage and admits he wishes he could have done more. The conclusion of Kesey's ordeal reaches its highest moment of eclipse when Kesey is informed that Ginsberg has testified that the crowds of drug-taking hippies in Haight-Ashbury were part of a CIA experiment to find out what would happen if people took LSD.[31] *Magic Trip*, more than other psychedelic documentaries, points roundly to LSD's eclipse and to how scientific studies and academic beginnings might stray far from their original purpose, easily and widely absorbed by the parent culture in an attempt to dissuade interest in their findings. Kesey as much as was true of Timothy Leary while in jail on a pot charge, must accept in theory Ingsoc's victory as in Orwell's *1984* and that one's stated purpose of building utopia had left him bare to the more pursuant charges of marijuana, more commonly used and so not a part of the decisive learning.

But Kesey operates his tryst with destiny and commemorates what he felt was the success of the bus trip by saying openly: "I wanted to be, I wanted to get back to the desert land, get back to history, but it wouldn't die."[32] As the entourage settles in to listen to and praise thirty hours of video footage, Kesey explains that he saw the Dead "as a sort of backup band." As the music plays and people dance and enjoy the experiments, a young Garcia says, "It sounded like a really interesting thing to go and check out."[33] As songs from the Coasters play, including "Youngblood," Kesey opines about the Dead, "They weren't just playing what was in the music, they were even playing what was in the air."[34] Thus, even vague responses told us that LSD-centered events were beyond the author's scientism and could open doors that appear to have been fixed in his imagination.

---

[31] *Ibid.*
[32] *Ibid.*
[33] *Ibid.*
[34] *Ibid.*

Magic Trip concludes the bus trip with a screenshot of Kesey's notepad, saying, "The World's Fair is NOT a cool place."[35] Kesey longs for popular change and remains a standard-bearer of a more uncontrived, unlimited scheme of invention that could either build or destroy psychedelic science or both within the growing rock spectacle. That the FURTHUR participants thought that ideas and experiences could root themselves together is visibly clear enough—culture and freedom from it are paired together as a tryst of specific meaning, connected to modern man's literature, traditions, and political ideas, rolled into one. "Cool" implied Kesey's Beat-meshed point, at which modern man, freed of his conditioning, could enjoy and communicate with worlds beyond the rational man's grasp. From this angle, we can easily see that *Magic Trip* ensured future visionaries greater husks of thought and introspection and greater scientism that has poured out of academic control.

---

[35] *Ibid.*

Chapter 21

The Tomorrow Show and the Grateful Dead: Guitarist Jerry Garcia's Explanations about LSD with Ken Kesey

I believe that it is fair, when we pose the longevity of LSD experiments happening in the 1960s and 70s, to also present Grateful Dead guitarist and singer Jerry Garcia as begetting a meaningful summit with the generation's destiny. This is because the Grateful Dead were a rock band who produced hundreds of music fronts friendly to the theorists' stated doctrines that were derived from thinkers and shamans and because the Dead enjoy a much wider audience, and so speed up crucial dissemination of acid facts, meant that the specific *genre* turns over itself to playing and participating instead of to the psychiatrist's quadrant with stats and instructions as key metaphors. Of course, we admit to the story's basic facts: Garcia was a drug addict who used heroin for a full twenty years, and enough of us could say that LSD's appreciable force spinning around their concerts competed and conflicted with his addiction to harder drugs destroying and aging his body, even to posit the "race against time" when creating psychedelic Being's livable forms.

Born on August 1, 1942, into a Spanish-American family, Jerome Garcia studied bluegrass music at an early age and was moved by his creative motions: he picked up the blues by the time he was 12 and studied art at the San Francisco Art Institute under the tutelage of Wally Hedrick. As was true of Doors lead vocalist Jim Morrison, the wisdom of Jack Kerouac's *On the Road* inspired him; thus, the clothespin of influences had guaranteed learning of American music and culture and was part of persistent impressionism, aided by drugs yet sympathetic with America's imagistic and memory roots that might transform psychedelic blues into refurbished American spiritual navigations and, when possible, their legendation. Before going into *The Tomorrow Show's* specific text, let us establish that Garcia was, too, interested in a wide range of folk styles and its lyrical tale-telling as the operative generating moment in modern consciousness, that these styles could be re-invented through LSD's christening powers. It was likely, too, that Garcia represents a generation puzzled and fascinated with Kerouac's road and its multiple texts and symbolism that drugs supposedly invigorated.

We might at least allow that Snyder had interviewed rock greats on his show and that late-night TV shadows the show's participants in a kind of offset grandeur that means praise for the artist. Still, there are important questions about why this episode befits anything in countercultural history when we target two factors: one, that the counterculture had by 1981 subsided a good deal, with neoconservative rock and pop attitudes for the time being relegating acts like the Dead to an underground amidst more pleasantly received pop stars and their more limited artistic examples. Because this episode aired during the Reagan Era, we might add questions about the timely relevance of the band's meditations and those of Kesey. With the acid tests long gone, it was unclear what direction the band's specific minute of time signature would command in the viewing eye. Still, a wide-eyed Snyder professes his support, though no such platform exists in the general population for another drug-taking act. Certainly, fewer questions would abound when telling the Dead's story as it had been set in the 1960s, not the 1980s. Nonetheless, enough of us might call Garcia's comments lies; he was already addicted to heroin and so had himself "moved on" from the innocuous-sounding poetics of LSD.

I also think Garcia's dual expression of the deep responsibility for taking drugs and situating them to be derivable conscious experiences accomplished what host Tom Snyder hoped: an active experience with fewer boundaries. Hence, the transference of "science" onto *praxis* to fulfill what may have been the predominant thinker's goals. Snyder, for his part, took down notions of communalism and participation to engage burning questions about Garcia's mind, saying: "Was I correct when I said that you took some of the LSD for yourself that wasn't Uncle Sam's group?"[1] Garcia stokes the phantom of ownership for his part, saying that he guaranteed a wider context and a managed control of both the band and its creativity of sound and sight: "It's something I wouldn't do professionally. Now I feel more of a sense of responsibility to be able to be in command."[2] Certainly, Garcia's elucidation of rock's tale, with its massive behemoth of self-presentation and sound orchestrations, deserves equality with the theorists who arranged experiments in hospitals and quantified facts and findings. When distanced from the political specter of Vietnam, protests, and Woodstock, Garcia certainly found a much greater avenue for his music's expression. This shaded lens was important because Garcia notes in his interviews that the music's sound is the most important factor, not any intellectual ideas or composed theories that might state *praxis*. Of the famed "Acid Tests," Garcia told Snyder the following:

---

[1] *The Tomorrow Show with Tom Snyder.*
[2] *Ibid.*

But on the other hand, sometimes we'd play, and there was no pressure on us, people didn't come in to see the Grateful Dead, they came for the Acid Test. On the whole, that counted. So we were in the spotlight, the pressure wasn't on us. Not only didn't we have to fulfill expectations about us, but we didn't have to fulfill expectations about music, either. Being able to experiment freely is amazing.[3]

Garcia's dualism, or rather the dualism between idealism and corporate rock power, re-tracks the 1960s as a period of discovery and scrutiny: the Grateful Dead's "identity" contrasted with that of a group of friends playing within a controlled experiment's study and annals, one that Kesey had devised to simulate conscious growth. Kesey, who sits to Garcia's right in the interview, muffles commentary to discuss "conscious expansion" and "drama" to retread Garcia's statements about LSD and music by saying of the acid tests: "I think it was the beginning of a real, true revolution that's still going on."[4]

Still, Garcia's comment about drug expansions—and, presumably, the rebuilding of LSD venues and excursions by staging drug use, camaraderie, and music experimentation as part of a larger structure pervading serious modern imaginations, is not muddied and prevaricate to a greater structure mixing ideas and histories into the building of momentum and sense-derivations friendly to a spoken LSD consciousness that could have come from Huxley, Leary, Hofmann, or Kesey.

Introductions: Jerome Garcia

Of his group's music itself, a smiling Garcia admits that they "were never current,"[5] then points to the truth of the music as LSD messenger: "Well, it changes as we change. As a musician over the years, musicians have gotten to be better. There's more time to play, which we're getting to be almost good at."[6] For his part, Garcia states the trip's controlling concept but winds around that point by underscoring the music, playing, and the relationships in the band—things that were not controlled by any set form of conditioning nor tied to any one ritual form of self-expression. It dourly has to be admitted—rock, folk, and blues styles, strictly speaking, were *not LSD sonically*—though groups like the Doors had, as early as 1966, used Willie Dixon songs, including "Back Door Man"[7] as part of their musical tours. The conflagration of styles, music, and

---

[3] *Ibid.*
[4] *Ibid.*
[5] *Ibid.*
[6] *Ibid.*
[7] Doors, The. *The Doors.*

sonic textures speak to the LSD vehicle's building through interposed sounds and styles, lifting visual and aural translations into Being's common stance—still, Garcia notes the band's growth, maturity, and validity—becoming "almost good at it" meant that Garcia had started with a consistent vision of acid tripping, developing and enriching it over the years. Such comments expose the riddle about Garcia's form because, in previous interviews, the modernist ground was proudly and put in context, as Garcia says: "You can go hear me play—that's me, that's what I have to say; that's the form that my thoughts have taken."[8] While it is obvious that Kesey is too intoxicated to say much, he passively adorns his disciples' conception, targeting the movement's tenacity—true to form, as counterculture idealism had not died out by 1981, when the show aired—and underscoring late-night talk shows' collective responsibility to push the movement's contemporary relevance.

Equally noteworthy was the Grateful Dead's succeeding set, which included Bob Weir's song, "Cassidy." While the obvious metaphors of this paean star counterculture's generalities, speaking to marijuana in particular, "come to grow the starched ground green,"[9] the succeeding line collapses the twentieth century's penitent music history in a loose arrangement of sounds and intensities producing the positive spark of ideation and Being: "blow the horn, and tap the tambourine, close the gap of the dark years in between."[10] This was important and stars Garcia's positive adherence to ideas found with Jack Kerouac and not with Huxley or Leary, who occasionally scorned jazz and blues music. It was, and is, clear that the band members were avid readers of *On the Road* and *Dharma Bums*, paying positive attention to the metaphor of light and darkness when staging music's development during the twentieth century and then its less-than-traditional exercise with rock bands that ranged from saxophone-playing Traffic to flute-playing Jethro Tull. Without discussing the mechanics of music arrangements, an opportunity to close the gap between realization and industrial depression resonated in the band's memories about how they came to be who they were.

Psychedelic Rock's Survival?

It was not without some hesitation that we would grow LSD concepts away from their written origins. Traffic guitarist Steve Winwood had written several songs, such as "The Low Spark of High-Heeled Boys"[11] and "Shoot Out at the

---

[8] Jackson, Blair, *Garcia: An American Life*, xii.
[9] Grateful Dead, "Cassidy."
[10] *Ibid.*
[11] Traffic, *The Low Spark of High-Heeled Boys.*

Fantasy Factory,"[12] that either lampoon or criticize drug cultures symbolic of the counterculture. It is certain, however, that Garcia and his bandmates approved of the potential dynamism and the chance to see makings of history within this moment of positive uplift. Aside from the obvious—instruments had come from Black musicians, not from white classical music, and so would have stunted theoretical attempts to build sound into meaning—the song's syntax, at least, composes the generation's advent wielding positive entrenchments of the ideas, to surpass and solidify responses to industrialism-socialism.

In short, the May 7, 1981 airing of *The Tomorrow Show* included the Grateful Dead to attest meaning, sincerity, and decisiveness to the thrust of comments found in this one episode. While including advertisements and a smiling, almost sycophantic Snyder commemorating the band members, this episode of *The Tomorrow Show* successfully re-introduces the band and its minute of ideation that somehow might still permeate the world, speaking in many glancing metaphors of the movement's growth and maturity. Without discussing trends in music, Garcia rendered LSD's specific belonging very easily and with nuance. Twenty years after Timothy Leary's experiments, Garcia on *The Tomorrow Show* re-christens the presumed agency to grow minds and redirect sense-objectification through corporate rock forms and their penchant to grow sound and its overall effect. Warm, cresting, and happy faces re-bear the generation's ascent into commercialized Eras without trading away the ground of sound.

---

[12] Traffic, *Shoot Out at the Fantasy Factory*.

Chapter 22

Americans and the Quest for Psychedelic Truth: *Long Strange Trip*

Amir Bar-Lev's nearly four-hour replay of the lives of Grateful Dead members in 2017's *Long Strange Trip* includes concert material, interviews with the Dead, and their road managers and promoters. Still, thoughtfully enough, it focuses on how they "were American" and searched for their identity through their travels. There are enough cross-pokes of nostalgia beefing up this general effort—Beat Generation references, though not obvious, mirror the recording issues and inspirations that came from the road, from pluralism, from invention, and from the apex of sound that could fire rock generations with adventure's endless tale and its rewritings of what it was to "be" an American. It was not without Garcia's pensive criticism—he admitted his life's troubles, suggesting a blue-collar point of inspiration through horror film and maybe his evolving sense of how anti-theory could make rock a vehicle for truly psychedelic presentation. With footage heralding 1940s American comedians Abbot & Costello in a film featuring Mary Shelley's Frankenstein, Garcia talks about his particular crush on the horror film's legacies: "I used to draw pictures of the greatest monster, over and over. I think part of it has to do with being afraid. I think of the power of having fear."[1] While these reminiscences did not repeat a true cosmology, they once again opened the drama of rock and film speaking to mentally afflicted persons.

Owen Glieberman commented that this film was "an ardent piece of documentary classicism."[2] Our basic appraisal would be to rate this film on its expositions, or at least the development of the band's persona, tensions, and creative points from experimentation. We might then judge whether *Long Strange Trip* demonstrated a living psychedelic process, independent of scientific and theoretical elucidations that bind us to prize discovery with no learning of anything about the conditioned subject as an origination of expansive, many-texted theories that popularize psychedelic culture. There are several easy give-offs, as band manager Sam Cutler says, "They were children.

---

[1] *Long Strange Trip*.
[2] *Variety*.

Children in a man's world"[3] and then sermonizing ruefully, "Americans got this very strange interest in the discovery of what it means to be an American."[4] Easily available in Garcia's notation that the band members were not heavily trained, that LSD offered new prospects for playing never tried, and that the band hated the record industry. Bob Matthews, too, notes the band's unique trick of writing records "to go on the road touring" that they had no proper pop sensibilities. The band's pushy style of tripping and making music for that purpose was unfolded. Still, Garcia attests to its nuances:

> And I guess I thought, on some level, I do, I want to concern myself with things that are weird. I do things like fun.[5]

Commentary from Dennis McNally was equally ambitious and cutting: "If you ignore the rabid band and ignore the lack of expected television and American entertainment, then you will find the richness that fills your soul."[6] Un-targeted points of theoretical introduction, then, spoke to the band's concepts of freedom and self-introspected deviance, and the unclassified bogs of the unknown, the mysterious, the avenues of pleasure, to constitute a humanities development of ideas and immersions which ought to be beneficial for society. Garcia explores his pain, then turns over the proceedings to band members such as drummer Mickey Hart, who points out that the band would go to the zoo at night to film animals, then make films in the desert[7], and fellow drummer Bill Kreutzmann paired the absence of learning with the moment's true triumph: "I was never good at keeping time. I like to take the song so far out that you don't remember what song you're in, but this is fucking great."[8] Staging drug trips as the beginnings of performance and as a mainspring of the imagination met with Garcia's persistent teaching of meaning. Identifying the diversity of meanings, emblems of truth, languages, and perhaps the decentering of one's thoughts and perceptions, building truly psychedelic meaning into rock performances is useful. Naturally, the rock parable absorbs much of this melding process: producers were keen to state the band's adolescent mischievousness and total lack of preparation for the music business or "making money." Still, drawing comparisons to Nature, animals, silence, horror, and invention addresses questions of an enhanced modern Being.

---

[3] *Long Strange Trip.*
[4] *Ibid.*
[5] *Ibid.*
[6] *Ibid.*
[7] *Ibid.*
[8] *Ibid.*

Garcia's Psychedelic Talent: Workingman's Dead and American Beauty

But the most interesting content of this film is, perhaps, the staging of the LSD generation and its thoughtful ascension to rock membership and the use of technology, fame, music, and living senses to create the wide, powerful, and intense gradation of LSD community and its Being—concerts are crowded, and in some cases include thousands or even tens of thousands of fans. As the soldier stands up to clap at one gig while hippie participants remain seated, and an announcer tells audiences of the release of *Workingman's Dead*, "an album different from anything they've ever done before,"[9] the speculation grows as the band takes up simpler songs with the focus upon singing, anchoring playing to country and Western ideas and instruments. It should be said that Garcia's move towards folk and country was hardly unique, forming the basis for the gradual transformation of rock away from psychedelic colors and power-distortion tunes blaring rock's chaotic might. Still, as Garcia instructs Weir and Lesh, telling them to "sing out" on songs like "Candyman," we have enough advance of the notion that acid-head imaginations and social consciousness could pour their content into the bevy of unadorned, unspoken-of music forms that would bring the band fame and, in its truer instance, that told us more about Garcia's theory and his specific use of sounds and songs rebuilding improvisation and playing. With rock bands such as Crosby, Stills and Nash, The Eagles, and Eric Clapton warming to this sound, what attention did Garcia give that spoke to the creativity of rock avenues? Sourly, Cutler dismisses the band's LSD tripping, saying that many of the participants didn't know anything about LSD and surely did not know what they were experiencing. But producer Bob Matthews speaks proudly of the record: "It was a home run with two great singles, and it was called *Workingman's Dead*."[10] Garcia cues Weir and Lesh repeatedly to stress the singing above the notes, going through "Candyman" with an acoustic guitar; the studio cut reintroduces the instruments with more flair and louder playing. *Long Strange Trip*, of course, bridges the two seminal moments in the band's career by retraining and rebuilding the core sound of spontaneous, uneducated musicians from Garcia's specific emphasis on penning and playing rock songs bearing the classic stamp of rustic-trailed rock adventures through love, society, and humanity. Again, this path didn't have to be LSD's positive course, and to be sure. Other bands dropped much of the ballooning acid mythology to secure greater fame. In a recent interview, guitarist Bob Weir illustrates the common tension in these productions: "There is nothing quite as magical as

---

[9] *Ibid.*
[10] *Ibid.*

the American songbook."[11] This point of reference was seminal: band members learned and appreciated the form of Garcia's narrative and sonic decisions and acquired fluidity and maturity from those motions. But this was, in the realest sense, taught. Interchanges, in short, were dropped to favor the band's unswerving emphasis on popularizing folk and pop music forms. Warner Brothers, for its part, invited the Dead to tour Europe. If music is learned, and trained musicians will adapt tunes or write them, what is the outcome of a pop band that depended upon sound's power and acridity when writing country-flavored songs? *Long Strange Trip* depends upon the sound's free transaction, the idea that anyone could learn and use it, and the backdrop of working-class rebellions that spoke to a greater American humanity that guards the specific experience. I think it is evident that short songs and folk tunes proudly illustrated the psychedelic technique for turning the gears of the imagination and feeling—they are, as reconstructions of the original folk context, directed at opening tones and sounds of perception that are favorable to tripping and dreaming, carrying with them the dreamlike interstice between folk and blues that build Garcia's curiously enveloping sound. Without a microscope, then, we would affect the song's contents mired in the blues and romanticist blowing of notes from the guitar and bass as psychedelic music grew its tendency to activate the senses. Rock tunes aside, we should recognize the band's shaded moment of acoustic brilliance: these were released in the same year as Traffic's *John Barleycorn Must Die*, The Doors' *Morrison Hotel*, and Led Zeppelin's *Led Zeppelin III*. At this historical juncture, rock music effectively replaced classical with acoustic rock to fit the form of future psychedelic meditations.

It should be pointed out that this was *not* the direction of most bands that played acid rock—their path, it must be said, was technological, confirming sound's supremacy over song. Given these beginnings, and since Garcia pushed the band to play jams where all the emphasis was on playing, was this a sidestep? This movie partly tells Deadheads and lay citizens alike that vocal and sonic stresses outperform the music industry's expectations and rigors, as they might have hoped to keep sound and genres separate to make more money. Learning was meaningful—at least, we might unearth the deep catalog of Grateful Dead tunes to elicit the sense that music traditions, consistent with the idea that anyone could learn them, earn staying power among those who opted to broaden their influence, to suggest a greater Self orchestrating the conflicts, emotions, and specific feeling that had reached its main audience a generation before. Despite Cutler's grumbling and the glib happiness of Matthew's interest in the spectacle, Long Strange Trip zeroes in on Garcia's continued flowering of the pot of rock invention using a simple stress on sound.

---

[11] Ruggieri, Melissa. "Live Music Has to Rebound." *USA Today*, February 17, 2022.

While this was not the 1980s incarnation of the band, what is significant is that verbal and vocal *oeuvre* rebuilds the key attempt to stage sound from traditional roots. Drugs had been a part of popular music since Howlin' Wolf's "Spoonful,"[12] and acid-rock bands, including Led Zeppelin, had ripped off tunes from Willie Dixon in the pursuit of heavy metal power and expansion. But Garcia did not want to seek "complex psychedelic fantasies,"[13] here focusing his bandmates on *genres* that LSD consciousness could grow and politicize from their limited musical training. Rock critics agree that *Workingman's Dead* redefined the band's voice, attitude, vocality, and private reach into American imaginations.

Sam Cutler as Road Manager

Sam Cutler offers an essential tidbit of this rockumentary: he encouraged the Grateful Dead to be filmed for a movie. The move was unnatural and did not consider the band's comic indifference, which Cutler underscores in his estimation of the band members. He notes the problem of motivating the disorganized band to take their efforts seriously:

> So the film's crew slowly came under the influence of psychedelics. They start with a very formal idea, how do we film a band and slowly it got weirder and weirder. So easy, you know, now let's make a film here and ensure I don't show this. Well, that tends to go out the window. They just succumbed, they didn't know sufficient psychedelic experience to overcome the effect of the acid and, you know, make a film.[14]

At a glance, cinematography's lampooning would be frequently starred. A teasing Garcia stares into the camera, pointing his tongue at it, while Phil Lesh drinks a beer while being interviewed.[15] Still, as spokesman and prophet, Garcia does archly demonstrate the validity and cosmic necessity of tripping, supposing a trailer park to be like a valley. He warmly and confidently shares this vision with the cameraman and roadies parked outside the recording studio:

> I'll tell you what it is. The fact that these trucks are on either side of us. Making it seem as though on the horizon, it's kinda like being in a valley. And the human response to being in a valley is 'we're concerned'. But we're not, really, it's all an illusion because of these trucks. And if you can

---

[12] Howlin' Wolf, "Spoonful."
[13] *Long, Strange Trip.*
[14] *Ibid.*
[15] *Ibid.*

step out to where you can get a little bit of air around you so the horizon is kinda like below your vision, you'll feel much better, yeah.[16]

Garcia's prophecy is surefooted, pairing post-industrial society with the abiding power and direction of cosmic realities; it coincides with numerous hallucinatory tales where modern life's materiality was symbolic of more truly natural extractions from the de-rationalized mind, in that sense, and also in the sense that rock songs in this tenor re-equipped citizens for a more fantastic appraisal of data and sense-perceptions, Garcia opens the door to visions that partake of the elder's fantasies and hallucinations while stating the human problem of happiness to be situated against the powerful, postmodern urban materialism. "Tripping," and songs that re-interpret experience to favor the cosmos as a directing hand, is Garcia's supple style of linking ideas with a clear point of necessary reference in conduits of the brain, the senses, and the body. Naturalist re-directions may be as fantastic as sixteenth-century Spanish writer Miguel Cervantes' windmills in *Don Quixote*. What is likely is that tripping's dreaming power may revive man's instincts and attunement to the world's forces. With skill and ease, Garcia unveils the trick to defeat Leary's "games"— to understand nature's greater moment and its role in building sense-fulfillment through dream-interpretations. It could be said that, at least at this juncture, Garcia is casual when he re-arranges perception and meaning. It was apt that his concept would be extended through songs, performances, and lyrics about an endless maze of partial space-time directions. It is likely, too, that future Dead adventures emphasize the organ, synthesizer, and piano to restate dislocated transcendences that spell out the mind's truly rich replays and that Garcia encouraged what he saw as a way to expand the mind's hallucinogenic contexts and textures. The group's anthology of tales found in the songs would, in short, project an enhanced, complex, and interacting perception that grew and technologized the human experience. Realizing, then, that Garcia's imagination superimposed many moments of ideation and perception to advance future musical strategies that had grown in rock, blues, and R&B during the 1970s and 80s.

Abundant clips of the band playing before large audiences, the bandmates' penitent focus upon Garcia's cues, and overall sound samplings did much to attest to the counterculture's growing herald as a messenger of enhanced understanding and belonging. *Long Strange Trip* did, of course, include the rock counterculture's history as our beginning for understanding changes in the Grateful Dead and the abiding thought that sound and story would grow and that Garcia had masterfully planned for fans the sonic resonance that

---

[16] *Ibid.*

would adapt the growing legend. Cutler's general range of comments reemphasizes rock's basic tier as the antidote to psychedelic reasoning: the band was unprepared for rock's real world and needed structure and guidance. Still, Garcia's comments are light, airy, and sufficient, telling us how pop inundations sparked greater motions towards Being, situating the supposedly awesome machine of improvisation and folk abstraction within rock's basic dynamics. Rock tended to espouse an experimental form in goofy offshoots or simple commentaries. It had not considered all aspects of corporate rock production to be the necessary vehicle for social change. It could be said with certainty that Garcia's thesis that the music itself represented LSD's learning curve was replete in this film. Popular music supplanted science and study as our basis for understanding the acid generation. Garcia, Matthews, Hart, and Cutler are candid when visiting origins, and this theme structured a broader template of learning that scientists and Pranksters alike were less likely to realize during their times.

Chapter 23

Carlos Castaneda and Enigma of a Sorcerer: The Positive Value of Psychedelic Science

At the outset, in my eagerness to learn about philosophy and science, I found my father's water-damaged copy of Carlos Castaneda's 1971 work *A Separate Reality* while I was a college student at Vanderbilt. It did, in fact, open doors to new realities. Dreams, hallucinations, and non-ordinary arrangements of Nature, its creatures, and the natural media that constitute storytelling appeared visually and intellectually developed in Castaneda's books. Still, one must gravitate towards the subject's dour, vindictive scholarly bent: no one has proven Don Juan's existence, nor does a comparative ethnography establish the justice of those practices. In short, critics and commentators were always rife to appraise what was an invented cultural fantasy, an appropriation of naturalism that could free modern humanity from the Victorian *topoi* that enshrined capitalism and capital-object development of human psychology and meanings.

Mary Douglas, a respected researcher, expressed the tendency to embrace diversity while reading Castaneda's studies. She writes:

> It may be difficult to judge the spirituality of the religion revealed in this series because of the deafening clichés in which it is perforce rendered. But it would be more difficult to defend formally the view that their echoing contemporary philosophical concerns is proof of their bogus character. For they are consistently knitted into an attitude towards life and death and human rationality whose very coherence is alien to our contemporary thought.[1]

In all seriousness, opposition to Castaneda's general narrations of "non-ordinary reality" and shamanism was formidable and told us, among other things, that cult ritual and drug use could not be proven, experiences do not

---

[1] Braga, Corin. "Carlos Castaneda: The Uses and Abuses of Ethnomethodology and Emic Studies."

conform to the actual activities of tribes and subjects in Yaqui culture, and specific testimonies efface themselves in a world of pure, imaginative heresies. Calling upon the realms of psychological scholarship, Braga intends to prove that these experiments were not true, nor did they execute a truly systemic morphology. Still, Douglas's comments are appropriately toned to raise the debacle higher: would a religious consciousness depend upon rationalist objectivity to demonstrate the truth of its principle? Was it not likely that "non-ordinary reality" could be created from the imagination and its naturalist setting? Could these findings, too, corroborate agrarianism versus modern, urban, industrial makings of the Self and its role in society? We are given enough raw knowledge in the narrations of *Enigma of a Sorcerer*, and the humanist logic of the film's themes was meaningful enough to raise formal questions as to what could and could not be called *real*. In this 91-minute film, roundtable discussions about Castaneda and his invented science are telling, maintaining an active debate that seems relevant even today, twenty-five years after the author's death and the shuffling of his papers and experiences into the newfound obscurity. Specific testimonies from the narrator and commentators establish a counter-criticism that many aspects of shamanic culture, and the guarded framework examining rational/non-rational thoughts and perceptions, was wide and historically impactive enough to suggest their reality and the transference of meaning to possess some meaning.

Biography

Born Carlos Cesar Salvador Arana on December 25, 1925, in Peru, Castaneda immigrated to the United States in the 1950s, earning his anthropology degree in 1973 at the University of California. He authored twelve books before he died in 1999, including *The Teachings of Don Juan, A Separate Reality, Journey to Itxlan, Tales of Power, The Second Ring of Power, The Eagle's Gift, The Fire from Within, The Power of Silence, The Art of Dreaming,* and *The Wheel of Time*. What appears noteworthy was not simply Castaneda's authorship of these works but the recurrent attention to Yaqui shaman Don Juan's specific teachings and their positive conjugation of ideas and scriptural links among the Native American tribes of Mexico and Castaneda's specific passage into otherworldly states of awareness by using mescaline and psilocybin mushrooms as they staged reality and power. Castaneda did not exhume any new science but developed experiences and trips into narrated tales of the naturalist-visionary glory of recurrent metaphors for Being and Knowing in the supernatural world. That Castaneda is fictional separates his writings from his practice of *nagual*: his indoctrination's specifics canvas ideas and practices suggested or materially demonstrated in his novels. At the outset, it appears likely that Castaneda did not heavily reference earlier ethnology or studies, nor his specific studies and notes from the years spent in the Yaqui terrain, with the body of instructions and teachings that correspond to phonemic, anti-establishmentarian thrusts from naturalism and mysticism, told in a simple language and series of inferences that anyone could understand. Castaneda's positive skill appeared to be stating that non-ordinary experiences *could happen to people* and that there was no mystery in placing naturalism, earthen symbolisms, and societal codes into the categorical imperative for understanding the use of drugs to build hallucinatory realism.

In Context: Castaneda's Findings

After reading Castaneda's novels, it became evident: should we say that a non-ordinary psychology *could* exist, we would appraise its perceptual data and its deductions of meaning *without* physical proof, and so suppose the author to be the supreme anthropologist who might alter behaviors in pursuit of a kind of ascetic ideal, thus transposing our international focus from North American prophecy's narrow winds of degraded, sub-rational empiricism. A fact should allow for the basic transaction: there were, and are, many Native American mythologies that assume the practice of eating peyote and psilocybin mushrooms, and so our ethical configuration of philosophy as a single person's immersion may determine science, whether it was real or imagined. We might also get the steam of rebellion from Castaneda's authorship. Castaneda felt that anthropology was too limited and sought his development, tagging findings to the author, not to place or practice. Thus, Castaneda operated a kind of countercultural summit, where ideas were translatable without adherence to regions, history, or specific ritual practices, and so had propagated a greater idealism that comes from taking drugs, not from indoctrination. His method, quite naturally, was opted for as a sometimes goal of counterculture—to transcend study itself.

Commentary from Castaneda duly establishes the breadth of shamanic studies—and the totality of learning that escapes the humanist's magnifying glass and, thus, posits a positive science that is anti-rational, subjective, and calls attention to the non-rational nature of shamanic knowledge. Castaneda, we are made to believe, was not satisfied with academia's concept of knowledge, saying the following in the film's opening minutes:

> As an anthropologist, the reality of what one says is only a very small thing of the total range of what we could feel as real. We could learn to code the reality of stimuli the way the shaman does. That could elongate our range, real to a different interpretation. Good god, the only way we

have to recall it is as a hallucination, madness. We cannot conceive the one will do it.[2]

Of course, commentary from audio narrator Peter Coyote, "he used his brilliance to play tricks,"[3] and longtime lover and collaborator Amy Wallace, "I came to understand that the books were fiction,"[4] do not safeguard Castaneda's presumed temple of knowledge housed in things "non-ordinary." We may best surmise that non-ordinary reality supposed sets of knowledge and principles that did not correlate to ordinary psychological principles and may not be successfully described with attention to keystone notions of truth such as reality, power, and sorcery. Castaneda, by extension, took advantage of psychology's comparative lack of ideas and states of awareness to suit his anthropology, one which had welded the weight of many shamanic themes and aphorisms that could constitute a knowledge of body, magic, wisdom, and truth—ascetic concepts which, it must be said, imperfectly and narrowly told the details of one's experience. Castaneda, then, operated a synthesis for which he could not accurately describe states of being but could tie them to points of his self-realization in the living, physical universe. There is the suggestion of an enhanced Being consistent with countercultural philosophies and even some rough translations of fact that propagate positive knowledge's illusion. "Tricks" presumed the fact that Castaneda did take advantage of humanity's poor grasp of knowledge and quantification of hallucinations and visions—engagements of "non-ordinary reality" suppose a greater functioning, one stripping humans of their rational order and engaging physiological states that are, at best, imperfectly described or retold. "Brilliance," of course, supposed the generational rebel, a speaking conduit for his times, but the potential for *building* science anew was consistent and resonant.

Criticism and Praise for "Non-Ordinary Reality"

Perhaps we would be wise to harness Jiddu Krishnamurti's modern-fangled teachings to suppose knowledge's greater minute, and perhaps the seriousness of challenges to "non-ordinary" learning as the unveiling of ignorance instead of knowledge. Krishnamurti is especially nonchalant about this point; "If one does completely put aside every form of belief, then there is no fear whatsoever."[5] The adamant pose, whereby man is stripped of belief, religious faith and practices, and the fetishism of belonging to a particular belief system,

---

[2] Torjan, Ralph, *The Enigma of a Sorcerer*.
[3] *Ibid.*
[4] *Ibid.*
[5] Krishnamurti, Jiddu, *The Flight of the Eagle*, 92.

sharpens on the next page: "The mind must be free of every form of spiritual tradition and sanction: otherwise one becomes utterly lacking in the highest form of intelligence."[6] Challenges posed, in short, by the modern academic world might force us to estimate Castaneda's finding within the form of serious, rational inquiries as to what sorts of truth and power might unfold from the disparate, loosely organized structure of naturalist themes that Don Juan Matus espouses. We will have more questions about the veil of Castaneda's authenticity as a thinker and philosopher. Commentary by history professor Robert Moss did not, at our outset, establish the justice of Castaneda's hallucinogenic studies: "Our culture doesn't give us a training for what follows death the way that ancient cultures did."[7] In truth, there was not the grounding of specific teachings. Instead, it would spill over into mythology professor Daniel Noel's operative comment about Western humanism's positive truncation of forms of knowledge: "Not many people were scholars of shamanism because it wasn't out in the culture."[8] Speaking to the tenor of cult followers as bearers of ethnic and lifestyle liberations that cut out Western capitalism's positive fruit may give at least some note to specific teachings but fail to address those teaching's meaning—at least, when given Krishnamurti's quests for "energy" and "freedom" when appraising the modern subject. Sharply contrasting these introductions are the comments of lifelong anti-Castaneda scholar Richard de Mille, who points out the fact that "the days when Castaneda wrote these things come shortly after the dates when they were published in the literature or when their new edition became available, in the library or bookstore."[9] In addition, scholar Victor Sanchez abbreviates the power of "non-ordinary reality," stating that "the force of the spirit was following through, and that was from the spirit, through the people, to this writer,"[10] and swift and thoughtful intermediary comments come from Richard Jennings concerning the *nagual* (non-ordinary world), which Jennings claims Castaneda used as "a quite different use from the way that native peoples in Mexico or other parts of South America use the term," stating instead that Castaneda used the concept to set up the mythology of Don Juan and used *nagual* "to produce energy."[11] Support in the biographical form did come from girlfriend Amy Wallace: "When I was alone with him, it was an experience of pure intensity."[12] Castaneda's intactness of

---

[6] Krishnamurti, Jiddu, *The Flight of the Eagle*, 94.
[7] Torjan, Ralph, *The Enigma of a Sorcerer*.
[8] *Ibid.*
[9] *Ibid.*
[10] *Ibid.*
[11] *Ibid.*
[12] *Ibid.*

philosophical purpose also came from his workshop participants, including Felix Wolf:

> I remember certain workshops when there was just a magnificent energy of a thousand people, and the *nagual* had a magnificent speech, something happened, and he was so infused with the energy, he was basically floating, speaking and perceiving energy.[13]

It could be said with some sureness that, despite Moss's thoughtful commentary, we cannot say that hallucinogenic membership was consistent with preservations of the environment, as Kerouac did make modern capitalism and its phonemic control admissible to the worlds of knowledge. It is more likely, then, that *Enigma of a Sorcerer* returns to prove, through Wallace in particular, that the entourage of followers and devotees did posit something that possessed serious parapsychology and that motifs for discovery and belonging were and are meaningful from beneath the positive construction of hallucinogenic fictions pulling the metaphoric adherence to naturalism as a guiding force when organizing perception, imaginations, and the symbolism of resilient lives during twentieth century times. Notwithstanding Sanchez's pointed and excited comment that Castaneda was "devoured" by the positive falseness of self-presentation, we are likely to posit energy and intensity to resource future excursions into hallucinogenic territories, condensing memory, feeling, and imagination to comprise the potential loop of mental ascension and self-governance that Mescalito might provide to a human subject.

Critical Perspectives on Shamanism

When we consider readings of Castaneda's primary works and the enshrined literary parable navigating drug hallucinations and the meanings of deducible experience, we find the seed for more questions than answers. *Enigma of a Sorcerer* pays considerable attention to Castaneda's life and the formal details of his specific cult from his followers: we are given accounts as to what drugged inferences mean. There are some instances of the scholarly reception for the specific, derived parapsychology, but the film does not grant the written works any strong legitimacy after Castaneda's initial comments. Instead, we are given two opposing sides of the coin. Coyote, who in short defends Castaneda's record; Wallace, who attests to the peculiar derivation of meaning and social focus; and scholars including Sanchez, Jennings, and Wolf, who tear apart the sincerity of such endeavors in the cult and who even question the scriptural basis for these experiences. Therefore, it is worthwhile to categorize drug

---

[13] *Ibid.*

experiences from beneath this conflict: Castaneda's writings, including *The Teachings of Don Juan*, identify a benevolent spirit, Mescalito, who is "a protector and teacher." Other written Don Juan synopses paraphrase the persistence of visions with falcons and eagles and, in general, hallucinogenic hallucinations; they, too, catalog a radical agrarian spirit dissolving Castaneda's pretense to be an intellectual. Parables involving vision are included in *Enigma of a Sorcerer*. Still, commentator Victor Sanchez made his ringing point that the symbolisms of the eagle and the serpent, clear to Mexican cultural aesthetics and symbolic of the moral perspective, identify Carlos as a traitor and a sinful being.[14] While Coyote defends popular cultism, girlfriend Amy Wallace points to the organization of parties, the hierarchical arrangement of functions designed to gratify Carlos's sexual desires, and the private anxiety that his work would not be understood.

Participants Melissa Ward and Felix Wolf attest to the specific transformation through energy and belief through the sessions. Ward recalls a specific experience at dinner with *Datura* and the feeling of "flying."[15] The point was not culturally unique, nor did it establish a vein of truth in our findings about "non-ordinary reality"; Mohammed Mrabet had staged *Datura* in a tale where the drug incapacitates a man, who another man then rapes.[16] William Faulkner, too, featured Black sharecroppers smoking or eating jimsonweed in 1929's *The Sound and the Fury*. Ward's experiences, then, were not unique and proposed no universal membership; they were conditioned and thus related to no specific parapsychology. Gathering the stored data about the parties in context does not offer any real concept of what took place or the specific gradations and hierarchies of meaning connected to the *nagual* mean. Instead, they form a backdrop for a considerable, exploitable heresy at the progenitor's hands. Linking Castaneda to existing drug parapsychologies will at least assure us that Castaneda's technique was not new. Still, *Enigma of a Sorcerer* describes in some fluidity that such experiments carried with them the physical and sensual dimensions of real consciousness, and thus something that may persist in anthropological redrawing.

Enigma of a Sorcerer did bear the assumption that non-ordinary reality realizes the transcendence of ordinary perceptions in its translation of the written text. It tells us that our hallucinations define our reality, not our normal perceptual or interpretive dynamics: we are told to fly even with the instance of a rock chained to us.[17] In truth, much more could be said about the non-

---

[14] *Ibid.*
[15] *Ibid.*
[16] Mrabet, Mohammed, *M'Hashish*.
[17] *The Enigma of a Sorcerer*.

ordinary transcendences earned at parties, and no objective corollary exists in this movie, save the testimony of those probably blinded by those experience's meaning. It could be said, at the very least, that Robert Moss redeems the controversy around his initial statements:

> Don Juan was a form of scientism, an ideology of science. A form of silence causes us to distrust the inner experience, to distant visionary experience because it's awfully difficult to quantify and prove. [...] The true science of the 21st Century and beyond is going to be a science that has dreaming at its heart.[18]

Contentions about "enigma," in short, are put down with objective truthfulness—understanding experience meant accepting more subjective determinations of what experience was and giving validity to the brain's interactions with experience. In this reading, Moss attributes the literature to signal changes in how science observes and analyzes its subjects, giving legitimacy to hallucinogenic studies as meaningful, cultural, and philosophical. Moss's statements in this section tackle a much more realistic anthropological goal, building an ultimate significance without defending Castaneda's ritual excursions. Unfortunately, and in contrast, accounts of Castaneda's parties and the transpositions of *nagual* are not objectively detailed, and we are left to conjecture what indoctrination took place, what aural or experiential characteristics were part of the proceedings, and specifically what idea-synthesis took place among the devotees. Vapid responses include those from Goldstein:

> You know, sometimes I tried to focus on and listen to every nuance of what he was saying. And then sometimes I realized his lips were moving, and it was irrelevant what he was saying cause something else was happening, but I could never put my finger on it.[19]

The text of *Enigma of a Sorcerer* includes a three-minute audio of the instructions commonly given in the meetings to relax and accept the non-ordinary reality as one's Being.[20] It must be said that psychedelic thinkers, including Timothy Leary, operated a much longer instruction, and we should be apt to criticize pundits who cannot fully explain what it was that they were doing. Goldstein's comments cause us to question "learning" because they cannot relate the details of that specific knowledge. Testimony from Andrea

---

[18] *Ibid.*
[19] *Ibid.*
[20] *Ibid.*

called to interpret a pigeon as an "extra-terrestrial animal,"[21] does not establish a durable tone, as she is led away on a gurney while hallucinating. We are, in short, given accounts of how something *could* be true, but nothing that states that Castaneda's indoctrinations are, in any way, true. Generalizing the instructional form might lead us to less academic conclusions, even betraying commodity fetishisms that are common to pop culture—but, in the least, the specter of belief in *Enigma of a Sorcerer* is not challenged.

Valerie Kadium and Viewpoints from the Devotees

Questions arise about the importance of the teachings, and commentators attempt to answer them in some form or other to state authoritatively what kind of positive learning may arise from it. *Enigma*'s narrator states this clearly: "The goal was ultimate liberation from dogmatic ideology imprisoning us both in life and death."[22] Simple questions may then arise about the specific content of that liberation and what that might mean for those who had followed and believed from the depths of Castaneda's special nuance that traversed three decades of notoriety. *Enigma of a Sorcerer* spelled out these ideas in context clearly and in a fashion similar to the concepts expressed by Leary: "To drop the pretentious programming and finally find true freedom."[23] What was this liberation, and did its contrived, positive minute of finding refuge in non-ordinary reality depend upon? We might then evaluate these ideas with the tone of sincerity and the common dictum that personal experiences give us the leverage to re-evaluate existence, therefore spelling out Castaneda's positivity. Of course, commentary from devotees such as Valerie Kadium does not tell us much about hallucinogens or the specific alterations of the brain, memory, and perceptions. Still, it may give us an inkling of a clue to what the indoctrinations might tell us in the psychedelic form:

> The idea of closing my eyes seeking my house and moving up from my backyard, who did I play with in the backyard when I was a little kid, that brought back all kinds of memories and feelings, you know, but the whole idea is to create, to pick a person that you're focusing on, to create a scene and then move into that scene, and to me it's—you breathe in, everything from the scene that you can remember, all the stuff that's put on you that isn't you, you breathe yourself back in from the scene, you let go, you breathe out those judgments, let them go, breathe back in the pieces of yourself that get scattered when those judgments come down

---

[21] *Ibid.*
[22] *Ibid.*
[23] *Ibid.*

on you, that's the—my understanding, the intent of recapitulation—pulling back the pieces of yourself, and letting go of the things that are put on you that aren't necessarily who you are.[24]

In short, concepts and ruminations such as Kadium's aren't new, touching basic points of sympathy rather than perceptual data and moments of transcendence. The indoctrination, steeped in self-examinations, was very far from Don Juan's specific form and the ideas that color his indoctrination in the primary texts. Kadium expresses nativity as a point of realization and continues to note the positive ecstasy of filtering through the reality of a childhood long gone as a beginning for understanding the Self. This was not the opinion of the primary psychedelics, who may finger Castaneda to be a kind of counselor rather than a scientist, and correlates with other psychology practices that aren't focused strictly on perception. Still, the basic idea coincides with Leary, at least in theory: escaping and rebuilding oneself away from the "games' that constitute ordinary psychology may give us the details of graduating away from the stigma of living an ordered life within the military-industrial-capitalist system, and therefore refresh the ideas that make us living entities, connecting us then to the positive ecstasy of hallucinatory Being that is, then, a memory and a memory point of what is "real." Of course, this, then, is *not* new and is the subject of several pages of Kerouac's novels and letters: seeking meaning and focus from childhood and then filtering out details that don't constitute "who you are" may then build psychedelic thinking from a peculiar naturalism that shadows memory and then calls drug trips that which is "real." But Kadium operates these points ably, at least in the abiding thought that drug indoctrinations were and are Real, and so diffuse biography in ways common to Don Juan's scolding of Castaneda in his novels. The populist tone will tell us that ideas operate far outside the political-social vacuum that constitutes our traditional ordering of reality. In that sense, Kadium may ably answer de Mille's straight criticisms that nothing ever happened or that the basis for non-ordinary reality was and is false, a contrived moment of pretension.

Because Torjan's film staged opposite sides of the Don Juan-Castaneda legacy, we are apt to grow the number of philosophies that may match or at least color the shamanic philosophy as it was written in Castaneda's novels. We are also, conjecturably, less likely to dismiss or praise Castaneda for the legacy of his rituals or even his books because of the positive ambivalence of his ethnography as we might uncover it. At least, it appears that strict valuation limitations would be put on the exercise, which possesses less objective development of the experience's idea. No proof of the positive findings may

---

[24] *Ibid.*

activate literary readings tying Castaneda to prehistoric agrarian traditions and their philosophical intimations. Transpositions of the possible ethnography are grown and encouraged by this film; it is more likely that the film answers a much broader criticism fangled by the charge of illegitimacy.

Chapter 24

The Gospel According to Philip K. Dick: Narcotheorist Projections in the Science Fiction Era

The Gospel According to Philip K. Dick features a cast of friends, publishers, and thinkers and exposits, at length, the life and times of a famous science fiction writer who took drugs. To imagine greater possibilities and express, along with the many authors who talked with him over the years, postmodernism's crippling anxiety and the sterilization of souls. What appears most interesting about this film is that many. Possibilities of science fiction journeys are explained curtly and with meaningful intention, pairing Dick with several writers who took drugs such as heroin and cocaine. Though this is not our book's main focus, examining the contents is worthwhile to pronounce the futurism Huxley had intended thirty years before. Produced by Mark Steensland, *The Gospel* explores Dick's heroin addiction, his inscribed tales of conspiracy, and his deep, unyielding thirst for revelation's details. An author of thirty books and a widely regarded writer and socialite, Philip K. Dick bore the testament of many young people and journalists and, like the Beat Generation writers, used his fictional pretense and supposed agency to build communities for drug use. It's likely, as critics and audiences, that this paradigm will reduce his importance: it is more likely that Dick's specific quest for meaning puts him outside the predated role that the Beat Generation, and many writers from the 1950s, lived within and caused them to resurface a brilliant, if moth-eaten, romanticism during these times. Author D. Scott Apel summed up the terminological axis most favorable to our inquiries: The unknown side of Phil was that he probably was a philosopher in a world where philosophy and philosophy had been replaced by technology. Now we have science, what do we need philosophy for? We can find out what works and what's real. Nobody needs to speculate about it. If you want to be a philosopher, be a physicist. But Phil was a traditional classical philosopher.[1] Statements like these own up to modernism's obvious truth—cosmic dreams and projections and diminutions of the Earth's contents—and cause us to believe that modernism is dead and

---

[1] *The Gospel According to Philip K. Dick.*

our geopolitics are inferior to the mind's endless speculations. Full-length novels that boast loudly of technology's conquests and communist superimpositions upon the universe, as in 1964's *The Penultimate Truth*, gave us socialism's deeper fabric when it neutralized aesthetic and pastoral tones that could offset industrial deadness. They also, when restating communist conspiracies in technology, media, and weapons, place the drugged and divine powers of humanity, found in World War II's times, into the hands of reactionaries sworn to preserve the world and its Christian covenant.[2] Still, Dick cross-references and takes down Robert Coover, who had written *The Public Burning* to proclaim fascism's injustice: according to Dick, Julius and Ethel Rosenberg gave the Soviets the atomic bomb. Clearly, and with deep, if fetishized and postmodern, utterances, Dick had intended to rewrite stoned formats to stress conservative and Christian notions of truth that he appended to his characters. If he is a philosopher, we might surmise that his examples, beings, and gadgets are the stuff of theory meant to forage a greater union between the universe and the Earth.

We also divined the obvious fable: "futurist" writers, the characters' imaginative relapse was maintained in the 1940s, not the 2000s. Conceptual anomalies in print are not futuristic but frame humans, bound to their history and its examples, who enjoy a difficult universe they cannot conquer. The resultant dystopia, then, is an admixture of postmodernism and futurism; Dick's material examples subjugated humanity, thought, introspections, and beliefs. Still, Apel gives us a taste of Dick's positive tone when addressing drugs and our potential to rediscover existence through them. Shorn of pure comic moments, Dick is roundly compared to William Burroughs and Allen Ginsberg, both of whom had used cocaine and heroin alongside their taking of hallucinogens. Because of this, we may admit that gateway theory logic caused us to lump hallucinogens with other narcotic drugs. Would we then appraise Dick's specific path differently, or as though the amalgamation of drugged experiences and conscious vortices could tell us anything about the greater universe, or at least how modernism had delimited many ideas that could be expressed with greater force? Of course, Dick came alongside a fairly large number of science fiction writers and so had borne testament to things that were not aesthetically determined nor held within them any religious traditions. The commentators, naturally, admired Dick's characters; seated in places around the world, they give nothing but warm praise to the fictional moment, broad and filled with introspections.

---

[2] Dick, Philip K. *The Penultimate Truth*.

To get a sense of the expanse of Dick's writings, we turn to the literature: several novels detailed disease, addiction, and the compensation of poor societies. While this may not link us with Beat idealisms or the fore of the countercultural *nexus*, let us turn to a solstitial moment during the 1970s, when the fruit of Dick's psychedelic engagements had produced a pandemic. In *A Scanner Darkly* (1977), Dick outlines our decrepit possibility as humankind's salvation and self-understanding. At the novel's beginning, Dick frames a character ranked with disease: "Once a guy stood all day shaking bugs from his hair. The doctor told him there were no bugs in his hair. A month later, he had bugs in his hair." After the novel's main character is interrogated by his friend Charlie, he drives up to a drugstore front. He surmises what seem like ancient narcotic possibilities, in a tune familiar to those reading Beat novelist William S. Burroughs: In his fantasy number he was driving past the Thrifty Drugstore and they had a large window, and they had a huge window display, bottles of slow death, jars and bathtubs and vats and bowls of slow death, millions of caps and tabs and lots of slow death, mixed with speed and junk and barbiturates and psychedelics, everything and a giant sign, YOUR CREDIT IS GOOD HERE.

To begin with, it is clear that Dick did not invent this form, and novels and short stories by Burroughs and Kerouac establish the denigrating tone, whereby the lust for excess and addiction was narratively redemptive and assuring. It is not a matter of knowing what drugs "do," but rather an expansive statement of their availability and, therefore, the thrust of knowing from experiencing them. Psychedelics are linked with hard drugs, to the tune of Thompson: still, there appears to be cinematic luster in the passage, akin to Matt Dillon's starring role in 1993's *Drugstore Cowboy*. The material and capitalist possibilities might, then, be deduced from American angles and so were not tied to any Orientalism.

More, I believe that these introductions conjoined Dick with a host of writers who equated drugs not with disease and sickness but with American humankind's redemption from it in these forms. To state the positive parable through these resonant factors was not "science fiction," but instead nicely shuffles modernism and postmodernism in an engaging moment of self-contemplation. Dillon's Minute, by contrast, is probably shorter, and later narco-movies like *Requiem for A Dream* may spell anxiety's denouement. With these ideas in mind, could a documentary film render the tension between local and supernatural environments like space? Further, what moments of self-reflection aren't social and, therefore, "free"? It appears that Dick exercises a specific compassion, or rather the drug dealer's compassion, to pair personal meaning with drug taking.

The film's cast includes discussions of author and text from notables such as *Rolling Stone* writer Paul Williams, colleague Miriam Lloyd, editor Ray Nelson, and authors Jay Kinney and Scott Apel. When put strictly in context, *The Gospel According to Phillip K. Dick* hatches the winds of conspiracy theories around American drug subcultures while promoting the fictional and, ultimately, scriptural or supernatural brilliance of Dick's form and the testament to narrowly and hermetically designed visions or hallucinations that unveil storms of Christian piety. It should be noted at the beginning that Dick's revelations re-attach the domain of faith, and his role as an eternal messenger referenced and corresponding to others who believe. This cannot be documented as "proof" of Christ's existence but tends to the democratic impulse of Christian vision that could, it might be said, re-write and so affix its necessity in the human sphere. We aren't given many clues as to what Dick's visions meant: instead, the faithful friends and followers admire Dick's form and the vicissitudes of his drug-addled engagements of what lay beyond his immediate realm. Since they spindle the quest with meanings and human destiny, these defenses again revive the case that Western history and counterculture might re-affix the template of human redemption through drugs as Allen Ginsberg had done for the Beats.

Before we inveigh the muddled paradigm, whereby wisdom could be gained by taking heroin and amphetamines, we turn to the historical portrait as that which could gainsay revolution's dynamics. From the standpoint of "the scene," where young college-age teenagers frequented Dick's home and sought the company and fellowship of souls who took drugs, Dick is a missing link and an afterthought to the ribald tale of drug addicts seeking their self-realization. Dick, then, operated on the strength of positive hallucinogenic inquiry, and his inferences were additional, not solitary: the crest of speculation had produced his annotated wisdom, and thence the attachment of Christian faith and mercy to deeply introspected drug dreams and the fears that were prominent in his exercise. Author Robert Anton Wilson is commendatory from the outset: "Phil was extraordinary. And he had some super-extraordinary experiences."[3] *Rolling Stone* columnist Paul Williams lends the collaborative tone to identify the community where intoxication produced meaning:

> And these people knew that you go to this guy's house, that someone will let you there, you'd take Benzedrine, bennies, and you'd get some from him sometime. Even for Marin County, California. Everyone knew that his house was a place you could go to.[4]

---

[3] *The Gospel According to Phillip K. Dick.*
[4] *Ibid.*

Similarities and imagined correspondence with the Beat Generation call upon our memory of counterculture's past: Dick had absorbed Beat anxieties and the depressive tone of hallucinogenic inquiries that seemed to cloud the dimensions of revelation. Dick, in his estimation, did not succumb to the burden of this process: he declared himself a Christian messenger like Elijah and foresaw the realization of Jesus as truth. With the positive addle from commentaries and friends, it becomes necessary to underscore revelation's positive details, perhaps not just to demonstrate narcotic faith but also to trace the future's supersession or the assumption of much greater responsibility in human experience. Dick was, by his accounts, highly pressured: his house was burglarized, and he came upon a vision in 1974, eight years before his death.

Ray Nelson's identification of a letter, the "Xerox missive," that upon receipt would kill Dick, is perhaps the summary of a decade of private, self-endowed conspiracies that haunted Dick until he died in 1982. The opus of speculation about Dick's mythology, or rather of Christian adoption of visions into truth and human revelation, points to not only science fiction's scope but also to those of environment, ethnicity, economy, and philosophy. These additional summits will ask us to bring detail to Dick's sparred visions that could either represent an inscription of truth or the depressed branch of a dying modernism.

The cast of *The Gospel According to Philip K. Dick* enjoins a heartfelt endorsement of the author's writings and peevish witticisms recasting modernism's storied archaeology, or at least the fashion for deeply annotated meditations that speak to our refreshed purpose. Commentary by author Jay Kinney established the scholarly ton. Dick was paranoid, he was a genius, and his findings tormented him. Kinney recalled the author's intended fate:

I think that what occurs with mystical experiences is positive paranoia. The unseen forces are there but benign in that it's ultimately going to work out—ultimately, there's a sense that all of this is coming together, and that—you know, what I think, Phil was right on edge between those two things, you know. Ultimately, it came to a peace.[5] Robert Anton Wilson, appearing more circumspect, alternately praises Dick's "warm and friendly" tone when talking and stokes the speculative tone for modernism's new witchcraft, conceived out of space's illusions: "The CIA was giving LSD to people, and a lot of psychedelic bands were playing a memorable freakout."[6] Kinney offers an ameliorative tone: "In real life, for most people who have breakthroughs of an expanded consciousness, it's disruptive in their lives and destabilizing their possibility."[7]

---

[5] *Ibid.*
[6] *Ibid.*
[7] *Ibid.*

Dense commentary from Encyclopedia Dickiana webmaster Jason Koornick builds a considerable library compendium, with scholarly articles covering the computer's page and showing Koornick touting "an endless amount of reading."[8] The generational point is aptly made: science fiction would maintain its inquiry, its sources, and the severe anxiety spawning testaments to the truth. Viewers are given the omniscient module: Dick's studies and findings could have occurred at the onset of any drug culture, past or present, ideal or borrowed from the dark, decrepit streets. Dick's supposed conspiracy as it is followed in this film notwithstanding, Dick's inquiry is likely shared amongst the many, and that constituted a potential warming point of truth that drugs had encouraged. Questing is captured nicely: we are led to the annals of a much greater, long-standing inquiry that did not solely depend on fantasy's details.

Overall, *The Gospel* depends more on commentaries than upon the visual metaphor, and screened interviews recur comments from Apel, Wilson, Kinney, Nelson, Lloyd, and Williams about the details of Dick's subjectivities and his race against time, against the forces he could not control. With ample time given to the ruse of Dick's safe being robbed, the film focuses upon the author's anxiety as he encounters vision through drugs. We are given, it seems, no details about Dick's origins or anything close to an assemblage of childhood fronts and ideas that might mature into the chosen form. Still, these commentaries identified, too, the collaborative sense that Dick's characters and sketches represented the ideas and forays of a much greater multitude that had chosen narcotic inspiration to existence's unspoken dreams as we knew them. Preference is given to science, then ominously retracted as Dick matures into hallucinogenic form, an amalgamation of previous forms. Notes of Dick's death were not new: they were cataloged in Ginsberg's poems from the 60s onward. Still, the classic modernist attribute, dying but sparring for virtue, is ably reconstructed.

---

[8] *Ibid.*

Chapter 25

Truth, Doubt, and Penultimate Anxiety: Modernist Dictations of Future Truth in *the Penultimate Truth of Philip K. Dick*

When we attest to the courage, pitch, and intensity of fictional appraisals of "truth" through the use of drugs, we are at least likely, as with forerunner Aldous Huxley, to suggest answers and points of speculation from biographical minutes. Modernist analogs develop the use of drugs primarily through the author's unwashed, uncaged mind to forecast the peculiar meaning of "vision" and its attachment to modernist theory, which presumes thought and writing to have been organic. This is an important question in science fiction: where do ideas come from? From technology, ideology, or modern humankind's practical engagement of these? When visions arise, what importance are they, and how can we measure them to have been "true"? With this in mind, Emiliano Larre's 1 hour, 26-minute film may cause us to accept Philip Kindred Dick's partial defense of his activities and liaisons with drug-takers, to say that, with addiction and vision as a guide, that far-ranging and speculative concepts such as God could be known, and learned from, through drugs. *The Penultimate Truth About Philip K. Dick* staged this identity positively, and the movie's plot pairs interviews and trips to historic Berkeley sites where Dick lived and worked with a team of FBI agents, poring over Dick's documents, photos, and crucial works under the light of his study in his home. Key to this film was exploring the necessary minutes of Dick's childhood and early adult years: when we, for instance, pair Dick's story with those such as Paul Bowles, Ken Kesey, and Jack Kerouac, we attest to the author's anxiety, the absence of fatherhood, peculiar indoctrinations with music and short story writing, and the ingratiated nature of their inquiry—mainly, to answer terrors and uncertainties found in young life.

Dick, like Bowles and Kerouac, dropped out of college, found partners at work, and stressed music's meaning throughout their lives. Dick was married several times, and so the personal tale was integrated with family. The movie recalls, too, the death of Dick's sister at birth, posing a peculiar grain of similitude with Winston Smith in *1984:* Dick's sister dies because his mother feeds him more. The narrator continues: "You have been entrusted to determine the nature of these events."[1] Commentaries and crucial visits to places of literary inspiration, including Dick's home, the University of California, and the Art Studio where he met his first wife, are stalked by the narrative, with agents examining everything in Dick's file. Friend and co-author Ray Nelson notes thoughtfully Dick's attention to "all sorts of things that people called the feminine side of his personality,"[2] while Nelson intones, against the dictation of confidence and matrimony from Kleo Mini, his second wife: "I would say the main theme in Phil's fantasy life is the uncertainty of it."[3] The film's positive traction, between certainty and uncertainty, including visions, was captured in the printed documents that agents zero in on to locate Jesus's ministry in terms of "alternate realities."[4]

At some point, Dick embraces God. In contrast, Kesey and Bowles reject him, and then why other modernist authors purveyed the occult and its positive failure to tell the truth. In contrast, science fiction, based as it was upon visions, hallucinations, and operative twentieth-century cultural theories, tried to restrict in some form the "truth" of what had been found. This idea wasn't without fierce battling; Boujemaa's experience in Bowles's "He of the Assembly" included electric shocks and Aisha Qandisha in the masterful evocation of crimes and inventions. Ethical concepts, too, might be ably rebuilt to forecast society's success through visions: they, when compared to the onslaught of communist destructions, say that a world existed beyond humankind and that signs frequently appeared telling us to disbelieve in the left's corralling of culture and experience.

Moreover, neither is it true that science fiction, in Dick's eyes, was an entity separate from modernism. Through drugs, technology, and conspiracies, humankind sought his authentic, true universe and redemption for having understood. Dick's early studies did not correspond to any part of The Bible, and authorial reminiscences of his parents are studiously limited. Nonetheless, at least photographs and communications found in the agents' invasion hinted loudly at the placid lack of fulfillment during modernist times. "Uncertainty" does not belie the obvious: one cannot understand and then not understand. Instead, the necessary polarity suggests the physical pressures of two divergent worlds. One set today and the other in the future. To suggest the bargaining of vision with political realities and censorship might harbor resentment for classical modernism: science fiction developed its topography and mapping of issues and ideas, separate from the functioning of twentieth-century realism.

---

[1] *The Penultimate Truth About Philip K. Dick.*
[2] *Ibid.*
[3] *Ibid.*
[4] *Ibid.*

Did this suggest that Dick's meditations were wrought to be heavier and more pronounced than those of Huxley? Or did Dick propose, in the end, what was "unscientific" as the basis for understanding visions and God's prophecies? One must, in the end, hold Dick fully to the mantle; in this regard, colleagues could star key moments of his development and perhaps his splintering of "normal" consciousness in moves away from Scripture. It is without disregard that we may uniformly say that censorship was a persistent theme when talking about drugs and literature. There are frequent attempts to impede its peculiar logic and morphology as it may construe rebellion against the State. Kleo Mini would stitch the cloth for shrouding Dick's work in the heady steam of conspiracies, and thus modernism's loss of innocence, when it applied to our specific grasping of modern meanings: "a lot of [Dick's] writing has to do with ancient reality. So, what might have been the changing information we experience in this world is an unholy narrative."[5] To state, world consciousness's fracturing wasn't new. Still, it is apparent that Dick's specific terminologies and sketches of reality are meant to stage God's "alternate reality" and so deprive his faith and reasoning of its geography. In that sense, "real" experiences when in vision may be directly transposed onto a morphology that is conceived in the present: it, too, suggests futurism's anxiety about staging and giving place to "time travel," or rather our depressive advancement of opinions on what the world, and faith, might look like.

Still, the second wife, Tessa, provides the stabbing of guilt when it comes to Dick's mother: "Dorothy couldn't afford very much milk for them, and Phil was always so hungry that she gave him more."[6] Ray Nelson leaps upon this moment to chance science fiction's massive engines: "[Dick] felt a personality in his mind, of how [his sister, Jane] would be if she had lived, and into that personality, he injected all sorts of things that people called the feminine side of his personality."[7] To have a feminine side begs questions about authorship: Bowles was gay but had no feminine ideas; Kerouac was a classical heterosexual who aestheticized and romanticized women. Guilt, or rather familial guilt, might build the axis of one's social determinism, as it did with *1984*'s Winston Smith, or shut it, as it did with Kerouac's novels. Either way, Dick's alluded references meant that his nature was, in the modernist sense, compromised. So he sought adventure and hallucinatory reasoning to repatriate the chosen, fragile emotions that death and poverty had destroyed. In this sense, we may see Dick's novels propitiating a kind of creation, an alternate creation that survived socialism's thrusting sword of mind control.

---

[5] *Ibid.*
[6] *Ibid.*
[7] *Ibid.*

When I examined this film, I chose not to search solely for examples of text from specific works, which will appear later in this chapter, but to positively state the literary context's inculcation of drugs into form. Narratively, generatively, and socially, Dick was parallel to a very broad host of writers during his time: some of his visual choices exude ideas persistent among the generation's icons, as well. Returning to the first point, it becomes clear that Dick's genesis isn't unique, and shots of ambivalence between the writer's socialism and adopted Christianity meant to spell a kind of new revelation, one that could re-establish the traditional covenant against the tide of –isms that were staking ground in modern humankind's private consciousness. We have noted that Dick's early writing of short stories and deep immersions in music parallel Bowles: we are just as certain that Dick's assertion of prosaic forms retreads a specific re-tread of Jack Kerouac. Regarding drugs, Dick performed the same association—speed and "benny tubes" powered nights of writing, as it had with Kerouac and Ginsberg. In a nifty move, commentator Ray Nelson notes Dick's early choice of a New York City publisher who first published poet Allen Ginsberg; at other points, the expansive if dour premise for Christian re-calculation of spirit shadows Kerouac's more ambitious Catholic program.[8] There is, too, the parallel with Leary, who sought Catholic redemption from drug use; Dick's ongoing relationship with the editor's wife, Anne Dick, resulted in a kind of pandemonium, stimulating Dick's return to church.[9] *The Penultimate Truth*, too, locates Dick's prolonged association with Episcopalian bishop Jim Pike, who is featured in *Time* Magazine and pronounced a fringe cleric who faced the threat of excommunication for his views. Specific hallucinations aren't Dick's sole province and his "metallic image" vision that specifically powers his return to Christian theology had been reached at the same time with Kerouac, who on the *Steve Allen Show* in 1959 found "the great image of God" in the sky while inebriated.[10] What becomes clear is that science fiction writing would not "pay the bills," and Dick had turned to a more mainstream form of writing novels and wrote them with a tenacious speed. Commentators break down the point: Dick was never a famous, well-received writer and did not enjoy the fruit of fame in the public world. Cross-examinations of drug cultures by the FBI, too, weren't unique, and Paul Bowles and Allen Ginsberg spoke of its shadow at certain times. Of course, what is unique is that Dick, unlike even enemies of the Beats like Norman Mailer, directly spoke to the government and sought to clear his name by having their protection from criminals. The tension is much more dramatic: according to

---

[8] *The Penultimate Truth About Philip K. Dick.*
[9] *The Penultimate Truth About Philip K. Dick.*
[10] Jack Kerouac, *The Steve Allen Show*, November, 1959.

Barry Miles, FBI agents had given Kerouac "blow jobs."[11] Biography's sliding door, or rather the much bold pathway to power, was not miniaturized in this context: it is unclear whether Dick had sought power through his work or if he was very unlike Kerouac's visible and perverse subversion of national authority in his drunken, drug-addled times. At the historical moment of conflation, what becomes certain is that Dick's large following, plus the convincing tone of his very ambitious and skilled hallucinations, could create associations equivalent to a "society" or rather a kind of indoctrination performed through reading and contemplating Dick's many versatile forms of morphology and kinesiology.

Much attention was also given to the idea of a tormented genius whose work and personal life were always in question. Dick would have five wives, and the cast includes three of them. Commentary from them tends to emphasize the tones of modernist genius: Dick was novel, people liked what he did, and they were sympathetic to his organic, self-conceived "cause" to testify to drug miracles that spelled out the persistent doom of living under communist ideas. At the same time, the film notes Dick's occasional socialist leanings, setting up the massive change to Christianity in the last two decades of his life.

Wife Kleo Mini recalls Dick's stunt to spy on her for the FBI:

> Well, the FBI showed up at my door. I want information about the political meetings and save the date which I always went to, when they decide the political line. It was pretty scary, except that they were so inept. And you tended to like that.[12]

Still, Dick's penitent concept, replayed in several of his novels, of a "good god" and an "evil god" who had created the (bad) universe, is surmised in wife Tessa's observation: "Jesus didn't die on the cross," and that there were Christian cults that believed this.[13] At one point, the third wife, Anne, reads happily the lines from *Three Stigmata*:

> I do not find God in the prog system. I found something better. "God," Eldritch said, promises eternal life. I can do better. I can deliver it. "What's that?" Eldritch asked. "The [King] James Bible. I thought it'd

---

[11] Miles, Barry, *Jack Kerouac: King of the Beats*.
[12] *The Penultimate Truth About Philip K. Dick*.
[13] *Ibid*.

protect me." "Not here," Eldritch said. "This is my domain." He gestured at the Bible, and it vanished.[14]

Commentators such as Mimi, Nelson, and UCLA Professor Kay Hayles profess Dick's anxieties and his adventures with the unknown but stress the persistent possibility that all of his work came from his hallucinations. We can here note that "evil" supplanted the Christian God and that future works were meant to stage attempts to bring back this covenant. Still, the film's contents suggest it's doubtful that Dick had purveyed anything specific from The Bible, and we are more likely to redoubt Kesey's plan: that revelations happened today and could be counted as a kind of Scripture, just as the Bible was Scripture. This, of course, is heretical, but why? Why must we assume that only ancient men and women understood God, whoever this may be? Dick's supposition of "evil" and "good" gods is at least tenable: many ancient religions had not considered other civilizations and so banned them as being unreal. But clearly, the commentators note that Dick intended to quench humankind's thirst for legitimacy, for revelation, by pouring these experiences and moments into his works. Could we then imagine that an entire work was conceived as a hallucination, almost like Ginsberg's reefer on the rooftops of New York to write "Kaddish" in 1948?

We, then, tackle the obvious distinction: it is debatable to say that Dick's futurism was the same as it was for Huxley or Orwell: clearly, concepts and visions are negotiated with the languages and scientific imagination of their contemporary world. That, however, did not suppose that these entities could not anticipate change: machines would be more powerful, technologies could produce laser analogs that were more deadly, and robot entities could bear human adaptations. Therefore, a reading of Dick's central works would cause us to at least assume that the forces of the future, and not its human divisions, as in *Brave New World*, would determine human agency. Like many citizens, I watched the robot movies from childhood, including *Blade Runner*: stylizations of technology as socialist destruction and interdiction meant, then, to deromanticize the Earth, taking away from his true—and modernist—purpose.

Nelson affixes the decisive tension when re-examining the FBI as they tape family photos to the wall, read books in the darkness, and ponder documents in the office: "I don't think it was a delusion at all."[15] It is wise, as historians, to admit censorship against drug narratives was real and may even be today: when put into perspective, the inference that certain social traits and managing tendencies could be won in people by suppressing and criminalizing media is a part of democratic societies as well: our process, should we be in trust of this,

---

[14] *Ibid.*
[15] *Ibid.*

is then to find out what had been found out, and what specific ideas were dangerous to the governing authorities. Then, we might add that FBI-headed conspiracies were meant to suppress not just knowledge but communities: we will also say that Dick did not get his place in the public realm, as other others had, and did not get to sponsor his theories. Dick himself greatly expands the foregrounding of anxiety in the archiving of modern drugged genius and genesis at a conference in Metz, France, in 1977, recording in the public annals the following:

> I, in my stories often write about counterfeit, real worlds, as well as deranged, private worlds, inhabited often by just one person. In the meantime, the other characters remain in the world throughout or are somehow brought into the peculiar ones. This theme occurs in my twenty-seven years of writing. At no time did I have a theoretical, conscious explanation for my preoccupation.[16]

To say that he avoided theory yet knew reality, re-inscribes and re-textualizes Christian mysticism. Still, to profess worlds amounts to a recurrent hallucination that many drug users perform and excludes the associations and morphology that he instead pairs with a recurrent dialogue between reality and unreality, thus allowing room for collective societal growth. It is not to say that Huxley's model for humans in 1932 wasn't elastic—it was more likely that the volume of works and the specific notations of context meant to grow associations towards such a world and supersede pastoralism's historical necessity. That, in the final sense, made Dick's novels modern, not postmodern: there was the anticipation of the future man's thoughts, emotions, and sincerity.

With a strong cast and frequent trips to Dick's places of interest, *The Penultimate Truth* builds a meaningful bolus of ideas that could result in a greater valuation of Dick as a thinker and writer. Much work, in the offices and homes, is done to resurface Dick's modernist necessity, or rather the necessity of his inquiries. Fame, when denied to the author, may easily gain greater waves of appreciation in a film that situates the experiences of hippie communities in the Bay Area; we are given ample examples that attest to the living realm, or rather the fascinations of students with drug cultures. In these instances, conspiracy theories are visually and conversationally met in the author's remembrance.

---

[16] *Ibid.*

Conclusion: Literature and the New Dynamic for Studying Psychedelic Films and Culture

I believe that the basis for studying psychedelic drugs constitutes a form that has imperfectly developed over the twentieth century and that we ought to signal at least the basic transition of meaning: namely, that science does exist and that its collation and preparations of data and perspectives are real does engage the worlds of theory and criticism, and that evidence exists to justify broadening this discipline. What becomes recurrently clear, though, is that many psychedelic theorists *did not* uncover troves of psychedelic criticism and that firsthand accounts counted the study of the drugs' ethical interactions as often as they studied perception, ideation, and neuropathology. From the embryonic angle, then, it was as likely that psychedelic science would grow and develop, acquire a formative basis based upon generalizing themes of immersion and reflection, and that our first-hand accounts, roughly dating from the end of the 1920s, would cause us to pose questions rather than arrive prematurely at a summit of spiritual wellbeing that everyone could situate in the barren monotony of their modern lives. Studies of the authors, professors, doctors, and writers of the time, and their specific self-experiments and those performed on patients, plus those of rock revelers who could recall the details, will do more to re-bundle the vast multitude of drug trips as having an elastic, conceptual continuity, a theme by which trips could be theoretically and mentally understood in much more widespread terms.

At that point, it becomes necessary to separate science from its pretense, allowing that, of course, it was relatively clear that modern psychology had not given sufficient weight to these studies and that literature that involved the taking of drugs was experimental: lest we give lesser credibility for this factor, it is just as likely that psychedelic studies would develop from psychology's positive errata, from situations and ideas that had not been worked out appropriately in the complex, conflicting times of the twentieth century that gradually had disavowed Foucauldian, Victorian psychiatry as the standard-bearer for treatment and personal development as citizens. Thus, we give life and additional meaning to the experimental techniques and democratize ethical questions to pursue greater, more inclusive happiness.

I defend narrowing of the focus: in fact, it becomes obvious that, from the dialogues and commentaries of Aldous Huxley during the 1950s, we are wise to endorse the relative separation of drug interactions when considering hallucinogens—not, it could be said, "true" narcotics with a less studied pathology over time. This, naturally, enhances the special and specific parable that drugs could rebuild the human experience and reference a wide range of religious, literary, and popular histories and that studies might become more complex and studied over time. Positive aversions, it must be said, to psychedelic studies did not close the door on inquiry, and the examples of Huxley, Leary, and Kesey proudly attest to the form's openness and their special status away from Burroughs's microscope that was more patently focused on traditional narcotics such as cocaine, marijuana, and heroin. I believe that, too, examples from Huxley and Castaneda state the obvious gist of relentless modern invention: it would be possible to synthesize and develop neurology and psychology from the dimensions of an uncalculated and growing apparatus that could synthesize culture, experience, and invention at the same time. I will say, too, that the annals of time during the twentieth century forecasted drugs to be a persistent, penitent literary force that interacted and conflicted with mainstream Western cultures that still staged man's rationalist inquiries, or rather the annexed realm where reason and study could complement the massive capitalist-communist engine that built modern morals for billions of people.

In conclusion, I will also say that the potential to study drugs in this unique light need not mean that we shed the trail of nineteenth-century readings that may suggest a greater universe or man's imperfect calculations of it while countering the rise of Marxist interrogations of theory and ideas. It becomes evident that the twentieth century operated many ethical and personal details that coincide with the psychodramas of the nineteenth: questions of ethics, it must be said, interface with a much larger, theoretically rich world that, in its turn, depended upon literary immersions rather than the distinct temple of studies that may constitute psychology. Once again, psychology's errata–the scope of what was *not* covered and the limitations of the psychologist's study– were principles Huxley, Leary, and Kesey exploited for the positive gain of drug studies. Hallucinatory realism and its study, then, are a romanticist testament to human fighting against the pincers of socialist and Victorian control—they, suggesting a refreshed intellect that could map out new possibilities connected with perception rather than reasoned thought, may re-invigorate rationalist dialogue linked with the possibility of raising human freedom to a new level, empowering the arts, literature, and psychology to determine greater strides of feeling and self-internalizations that, as they are not repressed and are guided by brain-determinations of man's primarily aesthetic complexity, produce testaments to nature, imagination, and memory, three forces that could revive and renew the modern man caught in the chains of technological-capitalist vacuum. Because traditional parapsychologies have been proven to negotiate turns and developments in the relationship between the brain and nervous system, it is necessary to detail the world-view of the person tripping and the insight about Being that is non-rational to suppose this greater rationality, and hence the persistent literary mechanism that Huxley first identified in 1932 with the publication of *Brave New World*.

Lastly, the point tied to modernism is abundant: drugs almost certainly posited a robust, ambitious growth of syntax and its celebration. Examples throughout the twentieth century established a positive tenor for expressing "new consciousness" and the governance of that consciousness, from cocaine-addicted James Joyce to mescaline-taking Jack Kerouac. In the short run, such findings will revive humanist portraits of both authors and their literary works.

Works Cited

Primary Works

Barthes, Roland. *Mythologies.* Les Lettres Nouvelles, 1957.
Bowles, Paul. *A Hundred Camels in the Courtyard.* San Francisco: City Lights Books, 1962.
Burgess, Anthony. *A Clockwork Orange.* William Heinemann, 1962.
Burroughs, William S. *Junky.* New York: Ace Books, 1953.
Burroughs, William S. *Naked Lunch.* Paris: Olympia Press, 1959.
Capote, Truman. *In Cold Blood.* New York: Random House, 1966.
Cassady, Carolyn. *Off the Road: Twenty Years with Neal Cassady, Jack Kerouac, and Allen Ginsberg.* London: Black Spring Press, 1990.
Cassady, Neal. *The First Third.* San Francisco: City Lights Books, 1972.
Cassady, Neal. *Collected Letters, 1944-1967.* New York: Penguin Books, 2005.
Castaneda, Carlos. *The Teachings of Don Juan.* Los Angeles: University of California Press, 1968.
Castaneda, Carlos. *A Separate Reality.* New York: Simon & Schuster, 1971.
Chandarlapaty, Raj. *Seeing the Beat Generation: Entering Literature Through Film.* Jefferson, NC: McFarland, 2019.
Chesterton, G. K. "How Christ Would Solve Modern Problems If He Were On Earth Today." From *The Aldous Huxley Collection,* Harry Ransom Center.
DeQuincey, Thomas. *Confessions of an Opium-Eater. The London Magazine,* 1821.
Derrida, Jacques. *Of Grammatology.* France: Les Editions de Minuit, 1967.
Dick, Philip K. *The Penultimate Truth.* Houghton Mifflin, 1964.
Dick, Philip K. *A Scanner Darkly.* Doubleday, 1977.
Eliot, T. S. "Tradition and the Individual Talent." Originally published in *The Egoist,* 1919.
Eliot, T. S. *The Waste Land.* London: Boni & Liveright, 1922.
Emerson, Ralph Waldo. "Nature." James Munroe & Co., 1836.
Faulkner, William. *The Sound and the Fury.* Jonathan Cape and Harrison Smith, 1929.
Fitzgerald, F. Scott. "Babylon Revisited." Originally published on February 21, 1931, in *The Saturday Evening Post.*
Foucault, Michel. *The History of Sexuality.* New York: Penguin, 1998.
Foucault, Michel. *Madness and Civilization.* New York: Vintage, 2006.
Freud, Sigmund. *The Interpretation of Dreams.* New York: Macmillan, 1913.
Ginsberg, Allen. *Indian Journals.* San Francisco, City Lights Books, 1970.
Ginsberg, Allen. *Collected Poems, 1947-1980.* New York: Harper & Row, 1984.
Griffin, Mark. *Bardo Thadol.* Hard Light Publishing, 2008.

Huxley, Aldous. *Point Counterpoint*. New York: Doubleday, 1928.
Huxley, Aldous. "Good Conversation." Reprinted in Nash's *Pall Mall Magazine*, May 2, 1931. Aldous Huxley Collection, Harry Ransom Center, University of Texas, Austin, TX, Box 3, Folder 6.
Huxley, Aldous. *Brave New World*. London: Chatto & Windus, 1932.
Huxley, Aldous. *The Perennial Philosophy* New York: Harper & Brothers, 1945.
Huxley, Aldous. *The Doors of Perception*. London: Chatto & Windus, 1953.
Huxley, Aldous. "If Christ Should Come Today." From *The Aldous Huxley Collection*, Box 4, Folder 1, Harry Ransom Center, University of Texas, Austin, TX.
Huxley, Aldous. "The Mike Wallace Interview, May 18, 1958. "New York: CBS Productions, 1958.
Huxley, Aldous. "Matter, Mind, and the Question of Survival." May 10, 1960, University of California, Berkeley: "Foerster Lectures on the Immortality of the Soul."
Kant, Immanuel. *Critique of Pure Reason*. Johann Freibuch Bartinoch, 1781.
Kerouac, Jack. *The Town and the City*. New York: Harcourt Brace, 1950.
Kerouac, Jack. *Dharma Bums*. New York: Viking Books, 1958.
Kerouac, Jack. *On the Road*. New York: Viking Books, 1957.
Kerouac, Jack. *Desolation Angels*. New York: Random House, 1965.
Kerouac, Jack. *Visions of Cody*. New York: McGraw-Hill, 1972.
Kerouac, Jack. *Selected Letters, 1940-1956*. New York: Penguin, 2000.
Kerouac, Jack. *Book of Haikus*. New York: Penguin, 2003.
"Kerouac's Bad Trip." From *Beatdom*, June 25, 2011.
Kesey, Ken. "Letter to Gus Blaisdell." From *The Ken Kesey Archive*, Pennsylvania State University Library.
Kesey, Ken. *One Flew over the Cuckoo's Nest*. New York: Viking Books, 1962.
Kesey, Ken. *Sometimes a Great Notion*. New York: Viking Books, 1964.
Kesey, Ken. "Plans For Acid Ceremony." *San Francisco Chronicle*, October 6, 1966.
Koestler, Arthur. *Darkness at Noon*. London: Macmillan Books, 1940.
Krishnamurti, Jiddu. *The Awakening of Intelligence*. New York: Harper & Row, 1987.
Krishnamurti, Jiddu. *You are the World*. New York: Harper & Row, 1972.
Krishnamurti, Jiddu. *The Flight of the Eagle*. New York: HarperCollins, 1973.
Krishnamurti, Jiddu. "Jiddu Krishnamurti on Psychedelics," *Dipitum Magazine*.
Krishnamurti, Jiddu. *The Awakening of Intelligence*. New York: Harper & Row, 1987.
Lawrence, D.H. *Lady's Chatterley's Lover*. Italy: Tipographia Giuntina, 1928.
Leary, Timothy. "Escapade." From *The Timothy Leary Collection*, Box 1, Folder 9.
Leary, Timothy. Interview With Joe O'Sullivan. From *The Timothy Leary Collection*, Box 1, Folder 12.
Leary, Timothy. *The Psychedelic Experience*. Republished by Citadel Press, 2007. Originally published in 1964.

Leary, Timothy. "Religious Implications of Consciousness Expanding Drugs." From *The Timothy Leary Collection*, Box 1, Folder 10.

Lee, James S. *The Underworld of the East*. Originally published in 1935. Republished by Green Magic, 2013.

Lewin, Louis. *Phantastica*. Originally published in 1924. 1998, Rochester, VT: Park Street Press.

Lutyens, Mary. *Krishnamurti: The Years of Awakening*. 1975, New York: Avon Books.

Mailer, Norman. *Advertisements for Myself*. Cambridge, Massachusetts: Harvard U. Press, 1992.

Marx, Karl. "Alienated Labor." Originally published in *Economic and Philosophical Manuscripts*. Reprinted in McNeill, Willam, and Feldman, Karen, eds., *Continental Philosophy: An Anthology*, 215-224.

Marx, Karl. *Das Kapital*. 1867, Verlag von Otto Meisner.

Miller, Arthur. *Death of a Salesman*. New York: Viking Press, 1949.

Mrabet, Mohammed. *M'Hashish*. San Francisco: City Lights Books, 1969.

Nietzsche, Friedrich. E.W. Fritzsch, 1872.

Nietzsche, Freidrich. *Ecce Homo*. London: R.J. Hollingdale, 1908.

Orwell, George. *Animal Farm*. London: Secker & Warburg, 1945.

Orwell, George. *1984*. London: Secker & Warburg, 1949.

Orwell, George. "Clink." *The George Orwell Collection*. Housed at the University College London Library.

Pynchon, Thomas. *Gravity's Rainbow*. New York: Penguin, 1973.

Sailey, Jay. *Ko Hung: The Master Who Embraces Simplicity*. Chung Wen Publishing, 1978.

Solzhenitsyn, Alexandr. *One Day in the Life of Ivan Denisovich*. Originally published in 1962, *Novy Mir* magazine. New York: Signet Classics, 2008.

Stevens, Jay. *Storming Heaven: LSD and the American Dream*. New York: Grove Press, 1998.

Taylor, Kathleen. *Brainwashing*. Oxford: Oxford University Press, 2004.

Thompson, Hunter. *Fear and Loathing in Las Vegas: A Savage Journey to the Heart of the American Dream*. New York: Random House, 1972.

Vivekananda, Swami. *The Complete Works of Swami Vivekananda*. Advaita Ashrama, 2014.

Vivekananda, Swami. "100 Amazing Quotes by Swami Vivekananda." Found at: *The Famous People*, https://quotes.thefamouspeople.com.

Wolfe, Thomas. *The Electric Kool-Aid Acid Test*. New York: Farrar, Strauss, Giroux, 1968.

Secondary Works

Anonymous. "Review: The Gravity of Light," Imdb.com.
Aufderheide, Patricia. *Documentary Film: A Very Short Introduction.* Oxford: 2007, Oxford U. Press.
Braga, Corin. "Carlos Castaneda: The Uses and Abuses of Ethnomethodology and Emic Studies." *Journal for the Study of Religions and Ideologies*, 9.27 (Winter, 2010), 71-106.
Giffort, Danielle. *Acid Revival: The Psychedelic Renaissance and the Quest for Medical Legitimacy.* 2020, U. of Minnesota Press.
Glieberman, Owen. "Review: *Long Strange Trip.*" *Variety Magazine*, March 17, 2017.
Greenfield, Robert. *Timothy Leary: A Biography.* New York: Harcourt, 2006.
Hofmann, Albert. "LSD: Completely Personal." From *Newsletter of the Multidisciplinary Association of Psychedelic Studies*, 1996.
Horowitz, Michael. *Moksha.* Park Street Press, 1999.
Jackson, Blair. *Garcia: An American Life.* New York: Penguin, 2000.
Jones, Le Roi. "Lush Life." From *Music Reviews*, Le Roi Jones Papers, Box 2.
Prince, Stephen. "The Discourse of Pictures: Iconicity and Film Studies." *Film Quarterly*, vol. 47, no. 1 (Autumn, 1993), 16-28.
Ruggieri, Melissa. "Live Music Has to Rebound." *USA Today*, February 17, 2022.
Rushkoff, Douglas. "Most VR is Total Bullshit," *Medium*, August 26, 2019.
Szasz, Thomas, *The Myth of Mental Illness.* New York: Harper & Row, 1961.
Stage Raw, "One Flew over the Cuckoo's Nest."
Stam, Robert. *Film Theory: An Introduction.* Hoboken, NJ: Wiley-Blackwell, 2000.

DVDs/CDs

Doors, The. *Morrison Hotel.* CD, Audio. New York: Elektra, 1970.
Doors, The. *The Doors.* CD, Audio. New York: Elektra, 1967.
Drugstore Cowboy. Color. Produced by Gus Van Sant. Santa Monica: 1989, International Video Entertainment.
Dying to Know: Ram Dass & Timothy Leary. Color, Documentary. Produced by Gay Dillingham. San Rafael: Mill Valley Film Festival, 2014.
Grateful Dead, The. *Workingman's Dead.* Warner Bros., 1970
Huxley on Huxley. Color, Documentary. Directed by Mary Ann Braubach.
Howlin' Wolf, "Spoonful." Chess, 1960.
Led Zeppelin. *Led Zeppelin III.* Atlantic Records, 1970.
Long Strange Trip. Color, Documentary. Directed by Amir Bar-Lev. Culver City: Amazon Studios, 2017.
LSD: The Beyond Within. Color, Documentary. Directed by Max Whitby. London: 1986, BBC.
Lyne, Adrian. Movie, color. *Jacob's Ladder.* Culver City: Tri-Star, 1990.

Magic Trip. Color, Documentary. Directed by Allison Ellwood and Alex Gibney. New York: Magnolia Pictures, 2011.

Moody Blues, The. *In Search of the Lost Chord.* CD, Audio. Decca, 1968.

One Flew Over the Cuckoo's Nest. Movie, color. Directed by Milos Forman. Burbank: Warner Home Video, 1975.

Rain Man. Movie, color. Produced by Barry Levinson. New York: United Artists, 1988.

Steensland, Mark. *The Gospel According to Phillip K. Dick.* Color, Documentary. Directed by Mark Steensland. New York: First Run Features, 2010.

The Enigma of a Sorcerer. Color, Documentary. Produced by Ralph Torjan. Hollywood: Indican Studio, 2006.

The Gravity of Light. Color, Documentary. Directed by Oliver Hockenhull. Begumpet, India: Moksha Media, 1996.

The Manchurian Candidate. Movie, color. Directed by John Frankenheimer. Roselle Park, NJ: MC Productions, 1962.

The Tomorrow Show with Tom Snyder. Color, Documentary. Directed by Roger Ailes and Shelley Ross. New York, RCA Building: 1981.

Timothy Leary's Last Trip. Color, Documentary. Directed by O.B. Babbs & A.J. Catoline. Los Angeles: Shout Factory, 2003.

Traffic. *John Barleycorn Must Die.* CD, Audio. Island, 1970.

Traffic. *Shoot Out at the Fantasy Factory.* Strawberry Hill Records, 1973.

Traffic. *The Low Spark of High Heeled Boys.* Island, 1971.

Tripping. Color, Documentary. Directed by Vikram Jayanti. Merry Pranksters, 1999.

Weir, Bob, *Ace.* 1972, Warner Bros.

About the Author

Dr. Raj Chandarlapaty studied at the University of South Florida and taught literature, writing, and philosophy courses in the United States and Afghanistan for 17 years. In Kabul, Afghanistan, he was awarded the Most Promising Teacher award in his first year. Dr. Chandarlapaty has since authored four books: *Seeing the Beat Generation, Re-Creating Paul Bowles, the Other, and the Imagination,* and *The Beat Generation and Counterculture.* He is most interested in American and British authors who write in the fault lines between modernism, postmodernism, and postcolonialism. Dr. Chandarlapaty has published ten journal articles, including *ARIEL, The Mailer Review, Storytelling, Self, Society,* and *The Journal of Urban Education.* With articles on Norman Mailer, Mohammed Mrabet, James Baldwin, and Allen Ginsberg, Chandarlapaty is an accomplished essayist who studies books and articles from the perspective of critical theory and unconscious literary formation. Not borne of any one period, Chandarlapaty calls himself a modernist and refers to humankind's incomplete formation of ideas and culture.

Index

A

"acid tests" 172
Aisha Qandisha Moroccan goddess 224
Amram, David (1930-) American composer 79, 84, 89
Apel, D. Scott (author) 217, 218, 220, 222
Auden, Wystan Hugh (1907-1973) British poet 74

B

Babbs, Ken (1936-) Merry Prankster 135, 167, 182
Babbs, O.B.(1969-) American actor and narrator 135, 136, 138, 140, 142
Bardo Thadol (Tibetan Buddhist scripture) 68, 125
Beat Generation, (The American literary movement, 1944-1964) ix, x, xi, xvii, 11, 12, 16, 36, 79, 81, 82, 83, 84, 88, 87, 90, 99, 117, 121, 136, 150, 153, 157, 160, 171, 180, 183, 184, 197, 217, 221
Blewett, Duncan (1920-) Canadian psychologist 102, 105, 111
Bowles, Paul Frederick (1910-1999) American author, expatriate, translator, Moghrebi humanist 35, 36, 161, 163, 223, 224, 225, 226
Broad, Dr. Charlie Dunbar (1887-1971) British philosopher 36
Buddhism (religion) xiii, 3, 15, 32, 124, 125, 140
Burroughs, William S. (1914-1997) American fiction writer xvii, 83, 86, 87, 95, 131, 143, 150, 151, 153, 155, 160, 163, 165, 178, 218, 219, 232; limitations in his studies of drugs 36

C

Cannabis (drug) 39, 46, 72, 74, 163 (*see* marijuana)
Capote, Truman (1924-1984) American novelist 79, 81, 88
Cassady, Neal (1922-1968) American mystic, countercultural hero, co-founder of the Beat Generation vi, xi, xvii, 11, 61, 80, 81, 82, 83, 84, 85, 86, 87, 88, 89, 90, 91, 93, 94, 95, 97, 98, 99, 135, 136, 138, 141, 169, 170, 171, 177, 178, 179, 180, 181, 183, 185
Castaneda, Carlos (1925-1998) shaman, writer, anthropologist x, 6, 14, 117, 205, 206, 207, 208, 219, 210, 211, 212, 212, 213, 215, 232
Cervantes, Miguel de (1547-1616) Spanish novelist 202
Chesterton, G.K. (1874-1936) British anthropologist and Christian theologian 24
Christianity (religion) Neoplatonism and 23; Aldous Huxley's praise and criticism of 24; and

mescaline use 32; Friedrich Nietzsche's criticisms of 24; Timothy Leary's LSD use and 114; role in Philip K. Dick's science fiction 218, 220; Jack Kerouac and 226
Civil Rights Movement, The (1955-1969) 136, 182
Clapton, Eric (1948-) British rock guitarist 199
Cocker, Jarvis Rock singer 170, 167
Coltrane, John (Jazz saxophone player, 1926-1967) 74
Condon, Richard (1915-1996) American novelist 42
Coover, Robert (1932-) 218
Coyote, Peter (1941-) American filmmaker, actor, director 63, 208, 210, 211
Cronkite, Walter (1916-2009) American news anchor 68
Crosby, Stills and Nash (1965-2023) American rock band 199
Cutler, Sam (1943-2023) Road manager 197, 199, 200, 201, 203

D

Dass, Ram (originally Richard Alpert, 1931-2019) mystic, writer, assistant to Timothy Leary 63, 65, 67, 117, 122, 145, 146, 147, 148, 149, 185
Datura (drug) 211; in William Faulkner's *The Sound and the Fury* 211
Davis, Miles (1926-1991) Jazz trumpeter and composer 74, 89, 95
De Mille, Richard (cultural critic, 1922-2009) 13, 209, 214

Densmore, John (1944-) Rock drummer 65
Denver (American city) 84, 85
De Quincey, Thomas (1785-1859) British writer 37
Descartes, Rene (1596-1650) French philosopher 48
Dharmakirti (Buddhist philosopher) dual consciousness of 20
Dick, Philip K. (1928-1982) American novelist 217, 218, 219, 220, 221, 242, 213, 224, 225, 226, 227, 228, 229
Dixon, Willie (1915-1992) American blues musician 193, 201

E

Eagles, The (1971-) American rock band 199
Easy Rider (movie, 1969) 181
Eliot, T.S. (1889-1965) American-British poet xi, 73
Emerson, Ralph Waldo (1803-1882) American essayist, philosopher, activist, and theologian 46, 82

F

Faulkner, William (1897-1962) American novelist 211
Fitzgerald, F. Scott (1896-1940) American writer 41
Forman, Milos American filmmaker 12, 136, 155, 157, 158, 159, 162, 163
Foucault, Michel (1926-1984) French philosopher xiii, 155, 160, 161, 162
Frankenheimer, John (1930-2002) Filmmaker 42

Index 245

Freud, Sigmund (1856-1939) Austrian psychologist 6, 14, 33, 45, 49, 64, 75, 115, 119, 120, 125

G

Gandhi, Mohandas (1869-1948) Indian activist and political leader 10; Huxley's criticism of, 43
Gans, David (1953) Rock musician and radio broadcaster 12
Garcia, Jerry (1942-1995) Grateful Dead guitarist x, 12, 136, 140, 142, 143, 145, 187, 188, 191, 192, 193, 194, 195, 197, 198, 199, 201, 202, 203
Gillespie, Dizzy (1914-1993) Jazz trumpeter, big band leader 89
Ginsberg, Allen (1926-1997) Jewish-American poet 40, 79, 80, 81, 82, 88, 89, 90, 95, 129, 136, 140, 152, 178, 183, 185, 188, 218, 220, 222, 226, 228
Goldwater, Barry (US Senator, 1909-1998) 172, 173
Grateful Dead, The American rock band (1965-1995) 12, 13, 122, 135, 136, 138, 139, 141, 142, 154, 174, 181, 183, 187, 189, 193, 194, 195, 197, 190, 201, 202
Grof, Stanislav (1931-) Psychologist 102, 108

H

Hart, Mickey (1943-) American rock drummer 198, 203
Hawkins, Coleman (1904-1969) Jazz saxophonist 74
Heidegger, Martin (1889-1976) German philosopher 46, 50

Hinduism (religion) xiii, 1, 3, 10, 36, 116, 128, 131; *soma* and 39; Leary's comments on while in prison 130
Hitler, Adolf (1889-1945) German chancellor 76, 77
Hoffer, Abram (1917-2009) Biochemist 103, 106
Hoffman, Dustin (American actor, 1937-) 159
Hofmann, Albert (1906-2008) Swiss chemist, author, biochemical researcher i, x, xv, 5, 10, 11, 17, 45, 61, 101, 102, 103, 105, 106, 107, 108, 110, 112, 113, 114, 115, 117, 118, 120, 122, 123
Hubbard, Alfred (1901-1982) LSD advocate, drug smuggler 111, 112
Huston, Jean (1937-) American writer 14, 55
Huxley, Aldous (1894-1963) Novelist, essayist, speaker, philosopher ix, x, xi, xiii, xiv, xviii, 2, 3, 4, 5, 6, 7, 8, 9, 10, 14, 15, 16, 19, 20, 21, 22, 23, 24, 25, 26, 27, 28, 29, 30, 32, 33, 34, 35, 36, 37, 39, 40, 41, 42, 44, 45, 46, 47, 48, 49, 50, 51, 53, 54, 55, 56, 57, 58, 59, 60, 61, 62, 64, 65, 66, 67, 68, 69, 71, 72, 73, 74, 75, 76, 77, 79, 80, 83, 87, 88, 102, 107, 108, 110, 111, 112, 113, 114, 115, 116, 119, 120, 121, 122, 123, 124, 125, 128, 129, 132, 136, 140, 149, 151, 170, 171, 175, 188, 193, 194, 216, 221, 225, 229, 231, 232, 233
Huxley, Laura (1911-2007) Classical musician, writer, artist 63, 64, 65, 66, 67, 68, 102, 108, 122

I

India 2, 4, 8, 10, 20, 36, 39, 46, 60, 110, 130
Industrial Revolution, The (1766-1973) 19
Islam, philosophical tradition of 3

J

Jagger, Mick (1943-) Rock singer 171
James, William (1842-1910) American philosopher and psychologist 51
Johnson, Lyndon Baines (1908-1963), 36th US President xiv, 4, 8, 104, 172, 173
Jones, Le Roi (1934-2014) Black American poet and essayist 74
Joyce, James (1882-1941) Irish novelist 28, 223

K

Kadium, Valerie (Castaneda devotee) 213-4
Kennedy, John Fitzgerald (1917-1963) 35th US President 68, 173, 180
Kerouac, Jack (1922-1969) Novelist, traveler xi, 11, 24, 33, 34, 37, 41, 77, 80, 81, 82, 83, 84, 86, 88, 89, 90, 93, 96, 98, 110, 116, 118, 136, 140, 150, 151, 152, 160, 161, 176, 178, 179, 183, 186, 190, 194, 210, 214, 219, 223, 225, 226, 227, 231
Kesey, Kenneth (1935-2001) American writer, thinker, mystic, Merry Pranksters' leader vi, x, xvii, 10, 11, 12, 13, 80, 93, 96, 102, 125, 135, 136, 137, 138, 139, 140, 141, 142, 153, 154, 155, 156, 158, 159, 160, 161, 162, 163, 167, 168, 169, 170, 171, 172, 173, 174, 175, 177, 178, 179, 180, 181, 182, 183, 184, 185, 186, 187, 188, 189, 191, 192, 193, 194, 222, 224
Kinney, Jay (1950-) author, editor, cartoonist 202, 221, 222
Koornick, Jason 222
Koestler, Arthur (1905-1983) Hungarian-American writer 77, 131
Krassner, Paul (1932-2019) Yippie co-founder 174
Kreutzmann, Bill (1946-) 198
Krishnamurti, Jiddu (1899-1986) Indo-American philosopher 4, 5, 14, 15, 42, 48, 116, 122, 123, 128, 208, 219

L

Lacan, Jacques (1901-1981) French philosopher and theorist xii, 2, 3
Lansbury, Angela (1925-2022) Movie actress 42
Lawrence, D.H. (1886-1930) British novelist 28
Leary, Dr. Timothy (1920-1996) American mystic, professor, psychedelic thinker vi, x, xiii, xiv, xvii, 3, 5, 7, 9, 15, 16, 17, 45, 46, 54, 65, 80, 99, 102, 105, 106, 107, 108, 109, 110, 111, 112, 115, 121, 122, 123, 124, 125, 126, 127, 129, 130, 131, 132, 133, 134, 135, 136, 137, 138, 139, 140, 141, 142, 143, 145, 146, 147, 148, 149, 150, 151, 170, 171, 178, 185, 188, 193, 194, 195, 202, 212, 213, 214, 244, 250

Index

Lee, James S. British writer 130
Lenin, Vladimir Illych (1870-1924) Soviet premier 76
Lesh, Phil (1940-) Grateful Dead bassist 139, 199, 201
Lewin, Louis (1850-1929) German pharmacologist 22
LSD (psychedelic drug) vi, ix, xiii, xv, 4, 5, 10, 11, 15, 16, 21, 35, 64, 66, 93, 95, 96, 97, 98, 99, 101, 103, 104, 105, 106, 108, 109, 111, 112, 113, 114, 115, 116, 118, 119, 120, 122, 123, 126, 129, 132, 135, 136, 137, 138, 140, 142, 143, 146, 148, 151, 153, 167, 168, 170, 171, 172, 173, 178, 179, 180, 181, 187, 188, 191, 192, 193, 194, 195, 198, 199, 201, 203, 223

M

Mailer, Norman (1923-2007) Jewish-American novelist, countercultural critic, short story writer 41, 114, 226
Marijuana (drug) in student essays 10; Krishnamurti's criticisms of 5, 122; the Beat Generation and 16; Aldous Huxley and 35; Neal Cassady and 79, 83; in *On The Road* 119; Leary's reflections while in prison 130; at Harvard 139; Ken Kesey and 180, 185, 186, 188, 214; Grateful Dead, in songs 194
Marx, Karl (1818-1883) German political philosopher xv, 46, 67
Matthews, Bob (Grateful Dead producer) 198, 199, 203
Mayhew, Lord Christopher (British politician, 1915-1997) 118
Merry Pranksters, the (Ken Kesey's entourage) 93, 95, 97, 120, 136, 138, 139, 140, 160, 167, 168, 172, 178, 182, 186, 203
Mescaline (psychedelic drug) ix, xiv, 6, 13, 16, 22, 31, 32, 33, 34, 36, 67, 79, 80, 94, 101, 110, 111, 113, 115, 116, 120, 122, 137, 146, 149, 150, 180, 216
Mexico 10, 11, 79, 94, 107, 110, 114, 117, 137
Miller, Arthur (1915-2005) American playwright 59
Mini, Kleo wife of Philip K. Dick 206, 225, 227
Moody Blues, The British rock band 16, 139
Morrison, Jim (1943-1971) American rock singer 191
Mrabet, Mohammed (1936-) Moroccan storyteller 211
Murphy, Eddie (American actor and comedian, 1961-) 165

N

Nash's Pall Mall Magazine 22
Nelson, Ray (1931-2022) British science fiction novelist 219, 221, 222, 224, 225, 226, 228
New Orleans (American city) Merry Pranksters and 181
Nicholson, Jack (1937-) American actor xi, 154, 157, 158, 159, 160, 161, 162, 163, 164, 165
Nietzsche, Freidrich (1844-1900) German philosopher 3, 24, 25, 28, 47
Nixon, Richard Milhous (1913-1994) 37th US President 16, 129, 136

O

Orwell, George (1903-1950) British novelist, colonial traveler x, xviii, 2, 8, 20, 21, 43, 45, 57, 72, 77, 80, 83, 141, 186, 208, 228

Osmond, Dr. Humphry (1917-2004) Canadian psychiatrist at Weyburn Hospital 69, 102, 103, 104, 105, 106, 107, 108, 109, 110, 112

P

Pike, Jim (Episcopalian bishop, 1913-1969) 226; compared with Kerouac's interpretation of vision 226

Postmodernism xvi, xvii, 13, 35, 40, 93, 202, 217, 218, 219, 229

Psilocybin (psychedelic drug) ix, xiii, 13, 33, 35, 103, 110, 113, 129, 132, 133, 135, 146, 149, 150, 153, 180, 206, 207

Pynchon, Thomas (1925-) American novelist xvi, xvii

R

Robbins, Tim American actor 42

S

Sandoz Corporation xiv, 110, 111, 113, 114, 120, 146, 149

Savage Reservation (New Mexico) 75

Shank, Bud (1926-2009) Jazz saxophonist and flutist 185

Shelley, Mary (1797-1851) British novelist 197

Sinatra, Frank (1915-1998) American singer, actor 42

Smith, Dr. Huston (1919-2016) American religious scholar 58

Snyder, Tom (1936-2007) American talk show host 192, 195

Solzhenitsyn, Alexander (1918-2008) Soviet-American writer 131

Stalin, Joseph (1869-1953) Soviet premier 76, 77

Stevens, Jay (American writer) 113

Stolaroff, Myron Biochemist 111

Stravinsky, Igor (1882-1971) Russian composer 65

Sundsten, Paula Prankster groupie 177, 182

Szasz, Thomas (1920-2012) American psychiatrist 154

T

Taylor, Kathleen British biologist and psychologist 7, 40, 44, 45

Thompson, Hunter (1937-2005) American writer 12, 169, 173, 174, 219; interpretation of LSD 168

Traffic (British rock band) 194, 195, 200

Tull, Jethro (British rock band) 294

V

Van Sant, Gus American filmmaker xiv

Vedanta (school of thought, 1920s-) 5, 122

Vietnam War, The (1964-1973) 43, 136, 172

Vivekananda, Swami (1863-1902) Indian mystic and thinker 1

W

Wallace, Amy (Castaneda's girlfriend) 208
Wallace, Michael (1918-2012) CBS News anchor 6, 7, 10, 14, 15, 39, 40, 41, 42, 43, 44, 45, 56
Weir, Robert (1949-) Grateful Dead rhythm guitarist 194, 199
Weyburn Hospital (Saskatchewan) 10, 103, 104, 105, 111
Williams, Paul *Rolling Stone* journalist 219, 220
Wilson, Robert Anton (1932-2007) American author, futurist, psychologist 220, 221, 222
Wolfe, Thomas (1930-2018) American author 99, 139, 141, 182, 183, 187
Woodstock (festival, Yasgur's Farm 1969) 192
Wavy Gravy (1936-) American entertainer 135
World's Fair (1964) 185

X

X, Malcolm (1925-1965) Black political leader 131

Y

Yugen (American magazine, 1955-1963) 153

Z

Zeppelin, Led (1968-1980) British rock band 200, 201